European Security in the N

European Security in the New Political Environment

An analysis of the relationships between national interests, international institutions and the Great Powers in post-Cold War European security arrangements

JAMES H. WYLLIE

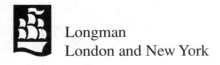

Longman
London and New York

Addison Wesley Longman Limited
Edinburgh Gate, Harlow,
Essex CM20 2JE, England
and Associated Companies throughout the world.

Published in the United States of America
by Addison Wesley Longman Publishing, New York

© Addison Wesley Longman Limited 1997

First published 1997

ISBN 0 582 24403-X PPR

British Library Cataloguing-in-Publication Data

A catalogue record for this book is
available from the British Library

Library of Congress Cataloging-in-Publication Data

Wyllie, James H.
    European security in the new political environment : an analysis
of the relationships between national interests, international
institutions and the great powers in post cold war European security
arrangements / james H. Wyllie
        p.   cm
    Includes bibliographical refernces and index.
    ISBN 0-582-24402-1 (hardcover). — ISBN 0-582-24403-X (pbk.)
    1. National security—Europe. 2. Europe—Politics and
government—1989- I. Title.
UA646.W9597   1997
355'.03304—dc20   96-35238
                                                        CIP

Set by 8 in 10/12 pt Times

Produced through Longman Malaysia, VVP

Contents

Abbreviations

ARRC	Allied Rapid Reaction Corps	LDP	Liberal Democratic Party (Russia)
CDE	Confidence and Security Building Measures and Disarmament in Europe Conference	MC	Military Committee (NATO)
		MTCR	Military Technology Control Regime
CFE	Conventional Forces in Europe	NACC	North Atlantic Cooperation Council
CIS	Commonwealth of Independent States	NATO	North Atlantic Treaty Organisation
CJTF	Combined Joint Task Force	OECD	Organisation for Economic Cooperation and Development
CMEA	Council for Mutual Economic Assistance	OSCE	Organisation for Security and Cooperation in Europe
CPSU	Communist Party of the Soviet Union	PfP	Partnership for Peace
CSCE	Conference on Security and Cooperation in Europe	PJHQ	Permanent Joint Head Quarters
DPC	Defence Planning Committee (NATO)	PKK	Workers' Party of Kurdistan
		PRC	People's Republic of China
EC	European Community	RAF	Royal Air Force
ESDI	European Security and Defence Identity	RUSI	Royal United Services Institute for Defence Studies
EU	European Union	SACEUR	Supreme Allied Commander Europe
FIS	Islamic Salvation Front	
FRG	Federal Republic of Germany	SHAPE	Supreme Head Quarters Allied Powers Europe
G.7	Group of seven leading industrial states	SPD	Social Democratic Party (Germany)
GATT	General Agreement on Tariffs and Trade	START	Strategic Arms Reduction Talks
GDP	Gross Domestic Product	
GNP	Gross National Product	UK	United Kingdom
IFOR	Implementation Force (NATO)	UN	United Nations
IISS	International Institute for Strategic Studies	US	United States
		WEU	West European Union
JRDF	Joint Rapid Deployment Force	WTO	Warsaw Treaty Organisation

Preface

The breaching of the Berlin Wall and the end of the Cold War belong to a previous historical era. They now seem a long time ago, and there is some impatience and frustration that a new, stable security regime for Europe is not in place. The experience of the Cold War, at least in the West, has led to expectations of cohesive, coherent multilateral behaviour which will deliver a new set of stable security arrangements to replace the old. The perceptions of the Cold War created images of cooperative and quasi-integrative international institutions where common interests resided and where the concepts and practice of national security and national interest were relegated.

This book argues that the Cold War was an anomalous period in European history, and that many of the images and expectations created by the Cold War are misleading. The division of Europe into two roughly balanced political and military blocs was an accident of history and produced, for a generation, a crude strategic stability which was quite abnormal for the European condition. It is much more normal for European security conditions to be characterised by fluid regional balances of power, occasional power vacuums, untidy alliance blocs and competitive national interests. The pursuit of national interests, of which national security is the highest, never disappeared in Europe during the Cold War. But given the nature and scale of the Soviet threat, Western cooperation and quasi-integration in defence and economics was undertaken to a degree never before experienced. In the circumstances such policies were deemed the best way for most Western states to address national interests. Now that the Cold War threat is gone, a more distinctive view of national security is reasserting itself. To those imbued with the spirit of international integration and supranationalism this may be regrettable and even short-sighted, but it is the reality of what has happened since the end of the Cold War and it looks like continuing in the near future. Perhaps, in the longer term, global warming, over-population, world trade, and other globalisation issues ought to be the salient international security issues. But now, and at least for the first decade of the new century, governments faced by the real responsibility of safeguarding their peoples are addressing hard, traditional national security issues such as stable frontiers, non-threatening neighbours, resource security, civil war spillover, balances of power and reasonable guarantees of security. It is not the West which is forcing NATO or WEU membership on the Baltic republics, Slovakia, the Czech Republic, Hungary, Poland and many other aspirants. The governments of these countries have given clear notice that they wish membership of alliances which address traditional national security concerns. Following the logic of their geography and history, some European states are convinced that it is a national security necessity that they win membership of NATO. NATO does not seek the political and strategic problems and sensitivities in, for instance, the Polish clamour for membership – but nor can NATO avoid them.

The issue of East European membership of NATO and Russia's response illustrates another salient feature of evolving European security arrangements – the role and influence of the Great Powers. In this book 'great' is not used in any nineteenth-century, global or imperial sense. But in contemporary European security it is clear that there are states whose role and influence are much greater than others. Individually, or collectively, these states set the tone of European security: they govern how the international institutions behave (not vice versa) and, individually, they have the potential to create high tension and crisis. Germany, Russia, the United States and, to a lesser extent, Britain and France, are these crucial, bell-wether 'Great' Powers. The national security policies of each of these states all contain elements of uncertainty as well as distinct change over recent years. In the depths of the Cold War it was relatively easy to predict the core tenets of United States national security policy or Russian strategic doctrine five or ten years hence. Today, who can be confident about predicting the central features of the national security policy of Russia or unified Germany early next century? For the foreseeable future it is politics and policy-making in Berlin, Moscow, Washington, Paris and London which will determine the untidy mosaic which will constitute European security arrangements. International organisation headquarters in Brussels, Vienna or New York will not dictate to these capitals on national security issues, they will respond. In an effort to appreciate the trends, to understand the risks, dangers and opportunities, and to glimpse part of the future of European security, this book examines the national security policies of the Great Powers and how these national policies relate to each other and to the web of international institutions covering Europe. The emerging picture is not neat, but it is being painted by many artists.

Over recent years, in North America and throughout Europe, I have benefited from long and often energetic discussions about European security with a wide range of academic colleagues, serving and retired military officers, foreign and defence policy-making officials and journalists. Their names are too numerous to mention, and some would prefer to remain anonymous. I thank them for their insights, stimulating arguments and valuable time. I am also grateful to Christine McLeod for the patient, highly efficient and pleasant manner in which she transcribed this text. However, I am responsible alone for the details and arguments in this book and for any errors of judgement or fact.

James H. Wyllie
Aberdeen

Chapter 1

National Interest and the Primacy of National Security

In the European theatre during the Cold War the potency of national interest as the core driving force of foreign policy, especially national security policy, was obscured by multilateralism. In the North Atlantic Treaty Organisation (NATO) military resources were pooled, some standardisation of hardware achieved and common strategies developed. In the European Community (EC) national policies which were normally in the hands of domestic governments on matters such as farming, fishing and the environment were, to a greater or lesser extent, integrated and subject to direction from the European Commission. In East Europe, particularly from the late 1960s, close interoperability between the Warsaw Treaty Organisation (WTO) armies was developed and the Soviet Union imposed common strategy and tactics. The WTO was run from a wing of the Soviet Ministry of Defence in Moscow. The Council for Mutual Economic Assistance (CMEA), the economic wing of the Soviet bloc, was much more integrated than the EC, and was centrally directed by the Soviet government from Moscow. Other organisations such as the West European Union (WEU), the Council of Europe and the Conference on Security and Cooperation in Europe (CSCE) achieved little integration and only limited, occasional cooperation between states in the West or the East or across the Cold War divide, but the high rhetoric was one of 'interdependence' and 'integration'. This blanket of multilateralism over Europe created the image of a Europe where national interests were, or should be, relegated below common multilateral interests.

But this was a mistaken image. In the West those governments that pooled their military resources and integrated certain domestic economic functions with those of their neighbours chose to do so because, rightly or wrongly, they believed it to be in their country's national interest to do so. Given the circumstances they faced in Cold War Europe – a divided continent, a hostile, threatening ideology and massive offensive military power poised against them just over the Elbe – it was deemed to be the vital national interest to multilateralise national security arrangements in the first instance and some economic matters later. Among the non-Soviet Warsaw Pact states the element of real choice was missing but for most of the Communist governments survival of the political system, which is what most of these governments perceived as their primary national interest, required close alignment with the policies of the Soviet patron.

Now, in the post-Cold War world, circumstances are clearly different. All the core national security exigencies which made a high level of multilateral cooperation, cohesion and sometimes integration vital to the national interest have gone. In foreign policy-making national interest now expresses itself in a different manner. Many of the political and economic costs of the last 40 to 50 years need no longer be borne, and Cold War vehicles of national interest such as NATO have lost their strategic salience and relevance to a different agenda of priorities. The disintegration of the Soviet ideological and military threat and related security anxieties has liberated the foreign policies of many European states and also the North American states with interests in Europe. The international environment is now conducive to a more flexible, pragmatic identification and expression of high national interests. For those who identify a long-term value in deeper military and economic integration beyond the interests of individual states, the Cold War ended much too soon. The apparent scope of the Soviet threat always provided a fundamental, credible rationale for the elevation of multilateral interests above individual state interests. But history cannot be stopped or put into reverse. Just as it was national interest considerations which created NATO and the European Community during the Cold War, it will be national interest considerations which will determine the fates of NATO, the European Union and other cooperative and integrative institutions in the post-Cold War era.

Even at the zenith of multilateral cooperation during the Cold War there were many instances when perceptions of national interest drove governments down divergent paths. Anglo–American differences over the Suez crisis in 1956, United States–West European differences during the October 1973 war in the Middle East, and later United States–West European disagreements on sanctions over Soviet gas exports to West Europe in the wake of the Polish military coup in 1981 were but a few instances when perceptions of national interests did not conform to multilateral cooperation. Since the Cold War, the trend in intra-Western relations has been the identification and pursuit of national interests which no longer interface the way they did in the Cold War. United States–West European differences over NATO's future status in East Europe, divergent policies and preferences in ex-Yugoslavia, and United States–Japanese trade disputes illustrate that the post-Cold War pursuit of national interest lends itself to division and competition as much as Cold War national interests were conducive to collaboration. The international collaboration of the Gulf War 1990–1991 was the exception rather than the rule after the Cold War. While this event occurred just after the Cold War ended, it could actually be viewed as the last great Cold War exercise of Allied cooperation. Yet even in this illustrious case it should be noted that in January 1991 President Bush won the US Senate's support for the war by a majority of only 5 (52:47), and that a number of West European countries were slow and reluctant to proffer any meaningful support to the coalition war effort in the Gulf.

Scepticism over the value of multilateral operations, especially United Nations operations, is widespread in US foreign policy-making circles. When the United States has worked as part of a UN force in Somalia or Yugoslavia, failure has resulted. When the US has acted alone or as leader, ostensibly under UN authority but clearly with Washington in command, there has been some success. A string of foreign policy successes in 1994 – the Haiti intervention, the rapid dispatch of large

US forces to Kuwait to deter a resurgence of Iraqi pressure, and the agreement with North Korea to curtail its nuclear construction programme – seems to confirm this view. In May 1994 the US government declared a limit to American involvement in UN operations. As well as laying down a range of detailed conditions before US troops could be committed, such as acceptable command and control arrangements, Presidential Decision Directive 25 (PDD–25) declared that the United States would only support (even without troops) UN peacekeeping missions that were backed by adequate means, had realistic criteria for effective operation termination, and that served United States interests.

The nature of national interest

It may manifest itself in different policies in different eras, but serving the national interest is the primary objective of foreign policy for all states. This is not to deny that often, for governments as well as people, what actually constitutes the national interest is unclear. Fundamentally, national interest is the basic term deployed by foreign policy-makers to describe the long-term, core, collective objectives of the state. Generally, in descending order of priority, the collective objectives are deemed to comprise the security and survival of the state, economic prosperity, and the sustenance of the social and political values of the society of the state.[1]

Normally, governments will claim that these objectives constitute the fundamental, immutable interests of all the citizens of the state, regardless of social rank, party political affiliation or wealth. These nationwide, collective objectives are seen to reflect the vital interests of the whole state whereas the sectional objectives of sub-national groups probably do not.[2] There may be occasions when the interests of some sectional groups could be in the wider interests of the collective citizenry of the state, but this is normally not the case. Often the interests of sectional groups compete, and the successful achievement of one group's interests damage another group. A simple example of this would be a tariff on imports to protect a domestic industry which would raise the price of such goods to the customers requiring that product. Such clashes of interests prevent any simple aggregation of sectional interests constituting the national interest.

Nonetheless, as the term 'national interest' is imbued with a high ethical condition, sectional groups like to attach the epithet to their side of any argument. Clearly, what is in the national interest in any debate over free trade versus protectionism in the case of any single industry is far from obvious and may be very ambiguous. Yet the alacrity with which protagonists in domestic political and economic controversies claim that the national interest is on their side contributes to the cynicism surrounding the whole notion and the suspicions about the validity of the concept even when deployed by national governments. Because of the supposed moral virtue of the condition known as national interest, governments throughout the international system are inclined to damage the integrity of the concept by attaching it to short-term foreign policies, which may be of less than vital interest to the state and may be mutually contradictory, in attempts to win popular support. National interest is a term liable to exploitation by governments and interest groups of all political complexions. How accurate an accusation of exploitation may be usually depends upon which side any commentator takes on any argument.

But even if the term national interest is restricted to perceived, core, long-term, collective objectives, there are grounds for controversy and debate. The so-called collective objectives may have inherent inner contradictions or be incompatible. In the realist school of international politics, national security is at the heart of national interest, and the quest for power is a perpetual national interest in order to address state security needs. However, more liberal schools would argue that the unceasing search for power advantage over other states may, in many instances, create more enemies than it deters. In other words, to assign national security priority as a national interest may be to the detriment of national security. Indeed, there may be incompatibilities between the core, collective objectives. The 'guns versus butter' debate in nearly all modern societies illustrates this point. To what extent defence spending, while enhancing military security, damages civilian economic growth and social welfare provision was a salient domestic political issue throughout the Cold War, and remains so to this day. Another instance of how problematic it may be to reconcile incompatibilities in the collective objectives of national interest is the question of individual freedoms in a national-security state. Sustaining the traditional freedoms of individual expression, freedom of movement and employment, and open, accountable government is normally deemed a national interest of Western democracies, yet the exigencies of total war and Cold War illustrated the incompatibility of these values with the survival of the state.

There is the assumption that the bland, core objectives of national interest have been constant throughout the evolution of the state system and are immutable. Some critics argue that this is a false impression and that there may be occasions when the interests of the citizens of a state may not be in the continuance of the state.[3] It is quite conceivable that it would benefit a national society more to integrate voluntarily with a neighbouring state than to continue as a separate state, as happened when Scotland chose parliamentary union with England in 1707 and the young republic of Texas supported annexation by the United States in 1845. The close strategic, economic and cultural links between many states in the contemporary international system makes the debate over survival of the state as a real national interest a practical as well as an academic issue, not least within West Europe.

Increasing economic and social regionalisation in the Western developed world does pose a genuine conundrum over the exact role of the traditional state in serving its citizens' needs, especially when the needs and demands of citizens are going through such a rapid transition. There is a respectable argument that free access to a wider employment market better serves the needs of a West European or North American citizen at the turn of the twentieth century than a strong national defence policy. There is a strong political lobby within the European Union, including many national governments, which chooses to interpret national interest as best served by increasing political and economic integration, aimed at the decline of the old European nation-states as viable sovereign entities. This liberal view sees the state as merely an instrument to satisfy the needs of the citizens, and if the citizens' needs can be better served outside the state then it is in the national interest for the state to wither. The contrary, conservative argument, which may be entitled the 'Hegelian' view, is that the state is the supreme guarantor of citizens' rights and prospects, and that any development which weakens the power of the state is against the national interest.[4] In their fundamentals, the two camps contribute to the confusion about what national interest really is, but sometimes compromise may be achieved. Conservative foreign policy-makers may identify some ways to strengthen the state by allowing some concessions to external organisations. To date, British membership of the European Union may be seen in this light, but clearly there is a strong lobby across British political life that would see further concessions beyond the 1992 Treaty of Maastricht as weakening the British state and hence against the British national interest. Liberal foreign policy-makers may pull back from the strategy that cooperation best serves the citizens and retreat to strengthen the state when dire threats against the wellbeing of the people are identified. In the late 1930s, after a generation of foreign policy-makers had put their faith in disarmament, appeasement and collective security, Britain hastily rearmed in the face of the Nazi threat.

However, generally, political leaders are guided by their intuitive notions of national interest. The conservative inclines to strengthening the state and defending against threats. If international conditions are hostile to core objectives, then power will be sought and deployed to attempt to change these conditions. Only in stable, predictable circumstances will a more liberal interpretation of national interest be considered. The instinct of the liberal, or 'Kantian', foreign policy-maker is to look to cooperation and association as an answer to threats to the values and needs of the citizenry. In modern times this world view is fuelled by the rash of transnational challenges such as environmental pollution, international terrorism and cross-border criminality which appear beyond the capabilities of any single state or even *ad hoc* coalitions to manage. Only in the most dangerous of circumstances is there an expedient retreat into a robust, nationalistic defence posture.

What constitutes the values of a state is another area of dispute over the nature of national interest. In the modern world of social movement and transition the exact, or even general, moral, religious and ideological characteristics – the protection of which contributes to a country's national interest – is more open to debate than ever. This is particularly the case in heterogeneous democracies, of which the United States is the best example. Whether or not the United States should proactively encourage the spread of democracy in the post-Cold War world or, automatically, combat militant Islamic revivalism wherever it challenges secular government are but two contemporary issues illustrating the quandaries that surround the values component of United States national interest.

Whatever the core, collective objective is deemed to be, who makes that decision is a further feature of the concept of national interest open to question. Critics often argue that a salient weakness in the concept derives from the narrowness of the élite who decide what constitutes national interest. The high foreign policy pursued in the national interest is determined by a small band of the politically influential. This is particularly so in non-democratic societies, but is also usually the case in democracies. Claiming special expertise and privileged access to information, determining national interest is in the hands of a small élite of political leaders and government officials, sometimes influenced by their peer group in business, the media and academic life. This élite has established and perpetuated the ranking of national security first, economic advancement second and national values third as the core, collective objectives of national interest for most states. An 'interested public' of no more than approximately 10 per cent of the population concurs with this framework and, most of the rest of the time, the vast bulk of the nation pursue their lives oblivious to what the élite has decided is in their national interest. Only in peculiar, rare circumstances, when the high costs of a foreign policy seem to outweigh any advantages, does a nation exhibit a mass influence on what is deemed to be in the national interest. Such an instance was the widespread opposition to the United States ground war in Vietnam in the late 1960s.

However, it should not be assumed that foreign policy élites always have coherent, lucid conceptions of what is the national interest. Most of the time they inherit traditional frameworks and view the outside world through prisms bequeathed by their country's history. Most foreign policy-makers are too busy responding to immediate pressures to work out new collective objectives and devise grand strategies to achieve them.[5] Some notable exceptions to this trend have existed. Arguably, Napoleon Bonaparte, Adolf Hitler, Charles de Gaulle and perhaps Presidents Reagan and Gorbachev devised their own distinctive, coherent visions of national interest, but most foreign policies are no more than *ad hoc* responses in the light of a general awareness of the national interest rather than major redefinitions of it.

The national interest is a vague, abstract concept, over which there has been prolonged scholarly debate. At first sight, the notion of a clutch of core, collective objectives for a state seems self-evident and self-supporting. But on closer examination, some inherent contradictions, incompatibilities, competing perspectives and mistaken assumptions permeate the general concept. Awareness of these conceptual weaknesses causes some observers to suspect frequent political manipulation of what may be an emotive symbol for the mass of the uninformed public. Nonetheless, despite conceptual inadequacies and accusations of ruthless exploitation, political leaders and foreign policy-makers insist that there is such a thing as the national interest – whether it is a set of vague ideals or a catalogue of vital objectives – and that they know it when they meet it. And it is over issues of national security and war that national interest becomes manifest in its starkest form.

The primacy of national security

In whatever kind of collective unit mankind has found itself, the safety of that unit from conquest, destruction or even partial injury has been the oldest preoccupation of leaderships. This has been the case whether the units have been small tribes, city-states, large nations or empires. Fulfilling the task of national defence is not only the most potent symbol of government, it is also a clear signal to the population of the unit and to neighbouring units that it is felt there is something worth defending. To relegate the duty of national defence to an inconsequential task of government would indicate little concern over the integrity of the political unit. This could have dire results for domestic political cohesion and the respect which a sovereign unit is accorded by its neighbours.

The classic maxim that national security is the primary responsibility of sovereign government was clearly illustrated by the behaviour of states engaged in the recent Cold War. The Cold War has been over for several years, and the present threats posed to the former protagonists are of a wide variety, of lower intensity and less well-defined. Public discussion, at least in the West, of issues pertinent to the vital protection of the state has diminished considerably since the collapse of the Soviet Union in 1991. Yet a major feature of the behaviour of most states has been the cautious, gradual readjustment of relatively high defence budgets, and the determination not to abandon successful security policies with imprudent haste. An absence of imminent threat has not been taken as any guarantee that serious threats do not exist or may not arise, perhaps in a surprising manner, in the future.

The 'Velvet' revolutions in East Europe in 1989 and 1990, largely bloodless and non-violent, raised hopes that a new epoch of international relations had dawned, at least in Europe, when issues of national security and war could be relegated to near the foot of any agenda of national interests.[6] Assumptions of peaceful change as the norm in post-Cold War relations among European states were prevalent in the early 1990s. The benign circumstances of German unification, and the democratic nature of the new Germany, were seen to reinforce such aspirations. Optimism about a revived United Nations having a central place in international security arose from its enforcement role in the successful liberation of Kuwait from Iraqi occupation in 1991, and also from the explosion of global UN peacekeeping opportunities. The high, moralistic tone of United States foreign policy, now the sole superpower and unopposed global policeman, held out prospects of a comfortable future for the world's satisfied powers. The vision of democracy as the political wave of the future, and the questionable proposition that more democracy means less chance of war, also contributed to widespread notions in the West that the traditional policy-making priorities of government could be adjusted to new realities.

But further analysis demonstrates the weak foundations of such expectations. The brittle Communist regimes in East Europe lost legitimacy in their own eyes as well as those of the governed because of their inability to provide social and economic progress. Chancellor Brandt's Ostpolitik of the early 1970s and the CSCE Helsinki Final Act of 1975 had removed protection against West German revanchism as the major source of any popular legitimacy the East European governments may have enjoyed. By the 1980s, these administrations had nothing to contribute. With no realistic policy visions except more of the same failure, East European regimes had little will to carry on.[7] The patron power in Moscow was in a similar psychological condition and was weary of its rule over half of Europe. One distinct measure of self-justifying progress for the Communist system would have been to incorporate more of Europe into the subsystem, but the firm, effective and relentlessly superior national security policies of the NATO countries and the neutrals denied that lifeline to the corrupt and decrepit Marxist–Leninist governments. The relative economic and technological differentials between either side of the Iron Curtain widened in the 1980s, not least in military technology. This compounded popular discontent with, and contributed to, the low morale of the ruling élites. Nonetheless, national security as a central concern of government continues in post-Cold War East Europe. This is demonstrated by the priority attached to constructing NATO links and to the canvassing for NATO membership by post-Communist East European governments.

Within a few years of the end of the Cold War the optimism of the early 1990s has given way to a more cautious, sometimes pessimistic, assessment of the continuing salience of national security in high policy-making. Politically, German unification has been successful and the severe economic problems of adjustment are being overcome. German economic and political power now dominate the European Union and the rest of the continent.[8] This contributes to an undercurrent of unease among its neighbours. The developing debate among the German policy élite over the relative virtues of further European political and economic integration – a policy over which there was virtual consensus in Cold War West Germany – adds to the anxieties felt by some contiguous states. One of the major attractions of NATO for countries such as Poland is that it provides American power as a balance to German power on the continent. This is a politically sensitive issue, but many East European policy-makers aspire to NATO membership as much for this reason as any future security provision against a reconstituted Russian threat.

The tragic war in ex-Yugoslavia, the inability of collective action by the EU to defuse the crisis, and the ineffectiveness of collective security in the shape of the UN to enforce an end to belligerency and to manufacture an acceptable political settlement, conveyed stark images of a familiar international system. The limited achievements of humanitarian efforts in the Balkans only put into sharp focus the failure of a clutch of lauded international organisations – EC, CSCE, UN, NATO and WEU – to resolve quickly a relatively peripheral, local war on the European continent. The great ideological divide of the modern era may be over, but it proved difficult to reconcile the interests of great and local powers over the future of ex-Yugoslavia. Other bloody conflicts on the very edge of Europe, in the Caucasus, or contiguous to Europe, in the Levant, have proved similarly resistant to multilateral mediation, and have contributed to the persistent sense of unease and anxiety about national security. Conceptual ambiguities surrounding the United States foreign policy during the Clinton Administration, and the struggle for the management of foreign policy with the post-1994 Republican Congress, have demonstrated that the United States can no longer be assumed to have the will or the interests to fulfil a patron-power role in all circumstances for the Western, democratic international system. Democracy is brittle in Russia and East Europe, and many economically advanced East Asian societies bridle at Western rhetoric which asserts that only the North Atlantic model is the proper one.[9] Meanwhile, militant, political Islamic revivalism poses a severe threat to a variety of secular, authoritarian and pro-Western monarchical governments throughout North Africa and the Middle East. Such are the deep differences between post-Cold War societies and cultures in the world that one eminent strategic analyst has warned of a 'clash of civilisations' in the future.[10]

It ought not to be surprising that, after the initial euphoria greeting the collapse of the Iron Curtain, the inherent instabilities of an international system composed of unequal sovereign states should assert themselves. Gross economic inequality pervades the system. More important from the perspective of strategic stability, gross economic inequality pervades the regional sub-systems. The Cold War may be over, but the clear economic division of Europe continues – and will persist for some time. EU members cannot agree on the conditions of enlargement towards the East, and there is disharmony within the EU on this issue as well as growing resentment within the poor post-Communist societies at being excluded from the prosperity of West Europe. In the Middle East the wealth disparities between the oil-rich, mostly smaller states and the contiguous, larger non-oil states are vast, and the problems are compounded by the population explosion in the poorer states.[11] As the Arab–Israeli relationship, the Gulf War of 1990–1991, and the long-running Indian–Pakistani dispute over Kashmir demonstrate, notions of just and unjust borders resulting in high tension and frequent conflict persist throughout the modern international system. Indeed, the end of the Cold War, regardless of the peaceful nature of its conclusion, has exacerbated and revived many international disputes over territory. Another salient, apparently immutable conflicting characteristic of the international system which mitigates against hopes of a real international community other than a competitive system is the tension between the principles of sovereignty and non-intervention in the internal affairs of state, enshrined in Article 2 (4) of the UN Charter, and the largely Western impulse to interfere in human rights issues, as defined by the West, in other states.[12] Articles 1 (33, 55 and 56) of the UN Charter may be used to justify the breaking of the sovereignty principles.[13] The privileged position of the five permanent members of the UN Security Council and their access to a veto within the UN framework, causes resentment. Pressures are mounting for the addition of extra permanent members who, since 1945, have risen to the fore in international affairs, either by economic prowess or as regional Great Powers.[14] Most of the present permanent members are resistant to change. Whatever the eventual outcome – and it is hard to envisage an effective, enlarged Security Council with or without comprehensive Charter revision – resentments will persist. There will be those who resist the dilution of their influence and those who resent not being selected as new permanent members. And there is the vast majority of the General Assembly who resent the continued political inequality.

Currently, it may be understated in the post-Cold War, Western developed world, but the constant quest for national security remains the primary and fundamental interest of government as much now as at any time in the modern era. Outside of the North Atlantic Area, for instance in the Middle East and among the burgeoning industrial societies of East Asia, the salience of security is not understated. Large defence budgets pursuant to the dilution of Cold War stabilities and predictabilities are testimony to that reality.[15] Between the end of the Gulf War and 1993, the Gulf States ordered $40 billion of arms from Western firms. Kuwait is committed to a $12 billion arms programme before the year 2003.[16] Between 1991 and 1994 the United States alone received $34 billion of arms orders from Gulf states.[17]

So far, the international system remains a competitive and basically anarchic system of states. Submersion of all security requirements in multilateral organisations which aspire to supranationalism, such as the European Union and the United Nations, has been shown to be ineffective for most states. Just as at Munich in 1938 and Yalta in 1945, the Great Powers still organise the international system to address their needs. German insistence on EC recognition of the breakaway Yugoslavian republics of Croatia and Bosnia-Herzegovina in 1992, and the subsequent balancing of the interests of the UN Security Council permanent members during UN–EC attempts to resolve the conflicts clearly illustrated this reality. There is no effective authority providing comprehensive protection against hostile intentions of other states higher than the government of the state. In all but the rarest exceptions, states cannot abrogate responsibility for their own protection. It is the policies which governments devise and pursue which deliver whatever degree of security is attainable. States seek power in order to address the need for security. Without security, other achievements and values of the state are vulnerable. Distrust and suspicion among states has been an unchanging characteristic of the ancient and modern worlds. The paradox is that as more power is sought to achieve a level of security which can never be absolute, the greater the degree of insecurity felt by other states. One state's relative security being another state's insecurity is the dilemma which produces vicious circles of anxiety about national security. Hence, states are preoccupied with security.

Turkish defence policy is a vivid illustration of the security dilemma in particular, and persistent anxiety over national security in general. The end of the Cold War has not brought any security relaxation for Turkey. On the contrary, the demise of East–West enmity has created a more varied and challenging security environment for Turkey than it has faced for more than a generation. The massive Soviet threat to which Turkey was exposed for 40 years collapsed in 1991, but its disintegration created a mosaic of strategic challenges for Turkey. Its traditional rivalry with Greece was held in check by the Cold War, but that discipline has now disintegrated. In this relationship disputes and resentments abound: Turkish minority rights in Eastern Thrace, Turkish occupation of North Cyprus, territorial water disagreements in the Aegean Sea, Athen's nationalistic policies towards Albania and Macedonia and its empathy for Serbia, past Greek reluctance to accept Turkish participation in an EU customs union. Any advancement in Greek national security is automatically considered a potential threat to Turkey. In real terms, the Turkish defence budget has increased every year since the end of the Cold War. In addition to security preoccupations with Greece, conflict and instabilities in the Caucasus region, contiguity with Iraq and the enforcement of the UN economic embargo, consistently delicate relations with Syria over territory, water and Damascus' sympathy for the Workers' Party of Kurdistan (PKK) Kurdish guerrillas and the bloody internal struggle directly against the PKK in Eastern Turkey at the cost of over 15 000 lives since 1984, aggravate a sense of national insecurity felt in Turkey exceeding that of the Cold War years.[18]

It is difficult for states to measure their real level of security. Security is a debatable concept: ambiguous, flexible and open to wide interpretation. There is a distinct psychological dimension to notions of security.[19] Feeling safe from attack against values and possessions is a vital element of security, even when objective criteria could suggest great vulnerability. Measured only by objective criteria, Canada ought to feel extremely insecure *vis-à-vis* the United States. It does not: it feels very much at ease with its giant neighbour. It is the unique history, for over 100 years, of benign United States' intentions towards Canada which induces that deep sense of security, regardless of the severe imbalance of national capabilities. In most parts of the international system, such an imbalance of capabilities as between the United States and Canada would induce a deep sense of insecurity. Usually, security is assumed to comprise an absence, or at least a manageable level, of physical threat, and the confidence that any level of threat to the state can be defeated or repulsed. But any appreciation of security enjoyed by a state hinges on a correct assessment of the character of the animosity towards the state, externally and domestically, and honest measure of the weaknesses of the state. History is littered with instances where states got this wrong and suffered terrible consequences, not least France in 1940. And, on the other side of the coin, perhaps there have been many instances when states misperceived threats and subsequently wasted valuable national resources on needlessly high defence budgets. On the whole, security is negative in nature in that it stops nasty things happening – and it is often difficult to prove that nasty things were going to happen anyway. Nonetheless, the historical record does show that while states may often be uncertain about the level of national security they enjoy, in times of jeopardy they certainly know when they feel unsafe, whether or not feelings are an objective measure of reality. On any objective basis the Nicaraguan Sandinista government of the 1980s did not pose any real national security threat to the United States. In 1986 Nicaragua's total population of 3.3 million was less than half that of metropolitan Chicago; its GDP was barely 2 per cent of the United States defence budget; and its regular army was only 15 per cent of the size of the US Marine Corps.[20] Yet, unquestionably, the Reagan Administration perceived a real threat to US national security from the influence of the Nicaraguan policies on central America. The White House's anxiety was echoed by many in Congress and a broad swathe of American public opinion. At the cost of severe political embarrassment at home and abroad, a variety of covert devices were used to undermine the Sandinista government and defeat the threat it was seen to pose to US national security.[21]

The highly subjective element to feelings of security explains why so many considerations may be incorporated in any measure of security. What makes one person or state feel insecure may make another feel secure. The public debate in the West in the 1980s over the virtues and vices of nuclear deterrence illustrated this feature of national security. Clearly, national security is an inexact concept. Many variables contribute to and detract from national security. Identifying all the relevant variables is problematic; measuring them is even more so. Traditionally, military considerations are deemed the most important element.[22] Military force is the only governmental instrument sustained directly for attack or defence against rival states. Military power ought to be, and usually is, the monopoly of the sovereign government, and it is only through the military instrument that one state may conquer another. A state may be secure in political, economic and social terms, but failure in the battlefield can expose all these achievements to absolute vulnerability. However, military superiority alone does not provide a high level of relative security. In the modern world a strong, vibrant technological and economic base is essential to provide advanced military hardware and the means to pay for it. A legitimate political system and a popular consensus in support of the security policy is vital for a robust, durable level of national security. If the state is homogeneous, normally there is a deeper sense of loyalty, and it is stronger internally. If multinational, it is more prone to internal divisions, it is weaker domestically, and a consequence may be a heightened sense of external vulnerability. Ancillary variables such as strong allies, access to crucial raw materials, sea borders or undefended borders with historically friendly neighbours, a free trading system and cultural interests similar to other, neighbouring states all have a role to play in national security.[23]

An holistic view of national security would argue that as well as defence policy and most foreign policy, large elements of domestic policy such as education and social welfare have vital national security functions. In effect, all government policy carries national security implications. This is a view particularly popular in the welfarist societies of Scandinavia. Indeed, all states have their own national security cultures which are reflections of their history and strategic circumstances but which, by way of reputation, govern the security perceptions of their neighbours. Some states, such as Russia, are seen as expansive, belligerent and proud. Others, such as Canada and Denmark, have collectivist, liberal, low defence-spending cultures. The self-perception of states as well as the prism through which the rest of the international system views individual states colour assessments of security.

To be effective a national security policy must be dynamic. Just as power is a relative concept – and meaningless unless related to countervailing power – then so is national security. A state's security is of a different quality depending upon the state to which it is related. And the strengths and weaknesses of all states are in constant, often rapid change. In the international system, nothing is immutable. The nature of challenges change, capabilities change. Opponents may become allies and old allies transform into rivals. National security is a condition, not a framed set of policies. Policies must be flexible to address the desirable condition called national security. States use a variety of policies to seek security, not all of which are military in nature. If there is insecurity over access to raw materials in unstable, faraway countries, then stockpiling reserves, the use of substitutes, conservation and diversifying suppliers could be a more cost-effective way of improving security than deploying a military expeditionary force to a hostile, distant environment.[24] If, when measured in objective capabilities, a state is relatively weak, then diplomatic arrangements with states which share a mutual view of how the international system should be shaped may be pursued. Alliances, collective security agreements, and balance-of-power manoeuvres all have preferred visions of security as the goal. Such security regimes survive so long as the interests of the members correspond. When they diverge in a serious manner, alliances and other collective defence and security arrangements disintegrate. Balances of power change character as partners are changed.

States are independent actors and, recognising that diplomatic arrangements once forged will not always address changing security needs, have often formed various short-lived partnerships with other states. Changing circumstances may even drive states to risk war for reasons of national security. It should not be assumed that national security always equates with peace.[25] States surrounded by coalitions of hostile powers may perceive war-making as a chance to deflect enemies and establish longer-term security. Such perceptions influenced German policy in 1914 and Japanese policy in 1941. Currently, opponents of NATO expansion eastwards to incorporate the former Warsaw Pact non-Soviet states argue that Russia would feel threatened and perceive that it was being denied a natural sphere of influence in Slavic East Europe by the formal extension of NATO membership to the Vistula. This could engender such a feeling of diminished national security and resentment that hostile anti-Western behaviour of a Cold War character would be revived.[26] Traditionally, nearly all states have seen independence and wellbeing as being more important than peace. Loss of sovereignty is seen as too high a price to pay for peace. Perceptions of national security do not always coincide with sustaining the *status quo*, and vulnerabilities may be addressed through conquest, creating buffer zones, seeking regional hegemony and forming redistributive alliances.

National security is an amorphous and elastic concept. It may be conceptualised in a narrow way, restricting it to military capabilities alone. It is true that the military element is the primary feature of national security, but in the modern world it is realistic to widen the definition to include, at least, economic considerations. But, however we define national security, one certain feature is that no state can ever be absolutely secure as long as it exists in a system of independent states. The requirements of national security never stand still, and the precise measure of the security that the state enjoys is impossible. But the constant quest for national security is the price to be paid by a state if those who constitute political authority and their supporters wish to exercise that abstract but real notion called sovereignty.

Notes

1. See P. A. Reynolds, *An Introduction to International Relations* (London: Longman, 1971), p. 49.
2. See Charles W. Kegley Jr and Eugene R. Wittkopf, *World Politics, Trend and Transformation* (New York: St Martin's Press, 1993), p. 537.
3. See Joseph Frankel, *International Politics, Conflict and Harmony* (Harmondsworth: Pelican, 1973), p. 104.
4. *Ibid.*
5. See K. J. Holsti, *International Politics. A Framework for Analysis* (London: Prentice-Hall International, 1974), pp. 131–2.
6. See Adam Roberts, 'A new age in international relations', *International Affairs*, Vol. 67, No. 3, July 1991, p. 516.
7. See Renée De Nevers, *The Soviet Union and Eastern Europe: The End of an Era* (London : IISS, 1990), Adelphi Paper 249, chap. 3.
8. See Frederick Kempe, 'Restless Germany rummages for a foreign policy', *Wall Street Journal Europe*, 2 February 1995, p. 6 and 'Germany's Europe', *Economist*, 11 June 1994, p. 35.
9. See Kishore Mahbubani, 'The United States: "Go East, young man" ', *The Washington Quarterly*, Vol. 17, No. 2, Spring 1994, pp. 5–23.
10. See Samuel P. Huntingdon, 'The clash of civilisations', *Foreign Affairs*, Vol. 72, No. 3, Summer 1993, pp. 22–49.
11. See James H. Wyllie, 'Inter-Arab security – The demographic challenges', *Jane's Intelligence Review*, Vol. 4, No. 8, August 1992, pp. 364–7.
12. See Anthony C. Arend and Robert J. Beck, *International Law and the Use of Force* (London: Routledge, 1993), p. 86 and p. 108.
13. *Ibid.*, p. 109.
14. See Annika Savill, 'US backs expansion of Security Council', *Independent*, 11 June 1993, p. 11 and Emma Matanle, 'Reform of the UN Security Council: Changing the seats at the top table', International Security Programme of the Royal Institute of International Affairs, Briefing Paper No. 15, December 1994.

15. See Geoffrey Kemp, 'Regional security arms control, and the end of the Cold War', *Washington Quarterly*, Vol. 13, No. 4, Autumn 1990, pp. 33–51 for a prescient analysis. See 'East Asia's wobbles', *Economist*, 23 December 1995 – 5 January 1996, pp. 81–83 for analysis which bears out Kemp's prognosis.
16. See 'Comfort blanket for the Gulf', *Economist*, 5 December 1992, p. 69.
17. Martin Walker, 'Clinton team at odds over plan to boost arms sales', *Guardian*, 4 February 1994, p. 11.
18. See James H. Wyllie, 'Turkey – Adapting to new strategic realities', *Jane's Intelligence Review (JIR)*, Vol. 4, No. 10, October 1992, pp. 450–2; 'Turkey's eastern crises', *JIR*, Vol. 5, No. 11, October 1993, pp. 506–8; and 'Turkey – renationalising foreign policy', *JIR*, Vol. 7, No. 2, February 1995, pp. 74–5.
19. See Charles W. Kegley, Jr and Eugene R. Wittkopf, *World Politics: Trend and Transition* (New York: St Martin's Press, 1993), pp. 389–90.
20. See *The Military Balance 1986–87* (London: IISS, 1986).
21. See Walter LaFeber, *The American Age* (New York: Norton, 1989), pp. 683–6 and pp. 690–2.
22. See Barry Buzan, 'Is international security possible?' in Ken Booth (Ed.) *New Thinking About Strategy and International Security* (London: HarperCollins, 1991), p. 35.
23. See Lawrence Freedman, 'General Introduction', in Lawrence Freedman (Ed.) *War* (Oxford: Oxford University Press, 1994), p. 4.
24. See Hans Maull, 'Energy and resources: The strategic dimensions', *Survival*, Vol. 31, No. 6, November/December 1989, pp. 511–12 for a review of alternatives to military force.
25. See Hedley Bull, *The Anarchical Society* (London: Macmillan, 1977), p. 18.
26. See Michael E. Brown, 'The flawed logic of NATO expansion', *Survival*, Vol. 37, No. 1, Spring 1995, pp. 34–52.

Chapter 2

Security, Disorder and the Role of the Institutions

The post-Cold War world is complex, unpredictable and dangerous. During the Cold War global ideological and strategic competition between the United States and the Soviet Union imposed a large degree of discipline on issues of international security. Alliances and spheres of influence drew clear lines of demarcation of interest and responsibility. Grey areas, which fell outside either bloc and over which there was uncertainty as to dominant interests and influence, were few. Defections from one bloc to the other were rare. Less rare were arguments within blocs over rankings of power and influence, but the threat from the rival bloc was a crucial aid to long-term discipline. Over 45 years, from 1945 until 1990, by default rather than by design, a roughly balanced, stable, bipolar international security structure developed. There were some anomalies, such as Yugoslavia from 1948 and the People's Republic of China from about 1960, but most states could identify to a greater or lesser extent with one bloc or the other.

War was not banished from the globe. Volatile regions such as the Middle East and South East Asia suffered from much blood-letting from conflicts which had their roots in the years preceding global ideological competition between the United States and the Soviet Union. Often, by choice or by circumstance, the Great Powers became entangled in local wars but, from the perspective of Washington and Moscow, these conflicts were controlled and limited. Escalation to a level that would bring global war and the risk of nuclear devastation was not allowed. Given the sensitivity of the issues, the political intensity of the rivalry and the scale and scope of the blocs' military machines, it is remarkable that the world did not pay a much higher price for the Cold War.

In particular, Europe was a beneficiary of Cold War discipline. Europe was the biggest prize in superpower competition and the arena where history's most powerful armies met face-to-face. Yet, from the construction of the first version of the Berlin Wall in August 1961 until the breaching of the final edifice in November 1989, Europe enjoyed an era of relatively minimal inter-bloc tensions and widespread peace. In the European theatre bitter propaganda rolled back and forth between the blocs, arguments over the details of arcane arms-control negotiations would go on for years, and human rights would peak and trough as a salient East–West issue, but for decades there was no serious war-threatening crises between the blocs.[1] In these years the greatest prospect of war was within the blocs, between Greece and Turkey within NATO, and between the Soviet Union and occasional recalcitrant Warsaw Pact members. But Cold War discipline held and Europe was war-free. For many individuals, especially in East Europe, the Cold War was a distressing period when intellectual, economic and social liberties were severely proscribed. But when measured in terms of interstate war in the twentieth century, the Cold War was a halcyon period of peace for Europe.

Today, East Europe is no longer under Soviet imperial control and, in the absence of the Soviet political and military threat, dominant American influence in West Europe is steeply declining. While the Cold War existed, sensitive trans-Atlantic issues such as trade competition were held in check. They were not important enough to challenge the necessity for a common front against the Communist enemy. This is no longer so. Nor is Germany any longer in the front line of the Cold War. For more than 40 years the Federal Republic of Germany was the supplicant of the United States. It needed political rehabilitation, economic recovery, defence and unification. Today it has all four and has become a rival to United States influence in Europe rather than a complement. The old order to European security – in terms of ranking, arrangement and mandate – has gone, and a new, stable framework has yet to be put in place.

That there is a search for a new security order is evidence of this relative disorder. Books, journals and newspaper commentaries have been replete with propositions for new European security blueprints.[2] Some propose the renovation of existing institutions, some the amalgamation of institutions and others the creation of new institutions. Common to most of these analyses is the desire for some kind of order – though whether or not it is order in terms of a power-dominance structure, or comfortable, neat, universal organisation, or a system of enforced, regulated behaviour is usually unclear. Only a few analysts have recognised that the truly deep significance of the disintegration of the Soviet Union is that 'order' – as practised during the Cold War – is no longer possible.[3] It may be regrettable but the much lauded 'international community', which has been outraged by horrors in ex-Yugoslavia and Chechnya and is expected to bring order to such chaos, does not exist even though the Communist dragon has been slain. On an *ad hoc* basis, when the stakes are high enough, selective multilateralism just about works. The coalition effort in the 1990–1991 Gulf War is the best illustration of such behaviour, though as a 'community' effort it nearly did not work. But there are many more instances, from Somalia through Rwanda to Bosnia, where multilateralism has been clearly ineffective or only partially effective. Even among the few real liberal democracies in the world there is only limited agreement on which political, economic and strategic conditions are best for international security. At a highly superficial level there is a consensus in Western capitals about how a benevolent system ought to work, but little agreement about how to achieve it. National interests get in the way. The astute commentator William Pfaff has described it thus:

> The new world order thus reveals itself to be the old one in which individual nations pursue their national well-being, cooperating in areas of clear mutual advantage but governed on all matters involving risk and sacrifice by national or domestic political interest alone. The rhetoric of liberal internationalism has been permitted to obscure this for too long. This is an unpleasant reality to face, but such is life.[4]

The reality is that Europe, and also the rest of the world, has moved on from the relative simplicities of bipolar bloc confrontation and balance to a condition reminiscent of eighteenth- and nineteenth-century Europe. There is no encompassing explanation of international security, nor are there concomitant global or regional strategies with which to manage the insecurities. In the short- to medium-term there are a range of individual challenges to the national interests of individual states. Some of these challenges are a greater threat to some states than to others, even though the states in question may be West European, industrial, liberal democracies. The challenges to mind are the debris of the collapse of the Cold War security system. For reasons of institutional salvation – giving NATO a *raison d'être* and preserving some national defence budgets in a world with no Soviet threat – challenges such as intrastate ethnic conflict, the illegal drugs trade, migration pressures and threats to Europe from radical Islam are elevated above their station. This is demonstrated by the fact that the Western democracies, most of whom are in NATO and the European Union, have been unable to agree over many years about how best to tackle them and are unwilling to devote meaningful resources to counter such supposed threats to national security. Such behaviour stands in stark contrast to the Cold War when there was a real threat. In the meantime long-term, core, strategic considerations of European security are misunderstood and mishandled.

For more than 100 years, since the unification of Germany in 1870, the objectives, policies and behaviour of Germany and Russia have constituted the core geostrategic challenges to security and stability in the modern European international political system. In the 1990s the strategic foundations on which NATO and the European Union were built, and which sustained the political and security order in East Europe, have suffered from two earthquakes, resulting in some debris among the poorer constructions in the East. The unification of Germany and the collapse of Soviet power have completely recast the core security issues endemic to European international politics in the twentieth century: the behaviour of a strong, unified Germany, the responses of a weaker, anxious Russia, their mutual relations, and the degree of commitment by the reluctant United States. Currently, Germany and Russia are not threats to European security; they are challenges which could easily become threats. The contrasting sympathies and interests of Bonn and Moscow towards the conflicts in the Balkans since 1992 have demonstrated the potential that exists for Germany and Russia, and the quality of their mutual relations, to become serious problems for European stability. Either as rivals or partners, German–Russian relations are crucial. If a real partnership is struck up in the years ahead, then there are fears of Western exclusion from any influence in East Europe, and of a political and economic division of the spoils between the two European giants. If nationalist politics takes a grip in Germany and Russia – and if it does so in one it will fuel the same in the other – the old battlegrounds of East Europe will experience great tensions once again.[5] Either of these developments – partnership or rivalry – is bound to have deep implications for NATO, the European Union, the role of the United States in Europe and the demands made upon it.

In this return to the 'usual disorder of history'[6] what can be expected of the great international institutions which sustained the European security framework during the Cold War? There are arguments that a European security structure manifested by

NATO, the European Union (EU), the West European Union (WEU), and the Organisation for Security and Cooperation in Europe (OSCE) is in place. This so-called architecture, born of the Cold War to address Cold War contingencies, may fulfil certain routine functions of contact and some coordination, but it is clearly inadequate to the core and auxiliary security challenges facing post-Cold War Europe. Across the continent the security stakes – in the medium-term – have been reduced from the worst that could have happened in the Cold War. But while the worst threat has disappeared for the time being, lesser threats which are more likely to lead to wars have multiplied. However, as they are lesser threats and not equally vital to all states with interests in European security, there is a much wider element of choice in how to respond and less prospect of any purposive consensus. This normal lack of agreement by states over matters of national interest is an echo of the early years following the Second World War, before the Cold War became institutionalised by perceptions of an overweening Soviet threat to West Europe.

No comprehensive blueprint for European security was agreed in 1945. Indeed, the opposite was the case. Such was the determination of the victorious allies to address their own vital interests that no compromise could be reached over the political and security arrangements for Germany in particular, and for Europe in general. The messy institutional security framework in place in Europe when the Cold War ended was the result of a haphazard, often reluctant, adaptation to the exigencies of the intense ideological rivalry, minimal political dialogue and sharp military competition and hostility which were the hallmarks of East–West relations on the European continent for 45 years. NATO, the Warsaw Treaty Organisation (WTO), the WEU, the Council for Mutual Economic Assistance (CMEA), the EC and CSCE emerged as the institutional instruments to the fore in a complex interface of military, political and economic efforts to protect and project preferred views of societal organisation and political sovereignty.

But these institutions are, or in some cases were, international organisations born of Cold War, developing out of specific crises or addressing particular threats. And central to any understanding of the efficacy and longevity of some of these institutions was the existence of the threat in the East: the Soviet Union. Without the tyranny of the Red Army in East Europe the creation and survival of the WTO from 1955 until 1991 would have been highly unlikely. The overlordship of Soviet political and military power held the uneasy partnership of Poland, East Germany, Hungary, Czechoslovakia, Romania, Bulgaria and the Soviet Union together. Where Soviet military power could not reach, as in the case of Albania, defection was possible. The collapse of Soviet power meant the demise of the WTO and its economic shadow, the CMEA. During the period of Moscow's imperium in East Europe from 1945 until 1990 its security partners were not sovereign states but vassal states. On the recovery of sovereignty, these countries decided that their security interests did not lie in any alliance with the decrepit Soviet Union, nor in formal military alliance with other East European states. The projection of Soviet power to the heart of Europe was the vital bonding agent in the Western security institutions. In the face of that great external threat from the East, West Europe was obliged to bury ancient quarrels and hang together. NATO was the primary institution, under whose comprehensive security umbrella secondary, economic and political organisations could experiment and evolve. Conducive to the cohesion of the West European states was the requirement to present a cooperative face not just to the perceived enemy, but also to the patron superpower ally across the Atlantic Ocean without whose participation meaningful defence was impossible.

Today, Europe is a very different security context. The old conditions and certainties of the Cold War have gone. Crucially, the Soviet Union is no more, and Russian conventional military power poses little conceivable threat to West and Central Europe for the foreseeable future. The nuclear arsenal continues, but strategic arms control has created a climate of expectations about considerable reductions. And, in the short-term, the political conditions when nuclear weapons could be brandished border on the inconceivable. Attempts have been and are being made to adapt and redesign the institutions with which Europe has grown comfortable over many decades. But there must be grave doubts if it is realistic to task these institutions with demands undreamed of even a few years ago. The political, strategic and often economic bases for these organisations were very different from the prevailing conditions today. These institutions, collectively or alone, were not designed to manage post-Cold War European security. They were designed for different tasks in a different era.

NATO: The primary institution

On 4 April 1949 the North Atlantic Treaty was signed in Washington. Within a year, prompted by American determination to see military aid used for collective rather than purely national purposes, the North Atlantic Treaty moved from being a multilateral guaranty pact towards the development of a semi-integrated military organisation known as NATO.[7] Up until 1991 NATO performed its collective duties and responsibilities well and to the international acclaim of the liberal, democratic word. For more than 40 years its core task was to stop something happening. Through the successive application of deterrence-based strategic doctrines and the deployment of capable military forces, alliance cohesion was sustained and Soviet communism in the North Atlantic and European region was contained to the limits it had reached when the North Atlantic Treaty was signed. In addition, the security bedrock provided by NATO facilitated the growth of a prosperous, liberal political and economic system in the West. The achievements of this system presented a stark contrast with the corruption and gross inefficiencies of Communist, totalitarian government in the East; a contrast which contributed so much to the delegitimisation and collapse of the Warsaw Pact governments.

Throughout the Cold War NATO's core security objective was clear enough, and anxiety over national security was high enough, to sustain fundamental, political harmony among the Member States within the large treaty area despite all the stresses and strains of the era. This was no mean accomplishment for an alliance as widely spread as NATO, and with Member States as disparate as Norway and Portugal and as competitive as Greece and Turkey. Externally, the Alliance was under perpetual challenge from an impressive Soviet military machine, complemented by disconcerting and contrasting waves of seductive and aggressive diplomacy over many years. Internally, it was often buffeted by periodic arguments over nuclear strategy, burden sharing and out-of-area issues. France left the integrated military structure in 1966, and Greek–Turkish problems have required sensitive management since they joined the alliance in 1952. Yet NATO survived and prospered. It is not unreasonable to claim that in 1989, the year of its fortieth anniversary, NATO was the world's most successful, multilateral, peacetime alliance in modern, recorded history.

That same year the Berlin Wall was breached, and the Communist governments in East Europe began to tumble. In 1991 the Soviet Union disintegrated. NATO's core objective disappeared, as did the acute national security anxieties of most of its members. The Alliance's central task was done, but by the 1990s it had become a political institution as well as a military alliance. Sentimentality, institutional self-preservation and natural political caution have created a deep reluctance to disband it. Attractive but secondary by-products of the Alliance's Cold War experience have been elevated into 'compelling' reasons for sustaining NATO, even though the core objective which spawned these by-products is no longer extant. Arguments regularly deployed include inhibiting the renationalisation of European defence policies, not least Germany's; keeping the United States entangled in European security and perpetuating Washington's large contribution to the European defence burden; maintaining trans-Atlantic solidarity against the prospect, albeit unlikely, of revived Russian expansionism in Europe over the near- to medium-term; maximising the decades of effort put into military force interoperability, which could be important for future, multilateral tasks; sustaining an organisation which could be a vehicle for pan-European collective security; utilising a standing mechanism for trans-Atlantic armaments cooperation; and having an effective military alliance in place for, as yet undefined, traditional defence tasks.[8] There is a feeling that NATO has accumulated capital which is worth strenuous efforts to protect, and that it would be foolhardy to dismantle such a security system.[9] However, while NATO does fulfil the functions described above, and in the views of many Member States fulfils some of these functions very effectively, not all states are equally enthusiastic and committed to all or even many of the Cold War by-products. This was ever so during the Cold War, but then there was the overarching common interest in defence against the Soviet threat which bound NATO together and controlled the diversity of views on lesser issues.

So there has been a search for a grand, encompassing purpose and a new military structure to keep NATO alive, vibrant and relevant to the post-Cold War world. But such a search immediately reveals a fundamental weakness in the enterprise. Viable alliances should not need to search for a *raison d'être*. That core purpose should be all too obvious, driving states to pool their defence resources – the most potent symbols of statehood – in support of a vital common interest.

Currently, NATO's core mission seems to be that of a military agent of the international community – a term often used but rarely explained – ready and, in the Balkans attempting, to stem post-Cold War instability by providing multilateral forces for humanitarian, peacekeeping and temporary peace-enforcement tasks. This vogue as well as vague mission has emerged from a set of amorphous objectives set at the landmark Rome NATO summit in November 1991. NATO's 'New Strategic Concept' announced in Rome contains one six-line paragraph detailing the Alliance's purpose in the most general of terms. The most specific it gets is 'to safeguard the freedom and security of all its members by political and military means in accordance with the principles of the United Nations Charter' and 'the establishment of a just and lasting peaceful order in Europe'.[10] In the 'New Strategic Concept' some military public administration is detailed to take account of reduced forces and to give the professional military a sense of some purpose in a new environment. But, when describing the threat which the new multinational formations and the Rapid Reaction Corps are to address, the 'New Strategic Concept' meanders over a range of risks and challenges of high and low probability.[11] And the issue of out-of-area operations (meaning anywhere beyond the borders of the 16 NATO members) creates confusion, puzzlement and convoluted analysis of the 1949 North Atlantic Treaty.[12] In practice, NATO can do little out-of-area unless the NATO Council concurs, but there is no unanimity over how to respond to the multivarious risks of the modern security environment as there was on how to deter the Warsaw Pact. The UN's haphazard and hesitant use of NATO forces as a limited, coercive support for humanitarian aid and air support for some 'safe havens' in ex-Yugoslavia exacerbated the arguments surrounding serious consideration of a major NATO out-of-area role without a UN franchise. The 'New Strategic Concept' is much more about creating some kind of political role for NATO. NATO is seen to be the centre of a 'framework of interlocking institutions'.[13] There are, it is suggested, three mutually reinforcing elements to the 'New Strategic Concept'. One element is dialogue, another is cooperation, and the third is collective defence capabilities.[14] Clearly, NATO's military purpose comes third to some broad, ambitious but imprecise political objectives.

Examination of the *Rome Declaration on Peace and Cooperation* for a specific *raison d'être* for NATO will also be in vain. The document talks about NATO being an 'agent of change, a source of stability and an indispensable guarantor of its members' security' and 'playing a key role in building a new lasting order of peace in Europe: a Europe of cooperation and prosperity'.[15] It also talks about meeting 'any potential risks to our security which may arise from instability or tension'.[16] Most of the rest of the document is about internal NATO reform, and NATO's relations with other actors in the European security arena, such as the Conference on Security and Cooperation in Europe (CSCE).

Apart from the survival of the institution, the years since 1991 have been a difficult and disappointing time for NATO. Whether the political aspirations of the Rome Summit are taken at face value, or even if some more concrete political purposes for the Alliance are divined from the rhetoric, profound questions about the purpose and role of NATO are as apposite now as in 1991. Efforts have been made to imbue the Alliance with a sense of purpose and activity. The Rapid Reaction Corps has been created and the concept of the Combined Joint Task Force (CJTF) agreed. The notion of a distinctive European Defence Identity within the Alliance has firmed up, and France has moved closer towards the integrated military structure which it left in 1966. The North Atlantic Cooperation Council and the Partnership for Peace have constructed fraternal links with former enemies in the East and NATO has adopted a peacekeeping and peacemaking role. But such small steps do not meet the Rome objectives for continent-wide security, nor do they define a *raison d'être* for NATO.

The debit side of the NATO balance sheet is discouraging: it suggests an institution – in effect, the Member States which comprise it – struggling to find a role and unsure of its future. NATO, the world's most powerful military alliance, has been relatively powerless over the tragedy of ex-Yugoslavia. In a search for military relevance, the NATO Foreign Ministers agreed in December 1992 that there was a worthwhile role as the peacekeeping agent for the United Nations, the CSCE or other bona fide international organisations. Unquestionably, NATO's multilateral operational and training experience make it very capable for power projection to crisis points. But there is clearly a confusion about the relationship between operational capabilities, the political will to use them and the political wisdom of deploying them. The powers which make up NATO do not wish to use NATO's military power in functions other than defence of NATO territory unless sanctioned by a body of apparently wider international legitimacy such as the United Nations. But this then gives that body, with other non-NATO actors such as Russia at a high level of decision-making, influence over the use or non-use of NATO forces at the point of crisis. To date, NATO has not had the cohesion or the will to escape from its self-made subcontractor role – though one attraction of this is that it gets NATO 'off the hook' of responsibility and blame for failures which can be attributed elsewhere.[17] The Great Powers in NATO lack the cohesion and sense of common purpose to ascribe a policy-making and implementation role to their own alliance. The long Bosnian tragedy was exactly the kind of European contingency anticipated by the authors of the 'New Strategic Concept' and, given the proximity of ex-Yugoslavia to the NATO area, the question must be posed: if not in Bosnia then where will NATO discover and demonstrate its new role? One lucid lesson of the Bosnian experience is that if the United States is not willing to deploy ground forces for either humanitarian or peacemaking purposes, then NATO's influence is of little consequence. But even if Washington had been willing to deploy ground forces for peace enforcement early in the conflict, London was not. Britain's experience in civil conflicts such as Palestine, Aden and Northern Ireland has made it dubious of peace-enforcement entanglements in uncertain and complex local political circumstances. In effect, in ex-Yugoslavia, NATO has found itself in a micro collective security situation involving non-NATO actors rather than the familiar, cohesive collective defence experience of the Cold War years. Beyond the occasional use of air power to punish aggression against some but not all UN-declared 'safe zones', such as Sarajevo in August 1995, effective use of NATO's power has been largely paralysed by the differing interests of the wide range of external actors involved in the tragedy. The time and operational limits under which the NATO implementation force (IFOR) had to operate in Bosnia in 1996–1997, as well as the political and territorial characteristics of the Dayton Agreement which the NATO force was supporting, clearly illustrate the high degree of compromise within NATO and between NATO and other states before the force could be deployed.

NATO's search for a mission outside collective defence has had a deleterious effect on trans-Atlantic relations within the Alliance. Some slackening of cohesion was to be expected in the absence of the Soviet threat. The gradual reduction of American troop levels in West Europe by over 60 per cent during the 1990s is a clear physical manifestation of changing circumstances. But differences of strategic opinion within the Alliance during 1992 and 1993 over NATO's relationship with non-Soviet former Warsaw Pact states gave notice of deeper fissures. Generally, in 1993 and most of 1994, continental West European NATO members, especially Germany, were more enthusiastic about incorporating East European states into Western security structures than the United States. Washington gave priority to its so-called 'strategic partnership' with Russia, and did not wish to sour US–Russian relations by pushing NATO borders as far as Poland's easternmost border.

In November 1994 NATO cohesion took a direct hit when the United States decided unilaterally to pull out of the enforcement of the NATO arms embargo on ex-Yugoslavia as it affected Bosnian government forces.[18] This followed a failed attempt at the beginning of the month to persuade the UN to lift its arms embargo against the Bosnian Muslims. This American move was blocked by Britain, France and Russia. The unprecedented breaking of ranks with NATO and with the UN, and the American abandonment of the Contact Group's rule of public unity, unleashed deep arguments between Washington and the leading West European NATO powers. It gave strength to the West European lobbies for a distinctive West European, integrative defence organisation free of persuasive American control or influence. This whole episode, and the intra-alliance animosity it engendered, even in Anglo–American relations, did not bode well for NATO's ability to manage future, sensitive conflicts as a cohesive body. Such doubts undermined the credibility of any projected deterrent threat by NATO in out-of-area crises and the effectiveness of the deployment of military forces. This wounding of NATO's credibility in November 1994 was aggravated by the fact that it was the Alliance's patron power and leading member which broke ranks, and attached a higher priority to short-term domestic political pressures inside the American body politic than to longer-term international commitments. The practical implications of the United States' withdrawal of its small contribution to Operation Sharp Guard, the joint NATO–WEU operation that patrolled the Adriatic enforcing the embargo from sea, was limited. Arms were entering Bosnia along a variety of other routes. But the severe jolt delivered to brittle trans-Atlantic political harmony was considerable.

It would appear that the United States was the culprit but it is best to consider this incident not in isolation but as part of a process of widening trans-Atlantic relations. For some years now the United States has seen the West Europeans put the EC requirements ahead of NATO. It was against Washington's pleas and advice that the EC went ahead and recognised the breakaway republics in ex-Yugoslavia, and then insisted it could manage subsequent problems on its own.[19] In the long debate over admitting Turkey, a staunch NATO ally, to the EC or WEU, West European views took little heed of Washington's preferences. Issues of immigration, trade and Greek sensitivities take precedence over wider international security considerations. When, in 1993, the United States Congress cut the Clinton Administration's budget request for NATO from $240 million to $140 million, there was little complaint in the American body politic. At the January 1994 NATO summit President Clinton reaffirmed a commitment to European security and promised to keep about 100 000 troops on the continent. He also proposed the new Combined Joint Task Force (CJTF) as an integral component of NATO's military structure. This will provide for identifiable personnel and equipment, used to working together, to be deployed at short notice to any NATO theatre of operations, and flexible enough to incorporate elements from non-NATO forces. In other words, some NATO members, without American participation, could use NATO structures and forces to fulfil tasks of particular import to them and perhaps also to some non-NATO countries. Clearly, the CJTF device facilitates the United States drifting away from secondary European security problems in the East or the Balkans, and leaving that responsibility to NATO Europe and whichever organisation or countries with which NATO European countries choose to collaborate.[20] This is not to suggest that the United States would hold back in the event of a major, direct threat to continental European security, but it does signal that, post-Cold War, Washington no longer automatically sees it in American strategic interests to have a role in all lesser conflicts and crises.[21]

Anxious about impending obsolescence as a collective defence organisation, NATO rushed into creating the North Atlantic Cooperation Council (NACC) in 1991. Membership includes NATO, former Warsaw Pact non-Soviet states, the Baltic republics and all members of the Commonwealth of Independent States (CIS). Meeting once or twice a year at Foreign Minister or Defence Minister level, the focus of NACC is on cooperation not military integration. The cooperation is at a low, functional level and seems to have a strong civic-education purpose. Topics of cooperation include democratic concepts of civilian–military relations, training and education methods and concepts in the defence field, and key aspects of strategy. Little practical military cooperation takes place. It was never the intention of NATO that much, if any, would occur. NACC performed a 'make work' function for NATO; it gave the impression that NATO was busy and had a distinct view of what its role is in European security. The contrary is the case: NACC was a poor attempt to disguise NATO conundrums about its purpose and role. What NACC did do was to create resentment in liberated East Europe while encouraging aspirations for closer links with NATO. These pressures and expectations, and the sense of incompleteness led to vigorous debate in 1992 and 1993 over formal extension of NATO membership eastwards. The Alliance was split on this issue, with the Clinton Administration at that time reluctant to upset President Yeltsin with whom a 'strategic partnership' was being constructed, while Germany was much less concerned with Russian sensitivities and worked to extend NATO membership to some neighbouring central European states.

The compromise announced at the January 1994 NATO summit was the 'Partnership for Peace'. In practical terms this is an upgraded NACC, with selective technical–military cooperation in areas such as defence planning, budgeting and doctrine development, and occasional, low-level military manoeuvres, but with insignificant resource allocation. Nearly every country in Central and East Europe and most of the former Soviet republics in South and Central Asia, have joined the Partnership for Peace, but the programme does little to allay real security anxieties. Indeed, NATO ambiguity and divisions over criteria for full membership seems to exacerbate insecurities in the East and contribute to further resentment. The intention in June 1994 to accept Russian membership, but with due acknowledgement of Russia's special, Great-Power status, was greeted with dismay rather than celebration in some East European capitals. One fear was that Russia would use its influence within the programme either to inhibit NATO expansion eastwards or to transform the organisation into a vehicle more responsive to Moscow's directions. The sudden Russian walk-out of the Partnership for Peace at the NATO Foreign Ministers summit in Brussels in December 1994 surprised the West, and delayed the endorsement of a complex series of agreements negotiated between NATO and Russian officials over the previous six months until the middle of 1995. NATO action in ex-Yugoslavia and the support of some NATO members for formal extension eastwards were attributed as the causes for the shock.[22] Whatever the causes, NATO's political policies towards the East have caused deep misgivings in Moscow while increasing the security anxieties in other East European capitals. An inherent weakness in the Partnership for Peace initiative is that NATO demonstrates no inclination to intervene in any conflicts east of ex-Yugoslavia. Azerbaijan, Moldova and the Ukraine are just three of the former Soviet republics which are members of Partnership for Peace. Yet there is no possibility of NATO exercising its considerable military muscle in any of the current or possible conflicts involving any of these countries. Although those countries have been accepted into Partnership for Peace, there is no consensus about any NATO role where there is actual war or high tension to the East. However, NATO members are not slow to criticise Russia for its active interventions in the 'near abroad'. Such ambivalent behaviour damages the Alliance's self-esteem and undermines its credibility.

Another region, much closer to the official NATO area, where there are deep instabilities and insecurities is North Africa. Militant and radical Islamic fundamentalist forces are applying great pressure against the secular governments in Algeria and Egypt. In particular, a bloody civil war is underway in Algeria, with at least 40 000 dead in the past four years. NATO Mediterranean members, such as France, Spain and Italy, perceive greater security threats emanating from North Africa than from East Europe.[23] NATO, however, appears largely irrelevant to this threat.[24] In February 1995, under pressure from France, Spain and Italy, NATO opened a 'direct dialogue' at ambassadorial level in a clutch of bilateral meetings with Morocco, Egypt, Tunisia, Mauritania and, at Washington's insistence, Israel. The meetings were low-key and at a political level only. By attracting widespread criticism from the range of North African countries which had been excluded, not least Algeria, the initiative seemed to do more harm than good. Unilaterally, Washington applies pressure on Algiers for political reform, and props up the Egyptian government with massive economic aid. France gives aid to the Algerian military government, and applies pressure on the European Union to redirect aid to the Maghreb from East Europe.[25] NATO is not a leading actor on this particular stage. Another major threat to Western security is the proliferation of weapons of mass destruction, particularly but not exclusively nuclear weapons. This is not a new problem, but one which is exacerbated by the breakdown of the Cold War blocs and the international security regime of that era. The drive against proliferation is being led, almost alone, by the United States. Some of its actions may be conducted under the mantle of the United Nations, but Washington is clearly in the driving seat. Efforts, with varying degrees of success, to inhibit North Korea's nuclear programme, to disarm Iraq of its weapons of mass destruction, to persuade the Ukraine to relinquish its inherited nuclear-weapons status, and to enact a global chemical-weapons treaty are directed from Washington. NATO has no meaningful role in post-Cold War arms control. If the United States cannot or chooses not to do something in arms control, NATO cannot do anything about it. NATO's role is also insignificant when it comes to tackling items on the so-called 'New Agenda' of international security issues. Transnational threats to national wellbeing such as illegal narcotics, other aspects of organised crime, and terrorism in West Europe are viewed as best fought by political, legal and policing methods. Cooperation under European Union auspices is the security route favoured by concerned states. Clearly a military alliance is not seen as the best instrument to achieve many of the objectives discussed above, which tempts the question 'If NATO did not exist, would anyone wish to create it?'[26]

Other secondary security institutions

The Organisation for Security and Cooperation in Europe, with over 50 members, covers an impossibly ambitious geographical area. In recent years there have been conflicts in the trans-Caucasus region and the Balkans over which OSCE had little influence. In its early stages, the war in ex-Yugoslavia was deemed within the remit of what was then CSCE. Unable to act effectively, it tasked the EC to manage the crisis.[27] OSCE has often been mooted as a possible successor to NATO, and a future institution for Europe-wide collective security. The irony is that the CSCE was designed for exactly the opposite. The CSCE came into being in the early 1970s at Soviet insistence and after many years of Soviet pressure for an all-European (preferably without the United States, but that was not to be) security conference. The central Soviet objective was to persuade the European international system to acknowledge, and at best to legitimise, the division of Europe along the borders unilaterally imposed by Soviet military power in 1945.[28] Without the security basket of the Helsinki Final Act of 1975, which delivered to Moscow the minimum of what it required, the CSCE would not have survived. In return for the 'legitimisation' of the East European borders, unilaterally imposed by Stalin in 1945, the Soviet Union agreed to the human rights and the economic and technical cooperation baskets of the Final Act. Contrary to Moscow's expectations and the pessimism of many Western conservatives, these baskets did play a significant role in the ultimate delegitimisation of the Soviet system.

The main achievement of CSCE between Helsinki 1975 and the Paris Summit of 1990 was the Cold War business of arms control. The Conference on Confidence and Security-building Measures and Disarmament in Europe (CDE) Stockholm Treaty of 1986 and the Conventional Forces in Europe (CFE) 1990 agreement were conventional arms-control accords which provided an impetus to the decline of East–West antagonism as well as reflecting changing political circumstances already underway. With the Cold War clearly over, the CSCE Charter of Paris 1990 attempted to set up the CSCE (from December, 1994, OSCE) as a post-Cold War European security actor. A secretariat was put in place in Prague, an electoral-data office in Warsaw and a conflict-resolution office in Vienna. But the scale of OSCE membership means a wide divergence of national interests. The unanimity rule and a 12-month rotating chairmanship make the institution unwieldy and preclude effective action on its core security role. In 1992, in an effort to address these problems,

Germany proposed a CSCE Security Council on the UN model. This proposal received little support, not least from Britain. Few states wished to see the CSCE's real institutional power changed in any way other than marginal. Many have high policy interests in which the intrusions of a Pan-European security organisation would not be welcome; for instance, Russia in its relations with some former Soviet republics, and Britain with its Irish problems. So, while the Helsinki Agreement of July 1992 allows the OSCE to cooperate with the UN, and to call upon NATO or the WEU to provide troops for peacekeeping, the document clearly prohibits 'enforcement action'. Any proposed peacekeeping operations may only go ahead given the unanimous support of all the Foreign Ministers and of 'all parties concerned',[29] and if NATO and WEU then agree how best to fulfil the task.

The West European Union arose from the ashes of the Pleven Plan and the European Defence Community – failed attempts at West European defence integration even in one of the darkest periods of the Cold War. The WEU was created to control German rearmament and to reassure West Germany's uneasy NATO European partners that, barely ten years after the Second World War, a re-armed Germany could be securely managed.[30] The WEU was not conceived as an embryonic replacement for NATO. It only emerged in that prospective role in the latter days of the Cold War, when it had been revived from 30 years of inaction to be a vehicle for West European defence cooperation in the light of burden-sharing and arms-control tensions between NATO, Europe and the United States in the period 1983–1987.[31] In some European political quarters, though not in the Conservative government in London, the WEU is viewed as a partner and, in the longer-term, potential successor to NATO,[32] and as a mechanism through which the European Union (EU) could acquire a defence function. There is clearly disagreement between and within West European governments on this issue. And there is hostility in Washington to any serious challenge posed by the WEU to the basic integrity of the trans-Atlantic defence relationship. The Maastricht Treaty does propose a more concrete role for the WEU as a defence agency working alongside the EU, perhaps leading to absorption by the European Union. If this does come to pass at the 1996/97 EU Inter-Governmental Conference, despite considerable opposition and the problems of asymmetrical membership of the EU and the WEU, the WEU would cease to exist and defence would become subject to the political vagaries of the new European Union. If not, then the WEU would continue in a kind of 'no-man's-land', as a vehicle for some West European defence discussion and organisation, perhaps under Combined Joint Task Force (CJTF) auspices, but without the political heritage, institutional clout and strong integrated military structure of NATO.

To date the EC, now the EU, has had one broad political security role – entangling and incorporating German power-potential into an integrative West European framework. The Maastricht Treaty continues that objective which began with the European Coal and Steel Community and carried on via the Treaty of Rome and the Single European Act. But the EU has no official defence or security functions and under Maastricht any future security role is semi-detached and disputatious. For instance, the French Socialist government insisted that the Maastricht arrangements mean the WEU is subordinate to the European Union. The British government argues that the wording means it is not. In the treaty the European Union is empowered to *request* the WEU to 'elaborate and implement decisions and activities of the Union which have defence implications'.[33] France wanted *instruct* rather than *request*, but British insistence won that particular battle. France is getting a review of European Union defence arrangements in 1996/97, but Britain got the treaty to say that any arrangements should be compatible with NATO.

The EU is essentially an economic and social organisation, with a poor record of cohesion on foreign policy matters of a security nature. In many ways the war in ex-Yugoslavia has been a litmus test of EU security competence. In June 1991 Jacques Poos, Chairman of the EC Foreign Ministers, declared 'if there is any problem Europe can solve, it is Yugoslavia'.[34] The sense in the EC was that if the EC was capable of dealing with an external security crisis, then one directly in the backyard of the new Europe could not be more opportune. Yugoslavia was in receipt of considerable EC aid and the EC was a major trading partner. If military force was required to back up EC mediation, then NATO military forces in Italy and on the Mediterranean would be readily available. Delay, uncertainty and prevarication saw the EC obliged to turn to the UN, and hand prime responsibility for any initiative to tackle the escalating crisis to the old patron power, the United States. This abdication of Europe's opportunity and responsibility, in its own sphere of influence, does not bode well for a cohesive EU security policy over issues of a less vital character.[35]

The conflict in ex-Yugoslavia has entangled the United Nations in a war on the European mainland for the first time in its history. Throughout the Cold War Europe was a 'no-go' area for UN peacekeeping activities. But now that the ideological obstacles of the Cold War are removed, does the UN provide a structure conducive to European security? If the harmonisation of national objectives and defence policies are deemed desirable, then a universalist organisation is an even less suitable vehicle for European security than the OSCE. Regardless of its title, the primary function of the UN is not to unite states, but to provide security and peace for a system of sovereign states.[36] If the dilution or removal of sovereignty was the purpose of the UN, then states would not join, especially younger states jealous of new-found freedom. Article 1 of the UN Charter makes it abundantly clear that the peace and security sought is among states. Article 2 (7) reinforces the concept of national sovereignty: 'Nothing contained in the present Charter shall authorise the United Nations to intervene in matters which are essentially within the domestic jurisdiction of any states or shall require the members to submit such matters to settlement under the present Charter; but this principle shall not prejudice the application of enforcement measures under Chapter VII.' This proviso at the end of Article 2 (7) is largely redundant because in practice the rare times Chapter VII is utilised is when peace is threatened or broken between states, not within states. Although, how to define the threat or breach of the peace – as an international or domestic concern – does reside with the sovereign states which make up the Security Council.[37] As the history of the Cold War amply demonstrates, the UN Security Council is governed by the perceived interests of the Member States, especially the veto-wielding permanent members. The ideological confrontation of the Cold War sharply distinguished the interests of the Great Powers and their respective blocs. But the end of the Cold War does not mean the end of competitive national interest. It just means that national interests are sometimes less distinctive and predictable and more flexible. The global remit of the UN further disqualifies it from serious consideration as a vehicle for European security. The complexities and sensitivities of UN behaviour in the extra-European world do not lend themselves to European harmony and cooperation. Nor does any assessment of the UN track-record and capabilities.

The UN has become much busier on the world stage in recent years as the Cold War spluttered to an end and sprouted numerous, messy local conflicts previously held in check by East–West competition. The Gulf War experience produced unrealistic high hopes for a liberated UN which, as the organisation is no more than the sum of its parts, it has been unable to fulfil. The UN is poorly funded and many states have the habit of falling behind with contributions. According to UN figures in October 1995 Russia owed $20 million, South Africa $61 million, Brazil $26 million, Argentina $5.2 million, China $4.8 million, the Ukraine $52 million and the United States $527 million. These figures comprise only some of the debts, and the constant financial uncertainty inhibits UN performance. But the UN's reputation for poor management of its resources does not provide confidence to Member States to make large contributions.[38] Yet the UN is going through a 'peacekeeping' explosion, with over 60 000 UN personnel in the field at a cost of over $3 billion a year. In November 1991, when Boutros Boutros-Ghali assumed the Secretary-Generalship the UN peacekeeping budget totalled only $700 million and used only about 20 000 field personnel.[39] The Secretary-General's 'Agenda for Peace' proposals of June 1992 were designed to bolster the UN for its burgeoning global-order role. Boutros-Ghali called for UN reserve forces trained beyond peacekeeping and with a command structure answerable to the UN; a regularised system of financial payments from Member States; and a broader political mandate facilitating a legitimate, proactive UN role in military, human rights and humanitarian crises.[40] Many years on, these proposals have come to nothing. The UN actions in Somalia and ex-Yugoslavia may be seen to reflect elements of 'Agenda for Peace', but the UN membership is most reluctant to contemplate any formalisation of the 1992 proposals. All members are reluctant to provide more monies, and the states which provide military forces cannot agree on any practical mechanism for a standing UN military force. Naturally, the final proposal for a broader political mandate strikes at the very core of the notion of sovereign statehood. *Ad hoc* decision-making for UN intervention in Somalia, ex-Yugoslavia, or parts of Iraq for humanitarian reasons seem to be as far as UN members are prepared to go on the issue of a broader political mandate.

Meanwhile the UN attempts to struggle with a rash of conflicts and crises.[41] In Angola about 100 troops struggle to broker a ceasefire in the revived civil war following the 1992 elections. Totally inadequate to the task, the UN force costs about $26 million a year. In El Salvador 34 UN personnel, at a cost of $29 million, are overseeing a fragile peace process after a 12-year civil war. In the Middle East, from the Iraq–Kuwait border to South Lebanon, on the Golan Heights, and in Cyprus, nearly 9000 UN peacekeepers are busy trying to police the respective conflicts at an annual total cost of over $300 million. About 300 UN peacekeepers are supervising the delicate ceasefire between Morocco and the Polisario Front in the disputed Western Sahara at an annual cost of $41 million. Since 1949 UN peacekeepers have been in Kashmir monitoring the Indian–Pakistani ceasefire. Currently there are 39 troops in the area, at an annual cost of $7 million. And in ex-

Yugoslavia, prior to the Dayton Agreement, more than 39 000 UN personnel, at an annual cost of over $1.6 billion, struggled with a variety of tasks. In Bosnia their role was to safeguard the humanitarian supply routes and protect Muslims in a few UN-declared 'safe-zones', including Sarajevo. In Macedonia there is a force of 600 to inhibit conflict and deter Serb encroachment. So far, the UN force in Macedonia has prevented conflict, but elsewhere the record is disappointing. In Bosnia, Serb and Croat advances and ethnic cleansing were not prevented and, until late 1995, Sarajevo suffered under periodic bombardment. Large supplies of UN and other humanitarian aid did reach desperate people, but about 40 per cent of it is reckoned to have ended up in the hands of the rival local armies. A UN arms embargo, in force since the early days of the conflict, met with varying degrees of success. Clearly arms, ammunition and even personnel evaded the embargo and reached all sides.[42]

The record of the UN as a global international organisation pursuing global order is patchy and hardly encouraging. In the Cold War, ideological conflict was the explanation for an ineffective UN. That characteristic of global competition is all but gone, but the new conflict environment is even more problematic. The ethnic rivalries, civil wars and low-intensity conflicts which plague the contemporary international system are not conducive to resolution by large, sophisticated modern armies on the model of the UN-authorised coalition forces in the Gulf in 1990–1991. The conflicts in Bosnia, Angola and Somalia often have many frontlines, which change frequently, or have no frontline at all. Of the 11 UN operations started since January 1992, nine have been concerned with domestic conflicts and only two with traditional interstate conflict. Distinguishing combatants from non-combatants may be virtually impossible in such situations, as may be establishing with whom to finalise a realistic peace settlement – assuming that the belligerents want the quarrels resolved. Planning and coordinating multinational forces is a testing task at the best of times. Among others, the Somali and Bosnian experiences have clearly demonstrated the UN's inexperience and lack of expertise.[43] Yet, given its founding objectives and the requirement to sustain and nurture its credibility as the institution devoted to global order, the UN cannot resist entanglement in problems regardless of the prospect of success or the absence of a realistic local political objective.

It has been suggested that the post-Cold War world now finds itself in an 'imperial situation but without imperialists'.[44] There is barely a continent where the breakdown of the Cold War international security regime has not created corners prone to civil war, ethnic conflict and interstate war. But, selective Russian revanchism aside, major powers are not persuaded that it is in their national interest to bear unilateral responsibility for good government and order in these troubled areas. In the absence of willing imperial powers the model being tested in ex-Yugoslavia is of a UN delegation of peacekeeping, peacemaking and humanitarian tasks to established regional international organisations. To date, the effectiveness of this strategy in the Balkans is highly questionable. Regional international organisations may be as susceptible to disharmony among members as the UN, and if countries are unwilling to risk lives and treasure for UN purposes they may be equally cautious over crises in their regions but perhaps distant from their own borders. The clutch of organisations within certain regions may create problems of institutional rivalry and ambiguity of jurisdiction. Europe provides the best contemporary illustration of such difficulties.

Prescription

NATO's primary achievement since the Rome Summit of 1991 has been its own survival as an institution despite the absence of a clear common purpose and despite limited success in pursuit of ambiguous and nebulous objectives. On the assumption that the Cold War by-products of NATO's experience discussed earlier remain of value, what course should NATO now follow to survive and to contribute to European security in the medium-term?

If NATO was to collapse in rancour, then many supportive elements to North Atlantic and West European security would be lost, along with the pressure points of disagreement. If for no other reason, the prospect of a return to something resembling the characteristics of international security in the NATO area in the half century before the Alliance argues for a NATO salvage operation.[45] The present NATO area is a 'peace zone'. This alone is to be valued and should be given very high priority. NATO expansion to the German–Polish border following German unification was enough of a challenge to the balance of internal alliance structures for the foreseeable future.[46] Members should look more to alliance solidarity and cohesion rather than seeking new members. The argument that NATO needs to enlarge formal membership to survive can and should be rebutted. External threats to the NATO 'peace zone' do exist.[47] The prospect of a militaristic, authoritarian, resurgent Russia is low, but Russian behaviour in 1994 and 1995 did provide some evidence that this prospect is now marginally increased in contrast to the clear decline in the years 1990–1993. The probability of more wars in East and Southeast Europe, which could involve a clash of NATO and Russian interests, is higher than in recent years. While within the NATO area conflict between major alliance members is highly improbable, NATO's management of intra-alliance rivalries such as between Greece and Turkey should not be neglected. With no current major threat to compel high activity, NATO will have to be content to operate at a lower gear and with a reduced budget. Institutional and bureaucratic impulses work against such retrenchment and consolidation, but political leaders must put Alliance cohesion first, and not allow countries like Turkey to drift away. Low-level, unobtrusive, cost-effective collective defence for NATO's 16 members is a proper, post-Cold War core objective. A sustained American commitment is essential for NATO cohesion. Addressing Washington's wider, trans-Atlantic security interests outside the NATO area should be another priority for NATO. This must be placed ahead of formal enlargement into a, by and large, quiescient East Europe. If NATO is seen to be relevant to American transatlantic security interests outside continental Europe, sceptical American opinion about NATO's value will be better countered than by offering membership of the Alliance to Poland.

One function where activity is proceeding with benefit to NATO in-area is the build-up of a coherent, cooperative West European defence pillar. Up until the Clinton presidency a distinct West European defence identity was feared as a challenge to the integrity of the trans-Atlantic link. Too little West European defence effort was seen as disaffecting Washington, but too much was seen as posing a challenge to American leadership and tempting American military withdrawal. While France was enthusiastic about diminishing the importance of NATO and elevating

West European defence cooperation, Britain and normally Germany were determined to sustain the pre-eminence of the Atlantic link in West European security arrangements. But now, since the Bush Administration, Washington has developed a different world view. This is to be found in both the Democratic Administration and elements of the Republican Congress. With the Cold War over and the absence of a clear, major military threat to West European security, the United States now expects West Europe to manage middle-level or minor security issues in its own continent without the habitual recourse to American military power. American policy-makers look to a European Union with aggregate population and GNP larger than the United States, and expect West Europe to bear more of a reduced security burden. Indeed, United States support for a coherent trans-Atlantic security relationship is based, to a large extent, on West Europe seriously creating a form of common defence identity. Since its revival in the mid-1980s, the formerly moribund West European Union presents itself as the obvious candidate for the vehicle for this defence identity – and is recognised as such in the Maastricht Treaty. Given the traumas of West–West relations in the final quarter of 1994, even Britain is evincing greater enthusiasm for a collective but cooperative European defence identity, including more intimate bilateral collaboration with France.[48]

West European will to galvanise defence cooperation was given a dramatic impulse by American behaviour over Bosnia in November 1994. However, at the January 1994 NATO summit in Brussels, President Clinton made clear his endorsement of a common European defence. The emphasis given to Europe's role in defence in the joint declaration issued at the end of the Summit was unprecedented. Within 26 paragraphs 'European security and defence identity' was mentioned seven times, 'European pillar of the alliance' five times and the WEU eight times. The new concept of the CJTF was created to link the WEU and NATO. It included France, and its flexibility will allow the WEU to deploy task forces where NATO, essentially the United States, does not wish to take part.[49] NATO Council must agree to such activities, so obviously CJTF could not deploy under WEU direction if Washington was set against it. Also, some quid pro quo arrangements, for instance, over American use of NATO structures for unilateral out-of-area operations, may be expected.[50] But the overall message of how Washington viewed part of NATO's future was clear, and this view is likely to survive into the following administration whatever its political complexion. It behoves the West European members of NATO to heed the message and cooperate closely and quickly on defence, not least in establishing a common West European strategic perspective.[51]

It is vital for NATO's future, as a low key, twin-pillar alliance, to eschew the temptations of collective security. It is to be hoped that Russia's prevarication over the 'Partnership for Peace' arrangements will induce caution in the lobby pushing for NATO's eastward expansion, rather than inculcate a mood of opportunism. With or without Russia, a NATO of 20 or 25 members would move from a collective defence alliance to a collective security organisation. If it is without Russia, then the weaknesses of collective security are compounded by having a paranoid, sullen and resentful Russia outside the system. How credible any American nuclear guarantee would be to Member States on the easternmost periphery of the system, contiguous with Russia or the CIS, is a debatable question. If those who wish to involve Russia in a European security system via an institutionalised OSCE of over 50 Member States, of which NATO becomes a mere agency, eventually succeed, then NATO's utility as an instrument of the current North Atlantic powers is blunted. Either way, collective defence is abandoned and collective security takes its place. The NATO which survived would be a shadow of its former self. In efforts to justify itself for the years ahead NATO would be 'committing suicide for fear of dying'.[52] NATO's experience in ex-Yugoslavia should stand as stark warning. Acting as an agent of the United Nations, it placed itself effectively in a collective security system. Without concrete common interests and perceptions among the great powers in the UN, NATO was unable to implement meaningful military action to stop the war and return political arrangements to something close to those of 1992. In a collective security system, everyone is notionally allied with everybody but no one is definitely allied with anybody. The requirement for near-unanimity normally eliminates the prospect for rapid, effective action. Real power lies with the biggest members of the system, who will exploit, manipulate or even discard the instruments of the system as and when it suits their own interests. It is unrealistic to expect international security cooperation to be based on goodwill. The history of the modern state system, not least in Europe in the twentieth century, demonstrates that fundamental, common strategic interests are required as the basis for effective international security cooperation. The December 1994 Budapest CSCE meeting aptly demonstrated this immutable reality. The 52-nation conference, at Heads of Government level, collapsed in disarray after almost two days. It failed to agree a declaration on the war in Bosnia, to overcome the procedural difficulties in dispatching a peacekeeping force to Ngorno-Karabakh, or to settle the general question of the role of Russian troops in former Soviet republics. The only substantive result of the largest gathering of world leaders in Europe was to rename CSCE as OSCE (Organisation for Security and Cooperation in Europe).[53]

In and around Europe an uncertain period lies ahead. Currently, it is much more difficult to foresee the condition of European security five or ten years ahead than it was in 1970 or 1980. Yet the great strategic issues which are central to European security and will influence the whole continent are taking a back seat while the peripheral debris of the collapse of the Cold War system drive strategic debate and analysis. The painful tragedy of ex-Yugoslavia illustrated important dilemmas and quandaries about UN peacekeeping, ethnic conflict, refugee management, sanction organisation and the provision of humanitarian aid in a hostile environment. But most important of all the Balkan imbroglio illustrated the key players in European security, and the costs – actual and potential – of ambiguous and opaque appreciation of the interests of the major powers. Serbia and its ex-Yugoslav neighbours constitute a subregion which is not of the critical strategic and political importance it was deemed to be in 1914. However, other parts of Central and East Europe, such as the Baltic republics, Poland, the Ukraine and Turkey, are perceived to be of critical importance. Misappreciation of Great Power interests and misapplication of power in such arenas could have consequences of greater danger for European security than those manifest in the political ruins of Yugoslavia.

Notes

1. For analyses of the development and character of the Cold War, bipolar, European security system, see Robert Hunter, *Security in Europe* (London: Elek, 1972); A. W. DePorte, *Europe between the Superpowers* (New Haven: Yale University Press, 1979); and James H. Wyllie, *European Security in the Nuclear Age* (Oxford: Blackwell, 1986).

2. For instance, see Richard H. Ullman, *Securing Europe* (Princeton: Princeton University Press, 1991); Gregory F. Treverton (Ed.) *The Shape of the New Europe* (New York: Council on Foreign Relations Press, 1992); and 'It can't be done alone', *Economist*, 25 February 1995, pp. 21–5.

3. See William Rees-Mogg, 'Disarming while anarchy spreads', *Times*, 7 February 1994, p. 18; and William Pfaff, 'Back to history as usual, which means genuine complexity', *International Herald Tribune*, 7 July 1994, p. 6.

4. William Pfaff, 'There is no world community', *International Herald Tribune*, 22 April 1994, p. 5.

5. See Henry Kissinger, *Diplomacy* (London: Simon & Schuster, 1994), pp. 820–2.

6. Pfaff, 'Back to history as usual', *International Herald Tribune*, 7 July 1994, p. 6.

7. See Robert Osgood, *NATO, The Entangling Alliance* (Chicago: University of Chicago Press, 1962), pp. 45–8.

8. See Jonathan Clarke, 'Replacing NATO', *Foreign Policy 93* (Winter 1993–1994) p. 23; and Trevor Taylor, 'West European security and defence cooperation: Maastricht and beyond', *International Affairs*, Vol. 70, No. 1, January 1994, pp. 37–8.

9. See Gerhard Wettig, 'Moscow's perception of NATO's role', *Aussenpolitik*, Vol. 40, No. 2, 1994, pp. 132–3.

10. See *The Alliance's STRATEGIC CONCEPT* (Brussels: NATO Office of Information and Press, 1991), p. 5, para. 16.

11. *Ibid.*, pp. 4–5, paras 8 and 12.

12. *Ibid.*, p. 5, paras 13 and 14.

13. *Rome Declaration on Peace and Cooperation*, Press Communiqué S-1(91), NATO Press Service, 8 November 1991, p. 1, para. 3.

14. See *The Alliance's STRATEGIC CONCEPT*, p. 7, para. 25.

15. *Rome Declaration on Peace and Cooperation*, p. 1, para. 2.

16. *Ibid.*, para. 4.

17. Illustration of the debate over NATO's relationship to the United Nations in Bosnia is the leading article 'UN irresolution', *Times*, 1 November 1994, p. 19, and the robust letter in response from Lt General Sir Michael Rose, 'Prime mission of UN in Bosnia', *Times*, 2 November 1994, p. 19.

18. See 'Patching up NATO', *Economist*, 19 November 1994, p. 18; and George Brock, 'Clinton's contempt for NATO', *Times*, 12 November 1994, p. 18.

19. See Mark Almond, 'The grand abdication', *Wall Street Journal Europe*, 27 April 1993, p. 6.

20. See Ian Davidson, 'Alive but ailing', *Financial Times*, 12 January 1994, p. 24.

21. See Mathias Jopp, *The Strategic Implications of European Integration* (London: International Institute for Strategic Studies, 1994), Adelphi Paper 290, p. 37.

22. See Mark Frankland, 'Russian rogue elephant slips into NATO camp', *Observer*, 26 June 1994, p. 16; and Richard Beeston and George Brock, 'Snub by Kozyrev to Christopher widens rift with West', *Times*, 3 December 1994, p. 15.

23. See M. Blunden, 'Insecurity in Europe's southern flank', *Survival*, Vol. 36, No. 2, Summer 1994; and Shada Islam, 'Security and Stability', *Middle East International*, No. 490, 16 December 1994, p. 12.

24. See Blunden, *ibid.*, p. 139.

25. See 'Something new out of Africa', *Economist*, 16 July 1994, pp. 31–2; and 'Mediterranean Blues', *Economist*, 14 January 1995, p. 15.

26. See Jonathan Clarke, 'Replacing NATO', *Foreign Policy 93* (Winter 1993–1994) p. 23.

27. See Hella Pick, 'Security conference fails to live up to promise', *Guardian*, 11 September 1991, p. 8.
28. See James H. Wyllie, *European Security in the Nuclear Age* (Oxford: Blackwell, 1986) pp. 127–9.
29. See John Borawski and Macha Khmelevskasa, 'The CSCE Helsinki Summit: New directions for Euro-Atlantic security', *European Security*, Vol. 1, No. 3, Autumn 1992, p. 256.
30. See D. W. Urwin, *Western Europe Since 1945* (London: Longman, 1972), pp. 184–8.
31. See Ian Gambles, *Prospects for West European Security Cooperation* (London: IISS, 1989), Adelphi Paper 244, p. 29.
32. See Amand Menon, Anthony Forster and William Wallace, 'A common European defence?', *Survival*, Vol. 34, No. 3, Autumn 1992, p. 105 and p. 111.
33. See Article J.4.2, *Treaty on European Union* (Brussels: European Communities, 1992) cited in *ibid.*, p. 113.
34. Quoted in Mark Almond, 'The grand abdication', *Wall Street Journal Europe*, 27 April 1993, p 6, which provides a robust critique of the EC role in the Yugoslav tragedy.
35. For an appraisal of EU difficulties in constructing and implementing a coherent, common foreign policy, see William Pfaff, 'Nations can resolve to act, but Europe isn't a nation', *International Herald Tribune*, 10 February 1994, p. 6; and Charles Goldsmith, 'EU's struggle to form foreign policy shows scant sign of abating', *Wall Street Journal Europe*, 22 February 1994, p. 1.
36. See Michael Akehurst, *A Modern Introduction to International Law* (London: Routledge, 6th Edn, 1987), pp. 206–7.
37. *Ibid.*, p. 219. For a lucid analysis of the obstacles inhibiting UN collective use of force, see Anthony Clark Arend and Robert J. Beck, *International Law and the Use of Force* (London: Routledge, 1993), pp. 56–60.
38. See Anne Applebaum, 'Is the UN really necessary?', *Spectator*, 31 July 1993.
39. See Richard Staar, 'UN peacekeeping costs are exploding', *Wall Street Journal Europe*, 22 December 1993, p. 6.
40. See Adam Roberts, 'The United Nations and international security', *Survival*, Vol. 35, No. 2, Summer 1993, pp. 3–30, for a detailed critique of 'Agenda for Peace'.
41. See 'Can peacekeeping survive?', *Economist*, 11 February 1995, p. 65.
42. See Paul Beaver, 'Behind the Bosnian army's new strength', *Wall Street Journal Europe*, 27 January 1994, p. 8; and John Pomfret and David Ottoway, 'Balkan arms smuggling: Wider than US acknowledged', *International Herald Tribune*, 13 May 1996, p. 1.
43. 'UN accused of deploying excessive force in Somalia', *Guardian*, 18 June 1993, p. 24; and Mark Huband, 'Operation disaster born out of a lie', *Observer*, 12 December 1993, p. 16.
44. Adam Roberts, 'Grim reality after an optimistic era', *Independent*, 16 July 1993, p. 21.
45. The flavour of these anxieties can be discerned from John J. Mearsheimer, 'Back to the future', *International Security*, Vol. 15, No. 1, Summer 1990.
46. See Lothar Ruehl, 'European security and NATO's eastward expansion', *Aussenpolitik*, Vol. 45, No. 2, 1994, p. 118.
47. See Charles Glaser, 'Why NATO is still best: Future security arrangements for Europe', *International Security*, Vol. 18, No. 1, Summer 1993, pp. 5–6.
48. See Andrew Marshall, 'WEU urged to form NATO pillar', *Independent*, 28 October 1994, p. 14; 'WEU seeks to enlarge its defence role', *Independent*, 16 November 1994, p. 13; and Douglas Hurd, 'Old foes but new friends', *Times*, 28 October 1994, p. 20.
49. See David White, 'Europe undergoes change in defence identity', *Financial Times*, 12 January 1994, p. 2.
50. See Mathias Jopp, *The Strategic Implications of European Integration* (London: International Institute for Strategic Studies, 1994) Adelphi Paper 290, p. 38.
51. See Trevor Taylor, 'West European security and defence cooperation: Maastricht and beyond', *International Affairs*, Vol. 70, No. 1, January 1994, pp. 9–10.

52.   See Gerhard Wettig, 'Moscow's perception of NATO's role', *Aussenpolitik*, Vol. 40, No. 2, 1994, p. 132.
53.   See Michael Binyon, 'Summit ends in fiasco over failure to find deal on Bosnia', *Times*, 7 December 1994, p. 1.

Chapter 3

Germany: Agent for Security or Insecurity?

Modern Germany conveys a benign image to much of the international system. To the world at large contemporary Germany, unified since 1990, has the image of a pacific, anti-militaristic, 'civilianised' state, more intent on economic achievement and domestic political harmony than the ruthless, determined pursuit of foreign policy objectives. The concept of 'civilian power' has been popular with the German body politic for decades as, from 1949, the Federal Republic of Germany (FRG) struggled to rehabilitate German status from its recent, terrible past and to persuade the wider world that a future, unified Germany would not necessarily pose the same kind of threat to European and world security as Germany had done in 1914 and 1939.[1] From 1949 there has been general consensus, to a greater or lesser degree, that non-military means should take priority as instruments to pursue limited German foreign policy objectives.

Military power is viewed as a last-resort instrument, to be used only for the protection of the homeland or to protect NATO allies who were committed to extending security to the FRG. Throughout the 1950s the SPD, the major opposition party at that time, even opposed membership of NATO, albeit a defensive alliance, and did not endorse FRG NATO membership until the 1960s. But ever since then, the character of the defence provided by NATO has been a persistent theme running through German domestic politics. The strategies of NATO, nuclear and conventional, the types of nuclear weapons deployed, the FRG's role in NATO, and NATO's out-of-area aspirations have been the kinds of issues which have often provoked national debates over many decades, and which have been crucial issues in some general elections. Nonetheless, it has been generally accepted that military power, except in the most extreme of situations, should take a distinct second place to diplomacy within multilateral institutions. Membership of the Council of Europe, NATO, the WEU, the EC (now EU), the UN, the CSCE (now OSCE) and many other international organisations was and is deeply valued. These institutions provide the vehicles for the quiet, diplomatic pursuit of German objectives. The term 'national interest' is rarely used as it projects the wrong image for a Germany which claims to be intent on accommodating German interests with those of its regional neighbours.

Throughout the Cold War the FRG never spent more than 3 per cent of GDP on defence.[2] Fellow NATO members such as the United States and Britain sometimes found themselves spending more than twice the proportion of GDP on defence as that spent by the FRG. Under the protection of the United States and NATO, and constrained in foreign policy choices by Cold War circumstances, the FRG prospered and nurtured its vision of how a modern European state ought to behave. Successive governments, conservative and social democratic, projected the model of the FRG as a democratic, commercial, non-threatening republic, with the objectives of trade and prosperity rather than territorial expansion and hegemonic political influence. Up until the early 1970s, West Europe and the North Atlantic region was the arena in which the German model was displayed. Following the Ostpolitik of Willy Brandt between 1970 and 1974, the non-threatening, beneficent, 'civilianised' image of Germany, underpinned by economic influence, was exported beyond the Iron Curtain to the Warsaw Pact countries.[3] The Helsinki Final Act of 1975 and the CSCE process provided a political environment and a multilateral organisation conducive to propagating in the East the image of the FRG generally accepted in the West. Indeed, the political and economic successes of the Brandt Ostpolitik, reinforced by the security provisions created by the CSCE, so transformed the hostile image of the FRG in Eastern eyes that a large part of the legitimacy of the undemocratic, inefficient Communist regimes was undermined. By the 1980s the ordinary people of East Europe no longer viewed West German revanchism as a major security threat, and accepted that Germans did not constitute the same threat to them as they had clearly posed to their grandparents. One redeeming feature of Communist governments for most of the Cold War era was the protection provided against yet another German invasion. As the final decade of the twentieth century approached that was no longer a valid reason for tolerating the corruption and ineptitude of the incumbent regimes.

This benign image of 'civilianised' power associated in Europe with the FRG of 1949–1990 has been translated to the new, unified Germany. As an image which has served Germany well, Chancellor Kohl, his Foreign Ministers and much of the German body politic wished to sustain it regardless of the dramatically different circumstances. Policy-makers are loathe to contemplate any significant change of tack which runs the risk of blowing Germany towards any position resembling its traditional condition in European security. Historically, Germany has been a source of instability in European international relations, either through weakness or strength. The popular, contemporary view is of a strong, unified Germany unable to live in peace with its European neighbours. The most vivid periods of strength were 1890–1918 and 1933–1945. During these periods a united Germany proved too large, powerful and dominant for a stable international system in Europe. The geostrategic position of Germany harnessed it into the heart of Europe where any expression of influence, deliberate or resulting just from its sheer presence, could not but affect its many neighbours. Russia, Britain, the United States and France could expand territorially and project influence to their flanks without challenging the delicate balance of the European state system. David Calleo notes that it is ironic that the one major European state without a significant formal empire should have been seen as abnormally aggressive and ambitious. It was precisely because

European states lived so closely together that the balance of power between them in Europe was deemed so vital. But, as Calleo argues, 'Imperial Germany was not uniquely aggressive, only uniquely inconvenient.'[4]

However, the spasms of German power between 1890 and 1945 ended in disaster for Germany, and there is no wish to pose, or be perceived to pose, challenges to the European international order such as occurred in the first half of the twentieth century. But, adopting a longer perspective into history, the defining feature of the German experience has been weakness, and the fate of the German people has often been to be the object of great power rivalry. From mediaeval times German lands have been fought over by powers from all over Europe, often with horrendous consequences for the local populations. It was only with the successful assertion of Prussian military power over the old European states in the second half of the nineteenth century that German strength became the problem for European security rather than weakness. Given this political and military heritage it is hardly surprising that the Cold War era should be viewed so favourably by German policy-makers, and that efforts should be made to perpetuate a successful foreign and security policy posture when the end of the Cold War produced a European state system with some characteristics similar to the nineteenth and the early twentieth centuries. German policy-makers have been anxious, since 1990, to avoid a replication of the security concerns felt by Germany's neighbours when it was a unified state between 1870 and 1945. Between 1949 and 1990 Germany was neither too strong nor too weak.[5] Paradoxically the superpower division of Germany and of Europe created the longest period of international stability in central Europe for a very long time.

Transformed geo-strategic conditions

But the reality is that Germany has entered a new era, and the unified country has started from a relatively advantageous position. Unification in 1990 did not create the overt resentments, anxieties and hatreds among Germany's neighbours that was so evident following Bismarck's success more than a century earlier. 'Externally, this unification was achieved by telephone and checkbook rather than blood and iron.'[6] For the first time in the history of the modern German state it has no territorial claims on neighbouring states, nor vice versa. Germany is encircled again, but in contrast to the Kaiser's time it is encircled by friends. To the north, west and south are fellow democracies and fellow members of the European Union, NATO and the WEU. To the east are Poland and the Czech Republic, both democracies and both enthusiastic to join the Western multilateral organisations, membership of which is such a core feature of contemporary German foreign and security policies. In a remarkably short time, Russian power, influence and threat have been expelled far to the east, beyond the Baltic republics, which yearn for a closer economic and political relationship with Germany, and beyond Belarus. The 40-year experiment with democracy in the FRG was an outstanding success. This has been transferred with surprising ease to the old East Germany, which acceded to the FRG rather than create a whole new constitutional arrangement. In 1994, 19 scheduled elections were held throughout Germany, including the national general election in October of that year. There is a robust liberal-democratic consensus running through the German body politic, which has, with relative ease and firmness, consigned racist, extremist politics to the fringes of German political life. Given that East German society had, since 1933, experienced only Nazi totalitarianism followed by Communist dictatorship, the success of its democratic assimilation into the West German brand of politics is remarkable. Economically, unification was very costly to West Germany and caused some dislocation to the whole European economy. But, by the late 1990s, it is clear that the huge subsidies from West to East Germany and the huge investments have largely succeeded. Old East Germany's transport, telecommunications and utilities infrastructure is one of the finest in Europe – and economic growth is correspondingly high. Unified Germany is the world's third strongest economy, and Europe's strongest. As well as being physically placed at the heart of Europe, modern Germany also occupies the moral, political and economic high ground.

For Germany this is a unique and extremely advantageous position; how long it can continue is a question of genuine concern. In the warm afterglow of the end of the Cold War, as Europe readjusts itself to new circumstances and Germany finds its feet, the salient characteristics of the old FRG linger. But the new Germany has the potential to be, or be seen to be, threatening and destabilising. Germany's population of 81 million, dwarfs those of all contiguous countries. If Austria is included, then Germanic-speaking peoples are even more dominant. The German GDP in 1994 was $1,834.9 billion, 19 times greater than that of Poland.[7] The sheer presence of Germany influences surrounding countries, and with the best will in the world Germany cannot avoid a dominant role in Europe. For geo-strategic, economic, historical and political reasons, German policy requires more delicate management than that of other developed, industrial democracies. The point has come when Germany can no longer avoid making crucial choices about post-Cold War foreign and defence policy. These decisions have been put on hold for much of the 1990s. As a consequence the shape of future European security arrangements are very uncertain. More of the same is inadequate for circumstances which are so different from the Cold War years. The new Germany maintains the foreign and security policy of the old FRG, firmly and comfortably locked into the Euro-Atlantic framework. For 40 years the *raison d'être* of NATO and the FRG were the same. The defence of the FRG and the defence of NATO were the same. The inner-German border between West and East Germany was the central front of NATO and the faultline between two ideological blocs. These strategic conditions allowed the FRG to exist 'in a neo-political "cocoon", sheltered from the broader security and geo-political issues dealt with by its major allies'.[8] All that was required of the FRG was to be a willing host for large NATO armies, keep a low and non-controversial political profile and not to appear belligerent. Such behaviour was apt during the Cold War, but today Germany is no longer a front-line beneficiary of multilateral security. With its increased size and capabilities it is now a considerable potential provider of security. There are natural expectations that the largest sovereign country in Europe west of Russia, with the world's third strongest economy, will make some meaningful contribution to the stability and security of the continent from which it draws so much of its prosperity.

The incorporation of East Germany has altered the strategic orientation of Germany. East Europe is of much greater significance to German politics and economics than at any time since 1945. The importance of the West is in relative decline. To Germany the value of security and stability in the East is growing on a daily basis. The tremendous developments in Berlin illustrate this and will accelerate it. The perspectives of familiar multilateral bodies are no longer confined to West European defence or economic integration. These bodies are projecting responsibilities and creating expectations across the whole continent and to the peripheries of neighbouring continents. For Germany to carry on as if nothing had changed stalls the policies of other states and of the multilateral organisations. The vacuum is creating uncertainty, instability and insecurity. The United States continues to play a crucial role in broad questions of peace and war in Europe, but self-evidently the US body politic is no longer prepared to allow its country to shoulder the same degree of burden and responsibility as during the era of the Soviet threat. The new post-Cold War rules require relevant German security objectives and doctrines. During the Cold War Germany was at the edge of the Western world. Now Germany is at the heart of a new Europe where, for the time being, political and economic instruments of influence are in the ascendancy in mainstream international relations. For most states in the East, Germany is the most important neighbour and partner. It is a century since Germany was in a position of such potential strategic influence across the whole of Europe in peacetime. Where Germany decides to put its strategic weight over the next ten years will determine the political shape and security character of Europe for a generation.

For Germany the old constraints are gone. For 40 years it was the classic model of a 'penetrated' state[9] whose foreign policy was not its own. Defeat in the Second World War, great power division, occupation statutes, armament and alliance regulations, four-power control of the capital city, and the locale for the largest concentrations of foreign weaponry and soldiers in history denied the Federal Republic sovereign authority over its foreign and security policies. Now the salient constraints are gone. Only a few residual, redundant ones remain, such as the armament regulations derived from the 1954 London Agreements and Paris Treaties which granted Germany membership of the WEU and NATO. This treaty expires in 1998. Real constraints have gone, but so have the props provided by the FRG's frontline, sharp-edge status in the Cold War. Western concern over the FRG being tempted into a unification deal by Moscow, on Soviet terms, did grant Bonn some leverage over its NATO allies. German sensitivities had always to be borne in mind over NATO's high strategic and political policies. Over highly disputatious issues, West German opinion had to be given due regard. Much of NATO's Cold War history is a record of shaping nuclear and conventional strategy, weapons deployment and arms control to accommodate West German domestic political requirements. From its entry into the Alliance in 1955 until unification, the FRG and NATO had an intricate, symbiotic relationship: each constrained the other and each required the other's support. The disintegration of the Soviet threat and the startling achievement of the old FRG's primary foreign policy objective – unification – have transformed NATO, the FRG and the international security environment in Europe.

German choices cannot be avoided, but since 1990 there have been mixed signals as to which direction the new Germany may take. One problem in discerning the direction of high German security policy is the difficulty in determining German national interest. Running through post-Nazi democratic German politics is a distinct unease and discomfort with the notion of national interest; a feeling that national interest could open the Pandora's box of nationalism. 'Post-national democracy' is a concept which receives support across party lines. It suggests that European union is the proper route for Germany, and that any consideration of separate German national interests is 'suspect, retrograde, even reactionary'.[10] Nonetheless, a debate is beginning and there is some evidence that, in practice, German national interests today are identified and pursued in a manner very different from the Cold War era.[11]

German foreign policy in ex-Yugoslavia yields instances of assertiveness in dealings with fellow European powers. In December 1991, against the better instincts of major EU partners such as Britain and France, Germany pushed for EU recognition of Slovenia and Croatia. Foreign Minister Genscher made it clear that Germany would press ahead without the EC if necessary. In January 1992 the EC fell into line to avoid a major split and to give some substance to the notion of a common EC foreign policy. Germany also played a major role in collaboration with the United States, in spring 1994, in establishing the tenuous federation between Croatia and Bosnia and ending that vicious war. This strategy created a stronger balance against Serb power and led directly, again with American and German assistance, to the Serbian military setbacks in the late summer and autumn of 1995. By and large, during the Balkan tragedy, Germany has kept a low profile, but at vital moments it has chosen to exercise national influence when deemed appropriate. In other EC (later EU) matters in recent years Germany has been determined to achieve its preferences. Admission of Sweden, Finland and Austria into the EU was a distinctly German preference. Doubts by Mediterranean countries, in particular Spain, were robustly squashed by Chancellor Kohl and Foreign Minister Kinkel. Such stubborn determination is evident from other features of German foreign policy in recent years. Germany is one of Iran's largest trading partners, not least in the provision of oil for German industry. Regardless of clear evidence of Iranian sponsorship of international terrorism, of the death threat against the British writer Salman Rushdie, of extensive human rights' abuses inside Iran, of probable Iranian attempts to build weapons of mass destruction, of European Parliament condemnation of the Tehran regime and of an American economic embargo of Iran, Germany persists in a close relationship with the regime. Germany has acted as a major obstacle to concerted EU action against Iran.[12]

That there is such a creature as German national interest was again revealed by the priority given to protecting the Deutschmark over other EU currencies when the economies of West and East Germany were fused. Naturally this put a great strain on the West German economy and finances. Despite the high rhetoric about German and European common interests, the economic regeneration of the East has taken clear priority over the needs of West Europe. Between 1991 and 1995 transfers from West Germany to the East have totalled Deutschmarks 750 billion.[13] Annually, about 40 per cent of eastern Germany's GDP is made up of monetary transfers from the West. To put the scale of such assistance into perspective it is interesting to note that, in the late 1940s, Marshall Plan aid averaged less than 2 per cent of West Germany's annual output. The high interest rate and low inflation fiscal policy of Germany in 1992–1993, pursued to sustain the value of the DM, under strain largely because of huge borrowings to fund economic adaptation in the East, undermined West European currencies; hence the crash of the much-vaunted EMS.[14] In 1993 Germany's public sector borrowing requirement topped DM 230 billion ($135 billion), around 7 per cent of GDP.[15] The European continent-wide recession in the first half of the 1990s owed much to post-unification German fiscal policy and the assertion of German national interest.

National interest is now a feature of German foreign policy, albeit politically incorrect for any German political leader to admit. But that national interest is still mixed in a fudge of attitudes and behaviour inherited from the pre-unification era. The salient, dominant attitude which is inhibiting a new German role in European security is the reluctance to transform defence policy and strategy to meet new needs. Safety first, in the sense of avoiding any accusations of militarism, has been the overriding feature of German security policy. Apart from very basic aims such as territorial protection, the sloganistic objectives of peace and stability within a multilateral framework persist as the official objectives of German defence policy. Distinctive national security needs are an issue high policy-makers prefer to avoid. A dramatic downsizing of the armed forces from 700 000 to 330 000 through the 1990s and the creation of a special crisis reaction corps of 56 000, are technical matters easily managed. The reaction corps is being prepared to operate in unfamiliar terrain, including deserts and mountains and to rely on minimal infrastructure for supplies and reinforcements. Multipurpose, small combat units are to be the cutting edge of the new Germany's military establishment. The strategic criterion, including how such policies address German requirements, are sidestepped and parried with declarations of commitment to multilateralism.

Crucial political questions about where, when and why such forces should or could be used remain unanswered except for reference to UN or NATO missions. What Foreign Minister Kinkel describes as the 'culture of restraint' still pervades German attitudes to the military. Germany has not been a traditional 'exporter of security'.[16] If it was to emulate British and French behaviour and adopt a worldwide role and perspective, it is likely that its close neighbours would feel somewhat uneasy. Some tentative moves have been made to lay the groundwork for a wider role in the future. *The Defence Planning Guidelines of the Bundeswehr* (*1992*) defined a role in conflict and crisis beyond the NATO area. There has been a clutch of high political statements on German willingness to support allies on international security duties. But the kinds of roles and duties are left unspecified. Up until 1994 German politicians could claim legal obstacles to a wider role for the German armed forces as the Basic Law (constitution) could be interpreted to forbid the deployment of German forces for any combat duties other than homeland or NATO area defence. After much political debate and wrangling within and between parties, the issue was finally settled by the Federal Constitutional Court in Karlsruhe in July 1994. It chose to interpret the constitution as allowing the deployment of German forces on authorised UN peacekeeping and peacemaking operations. But rulings of the constitutional court may regulate the law – they do not govern public opinion.

As German politicians are well aware, the vast majority of the German electorate are against any military role perceived to be adventurous and potentially expansive. Because of historical experience the military are not held in high esteem. Some opinion polls reveal that half the country believe military officers are unimportant or even superfluous to the country's needs. As an interest group, the professional officer corps have insignificant influence over national security policy.[17] A measure of public attitudes towards things military is that, in 1991, the year of the Gulf War, conscientious objectors to military service equalled those willing to be drafted. In a 'civilian power', political leaders have to give heed to what the civilian population wants. The German population clearly has little patience with matters military, is not tolerant of high defence expenditure and has little sympathy for German projection of military power far from the homeland.

This deep-seated public mood acts as a tremendous influence on senior policy-makers, inhibiting any inclinations to pursue a security policy more in tune with Germany's economic weight, geo-strategic position and modern political role. Such political leaders, products of their own cultural environment since the Second World War, may well empathise with the public mood and use it as a welcome excuse when pressed by other major powers to do more. The Karlsruhe ruling of July 1994 did remove some of the supposed legal objections to German forces operating out-of-area, but all that has happened is that a set of political criteria has replaced redundant legal excuses. The legal restrictions that remain oblige German forces to be under UN or NATO authority, to be used for peacekeeping or peacemaking and to have the approval of at least two-thirds of the Bundestag.

It is fair comment that the German public have little enthusiasm for the Karlsruhe 1994 decisions. Any enthusiasm is to be found with Germany's allies. Foreign Minister Kinkel is on record as opposing the 'militarisation' of German foreign policy and there are divisions within the government between the foreign ministry and the defence ministry. Nonetheless, in recognition of German domestic realities, Defence Minister Volker Ruhe has outlined five criteria for the use of German forces in the light of the Karlsruhe decision:[18]

1. Limited to Europe and the periphery;
2. No unilateral action. Deployment must be under a UN mandate, and operate only with Allies and friends in the Euro-Atlantic community;
3. In countries occupied by Germany in the Second World War, the Bundeswehr to be deployed only as part of the solution, not before it;
4. Broad, deep public support and a consensus between government and the public, are vital; and
5. A compelling reason must be clear for German involvement, such as a threat to German homeland security or European security.

In reality, restrictive multilaterialism is alive and well in contemporary Germany. Defence Minister Ruhe's rules would prevent German deployment in any repeat of the 1991 Gulf War, or the UN operations in Haiti or Angola. Only in specific circumstances and in Europe could German forces be used under these rules. Such an opportunity did present itself in ex-Yugoslavia in late 1995, when a NATO force of 60 000 was deployed to implement the Dayton (Ohio) peace plan for conflict resolution in the Balkans. As a contribution to the NATO force Germany agreed to send 4000 troops to perform non-combat duties. This unit consisted almost entirely of sappers, engineers and medical personnel, with a few soldiers armed to protect their colleagues. The 4000 included 2000 already linked to UN peacekeeping duties in ex-Yugoslavia. None of the 2000 were combat soldiers on the ground: they were medical personnel, fighter-pilots enforcing the no-fly rules and sailors on a frigate in the Adriatic assisting in policing the arms embargo. Prior to the Dayton peace plan, the limited UN involvement was as far as Chancellor Kohl dare go, after repeated UN requests, in deploying German personnel out-of-area. As contributions to the Dayton plan, Britain will deploy 15 000 ground troops, France about 12 000 and the United States around 20 000 to NATO forces.

Hard strategic choices

Multilateralism is attractive to Germany because, in the Cold War era, it was a policy which kept difficult choices at a great distance and eschewed the necessity to decide national policy. NATO, the WEU and the EC were collective, defensive, international organisations, by and large introspective. But today these organisations have a much more outward-looking, expansive perspective. They have interests in issues as diverse as political and economic reform in Russia, militant Islam in North Africa, civil rights in Turkey and nuclear energy in East Europe. Germany's 'restrictive multilateralism' runs contrary to the whole tenor of NATO in the 1990s and can only detract from the respect given to German civil initiatives in bodies such as the EU for reaching out to the wider world. In the shorter term, restrictive multilateralism in the security arena may work for Germany, but it has created resentment and ridicule among other major powers. It can only be viewed as a temporary, stop-gap security policy which must lead to a clearer, more concrete, security policy posture.

So, looking ahead to the next century, Germany needs to decide on a range of national interests and select foreign and security policy positions to serve these interests. Whatever it chooses will fundamentally affect the European security system, for better or worse, and must be practised with discretion. Ideally, Germany will face up to responsibilities, but not in such a manner that old anxieties are rekindled among neighbours. In a less than ideal world a legitimate debate on national interest ignites old-style German nationalism with all its attendant dangers. Or, more likely, German domestic will proves immutable after generations of indoctrination and German neutralism – 'Switzerlandisation' is a concept increasingly used – is the outcome. This introversion contributes to the steady decline of formal multilateralism in European security and opens a dangerous power vacuum east of Germany.

Five main options are open to Germany, most of which are in contradiction to each other.[19] To date, Germany has kept these options open by fudging policies and dabbling, to a greater or lesser extent, with all the major actors. Perhaps in the medium-term one or two contradictory positions can be juggled together while retaining influence, but to keep all options in the air all the time will prove a difficult act. There is the real danger of Germany ending up friends with no one by trying to be friends with all.[20] If that were to pass, then the 'Switzerlandisation' option would receive a great boost, perhaps by default.

Even closer collaboration with France and a corresponding deepening of West European integration is the clearest option. Up until the mid-1990s the West German heritage of intimate political and economic collaboration with France, rooted in the historic 1963 Franco–German treaty and expressed in the Paris–Bonn axis at the heart of the EC and EU, looked the most likely option. The Eurocorps, with the Franco–German brigade at its heart, could be seen as an embryonic West European army. Unification and the retreat of Soviet power removed much of the strategic and economic rationale for the continuation of this West-Eurocentric policy, but habit, a flow of Europhile rhetoric from German leaders, and reluctance to change a policy which had become a political totem, sustained this posture. The 1992 Maastricht Treaty institutionalised the economic and monetary union objectives and made clear the aspirations towards a common West European foreign and security policy. Incorporating the WEU as a defence agency of the EU is a declaratory objective. Implicit in this relationship, and more explicit since Jacques Chirac assumed the French Presidency in 1995, is the role of French nuclear weapons in protecting Germany – and thereby removing the need for Germany to acquire its own – and possibly the whole EU.

However, by the mid-1990s, the diminishing attractions of this course for Germany, wrought by the consequences of the end of the Cold War, became evident. In the field of defence, grave disparities in attitude, perspective and hard policy cannot be glossed over by high-minded Euro-enthusiastic rhetoric. Harsh realities fly in the face of such idealism. In late 1995, President Chirac temporarily resumed French nuclear testing in the South Pacific in the face of much international condemnation. Paris was grateful that Chancellor Kohl did not explicitly criticise French behaviour, but the general attitude of the German people and most of the body politic was deeply critical. This reminded the world that within Germany there is a very large anti-nuclear element, against not only nuclear testing but also nuclear weapons and the whole concept of nuclear deterrence. France may aspire to provide nuclear security for Germany but many Germans do not want it.[21] The majority of French people are comfortable belonging to a nuclear weapons state; most Germans have no desire to belong to one. Attitudes to conventional military power and its role in the modern world are also widely disparate. French conventional forces are multicapable and designed for a worldwide role, within or outside multilateral organisations. Historically and in contemporary times France has taken pride in its military actions in Africa and Asia. It keeps forces in Africa and the Indian Ocean, frequently intervenes unilaterally in the developing world and, post-Cold War, has been a UN peace-enforcer in the Gulf War and peacekeeper in ex-Yugoslavia. Within the European theatre the French position in NATO – as a leading political member but not part of the integrated military structure – is completely the opposite from that of Germany, whose forces are the most integrated into the NATO structure of any in Europe. Indeed, high German foreign policy faces a severe dilemma over NATO or the EU as the primary West European security body if the Maastricht foreign and security policy ambitions are ever realised. So far, Germany has played down the contradiction between deep loyalty to NATO and support for an EU foreign and security policy function.

France has no problem with this one – a European common foreign and security policy comes first. Unless there is a surprising change of heart in Germany, NATO will come first. France is a military power; Germany is a civilian power. During the Cold War Germany accepted that French military power was used to balance German economic power within West Europe. But with the unique conditions of the Cold War gone, a marriage of the two attitudes, cultures and outlooks on military power in modern Europe and the wider world looks unlikely to succeed, and the engagement grows more fragile. It is not only in the field of international security that Franco–German incompatibility is now manifest. There is a fundamental difference over widening the EU to the East. German official policy is both to deepen EU integration and widen membership at the same time. Germany has obvious economic and political interest in Czech, Polish and Hungarian membership of the EU in the near future. France is unhappy with widening to the East, fearing that the centre of political and economic gravity of the EU will move to Germany. This will undermine the current political balance and draw resources and attention away from the Mediterranean. President Chirac is more of a Euro-pragmatist than his predecessor and is not so wholehearted in pursuit of the Maastricht criteria for economic and monetary union. Indeed, despite Chancellor Kohl's enthusiasm for economic and monetary union, all German opinion polls show a considerable majority in opposition to the abandonment of the DM. The opposition SPD have hinted strongly that the tripartisan consensus in Germany for decades that closer European integration will save Germany from itself and Europe from Germany is open to doubt. The attraction of a common, single European currency is being questioned by senior SPD politicians.[22] There is no longer any certainty that economic and monetary union, with Franco–German economic and monetary union at its core, will ever come to pass. On matters of future political integration France supports members' right of veto while Germany wants to limit veto rights. France will accept more issues for majority voting, but supports a multi-speed EU based on cooperation rather than the German vision of a European federation. Paris supports a strong Council of Ministers and a meaningful role for national parliaments. Bonn's view is that the European Commission and the European Parliament should be strengthened at the expense of national governments.

Other serious issues of divergence include the Schengen Agreement and the notion of a transatlantic free trade zone. To Germany, the Schengen Agreement on the free, unhindered movements of people between Germany, France, the Benelux, (Belgium, The Netherlands and Luxembourg) Portugal and Spain is a practical illustration of European unity as well as a potent symbol. In practice, France continues with border controls, citing problems of Islamic terrorism, drugs smuggling and illegal immigration from East Europe. Conservative objections to the attack on French sovereignty which the Schengen Agreement represents probably plays a major part in French policy. There is also disagreement on the goal of a North American–EU free trade zone. Germany accepts that this is a long-term goal, but French political parties of both the right and the left have no sympathy for opening the whole EU to unbridled American competition.

France and Germany must and will remain close collaborators in security matters and issues of functional European integration, but international conditions are no longer conducive to a reinforcement of common interests. On the contrary, many features of the post-Cold War era exacerbate the differences and make it likely that the Franco–German relationship will not progress to further practical integration. Although Paris will always constitute an important partner for Bonn, a Franco–German bloc will not best serve German interests in the future.

Another option for Germany, regardless of French criticisms, is to push hard for NATO and EU expansion to the East. It is now more important for Germany to stabilise its central European hinterland than to keep EU integration in West Europe. West Europe is stable, democratic and generally prosperous. The extension of Western institutions, foremost NATO and the EU, to Poland, the Czech Republic, Slovakia and Hungary would provide the symbol of belonging to the Western bloc and some practical security and economic advantages. In many ways Germany looks upon the Czech Republic and Slovakia as its 'Mexico', with skilled but cheap labour. But to reap maximum benefit from the liberation of East Europe, political stability is essential. Between 1989 and 1993 Germany has given more government aid – over $25 billion – to Central and East Europe than anyone else. More than half of East European trade with the EU is with Germany and twice as much German private investment is now going to East Europe than to West Europe.[23] The German–Polish border area, where low-cost labour advantage is maximised by Western capital, is one of the most active investment spots in the developed world. Increasingly the Czech Republic is becoming an integral part of the Bavarian and Saxon industrial infrastructure. But not all Germans are delighted. Cheap imports from the east do not please trade unions nor many home based industrialists.

German political and economic activities to the east provoke grave Russian anxieties and also some American concerns. So far, Russia has been more sanguine about extension of the EU into East Europe, but very much against the formal extension of NATO. While less contentious politically, except for France, extension of the EU would be very difficult economically and is very much a long-term matter. Among other things, there is no compatibility between the needs of the Polish and Hungarian agricultural industries and the EU Common Agricultural Policy. For a long time, countries such as Hungary and Poland would be major drains on the EU budget. Russia, with whom Germany wishes to retain good relations, is vehemently opposed to NATO moving east. Former non-Soviet Warsaw Pact states are enthusiastic because, in theory, it brings an American security guarantee which balances both Russian and German power. Many in the United States are unsure about whether NATO's future is as a military alliance or a political club. The credibility of an American security guarantee east of Germany is doubted by many Americans and they feel it would be dangerously misleading to give it. Yet a NATO political club is not why East Europeans want it.

Russia is content with the NATO 'Partnership for Peace' programme, with which is has a special relationship, because the programme is no more than a loose political club. 'Partnership for Peace' does not have the legal or practical attributes of a military alliance and is not meant to be one. Germany's enthusiasm for institutional expansion to the East is a manifestation of the congenital multilateralism which permeates German foreign and security policies. Some East European states may, in the medium-term, become members of NATO and the EU and may also join other asso-ciate organisations, but the accommodation of such members must so change the multilateral organisations that they no longer fulfil the very functions from which new members, and also Germany, hope to benefit. However, an auxilliary benefit of pursuing a widening of the EU in preference to deepening would be to reinforce the so-called 'silent alliance' between Germany and Britain. It is clear that some German interests, such as free trade, are better served by close links with London rather than Paris – though too close a link with London would unsettle the long-standing core relationship between the old continental partners at the heart of the EU.

A major foreign and security policy option for Germany, to which most other options would be subsidiary, is that of a strategic partnership with the United States and a concomitant, wide regional role. Recent history, since 1945, and intimate mil-itary links within the NATO integrated military structure provide some firm founda-tions for such a German choice. Throughout the Cold War the FRG was firmly Atlanticist, supporting the American presence in Europe and keeping French entreaties to relegate NATO at bay. Long-term insurance against Russian resurgence and also the provision of reassurance to German neighbours that American influ-ence would constrain German behaviour, would be real dividends. It was gratifying that President Bush, in contrast to Prime Minister Thatcher and President Mitterand, was an enthusiastic supporter of unification. In 1990 George Bush declared Germany to be a 'partner in leadership' with the United States.[24] Germany is an attractive strategic partner for the United States. It provides a vehicle for American power in the heart of Europe and an excellent base *en route* to the Middle East, where both industrial democracies are heavily dependent on oil supplies. So far, the FRG has shown loyalty to NATO in preference to French attempts to persuade it to back the WEU as a replacement for NATO. In broad ideological terms, there is a common commitment to enlarging democracy. France and Britain, and some other Western countries, also wish to see democracy spread throughout the international sytem, but a certain faith in the healing qualities of democracy for other states is present in the United States and Germany. That faith is somewhat absent in France and Britain, where more sceptical attitudes prevail resulting from the experiences of their past imperial possessions. Modern Germany and the United States are powers who like to think foreign policy should have a heavy portion of principle as well as interests in its character. Defence, democracy and free trade are three principles which could underpin an American–German partnership.

But certain demands would be made of Germany in such a partnership – and not all interests are compatible. The United States would be seeking a partner which would bear a share of the world-order burden. This would require increased German defence spending commensurate with its economic power, an expansive strategic doctrine not locked solely into NATO structures and a global foreign policy per-spective. These changes would require a transformation of German public opinion on its role in Europe and the world, and the means acceptable to fulfil that role. All measures of the mood in the German body politic and public at large remain to the contrary and appear deep-seated. Germany's distinct preference for multilateral diplomacy contrasts with the clear American preference, whatever the rhetoric may be, for bilateral connections. While successive United States administrations have expressed support for the concept of West European integration, the prospect of a German-dominated economic and monetary union and common foreign and security policy in West Europe, with a much-diminished role for national parliaments, is not favoured in Washington. The long-standing American commitment to Germany is not designed to ease German moulding of a new Europe. Nor is it clear that the American military presence will always be welcome in Germany for years to come. There is the neutralist tendency in Germany which would welcome the absence of foreign military forces on German soil. American political opinion usually feels much closer to Britain, or even France, than to Germany. Washington was not impressed by German behaviour during the Gulf War, when there was no military contribution and the government gave official blessing to Willy Brandt's visit to Saddam Hussein. Germany did contribute DM 17 billion ($10.6 billion) to the war effort – equivalent to one-third of its defence budget – but the tenor of German politics throughout the crisis was not helpful. Psychologically, Germany finds it hard to be a junior partner. If it did choose the unlikely route of a world role alongside the United States, then as a consquence of means and geo-strategic position it would have to be an unequal partnership. This could produce deep resentment in Germany and result in the propagation of anti-American attitudes which are latent in German society.[25] One potential clash between senior and junior partners would be over relations with Russia. The United States has a record of suspicion towards German relations with Russia. Washington feels that it can best deal with Moscow and knows what is best for Europe and the rest of the world. Since the time of Willy Brandt's Ostpolitik, and throughout Helmut Schmidt's close relations with Brezhnev and Helmut Kohl's intimate links with Gorbachev and Yeltsin, the United States has harboured anxieties about German–Russian deals over the future of Europe which could leave the United States on the sidelines. During the 2 + 4 negotiations (West Germany, East Germany, the USA, Britain, France and the Soviet Union) over German unification the FRG went to great lengths to satisfy Soviet security concerns, which raised disturbing fears of too close German–Russian relations in the new Europe.

Striking up a close strategic relationship with Russia, the most powerful state in East Europe, is 'the classic Eastern option of German foreign policy'.[26] There are many attractions. Germany could trade its technology and financial strength for access to Russia's abundant raw materials. Russia is Germany's biggest trading partner and German trade exceeds that of Russia's next three biggest trading partners – Italy, China and France – combined. In Russian economic affairs Germany is the leading European actor. Since 1990 American private investment has exceeded German, but in government aid Germany is ahead. Between 1990 and 1993 Germany granted Russia over $50 billion; $9 billion came from the United States and $3 billion from Japan.[27] Between them, Russia and Germany could bring a high degree of security and order to the volatile areas of Central and East Europe. If a viable partnership could be constructed, then one of the great rivalries of Europe, which has brought it much pain, could be transformed into something of benefit to international security.

At first sight, the Moscow option seems a rational route for Germany to take. But for modern, sophisticated, world-trading Germany, Moscow is important but not central to its interests. Russia is no longer on German borders, nor even Polish borders (except for the anomalous, small enclave of Kaliningrad). Russia is further from Germany than the Sahara desert. On the ground, the Russian security threat which has perplexed and obsessed Germany since the two empires were contiguous in the nineteenth century no longer exists. Nonetheless, there is the potential for a German–Russian clash of interests. Moscow clearly expects special influence in the newly independent states in the East and in the old non-Soviet Warsaw Pact countries. German influence, especially economic, is growing by the day in countries such as the Ukraine which are viewed by Moscow as being of vital strategic importance. As Russia recovers, as it intends to, partly helped by close links with Germany, it will vie with its partner for influence in these areas. If it does not recover and remains much the weaker partner, the cultural, historic and political differences between the two different systems will be exacerbated. Assuming such problems could be overcome, a ground-breaking strategic and political marriage with Russia would not only upset the United States, but the rest of Europe would be aghast. Most of East Europe would see their hard-won independence under severe threat from a German–Russian condominium. In West Europe such a German strategic coup would be seen to unhinge completely the subtle political and economic balances which have sustained good Franco–German relations for more than 40 years and maintained harmony throughout West Europe. Politically, Britain would be driven even closer to the United States and West European integration and cooperation would halt in its tracks. Germany's rehabilitation would be severely dented by a strategic venture which, in all probability, would not long survive the inherent political and economic contradictions.

The final major foreign and security policy option and the one which most fits the largely inflexible public mood and dominant political culture over the last 40–50 years, is that of an increasingly neutralist position. External relations will be extensive, but they will be of a 'civilian' nature. Visible and invisible trade, aligned with a high diplomatic profile in selective multilateral organisations, will constitute the salient instruments of high foreign and security policy. The security posture which has served the FRG well for nearly 50 years will, with symbolic adjustments to acknowledge alliance pressures, persist. Any out-of-area contributions to NATO or UN operations will be carefully prescribed and kept to a politically acceptable minimum – just enough to satisfy the immediate demands of allies but not too much to upset political consensus at home. In the medium-term Germany's contribution to international peace and stability in the field of military provision will be far from commensurate with the benefits it enjoys from an international system sustained and protected by American, British and French military power. When required, minimum military contributions, as in ex-Yugoslavia in late 1995, will be accompanied by large financial contributions towards such *ad hoc* operations. But currency alone does not defeat aggressors in battle. There will be a distinct danger that the resentments and frustrations of the major democracies could tarnish German relations with these democracies. This, in turn, could feed latent nationalist sentiment in Germany, either deepening the neutralisation trend towards a replica of Switzerland, or the other way towards a strident, aggressive nationalism. Both carry great dangers for European security. Current trends suggest the former is the more likely course, in tune with the long-term German mood.

Most of the foreign and security policy options discussed above are in stark contradiction to each other. So far, since unification, Germany has pursued elements of each while avoiding firm selection of any. It would be possible, with good diplomacy, to pursue two contradictory paths, but more than two would achieve nothing except to alienate many people. As the post-Cold War order (or disorder) becomes clearer, Germany can no longer avoid some distinct choices. The current prevarication is understandable. On trade matters Germany is caught between Washington and Paris, on economic issues in Europe between East Europe and Mediterranean Europe and on security policies between Washington, Paris and Moscow. No option or two options are without costs and changing circumstances make the choices difficult. But choices have to be made to allow the rest of Europe and the United States to adjust their own strategies accordingly.

Because of the dilemmas Germany may, in effect, choose to do nothing and to drift. In practice this will result in the choice, by default, of the final option. This will pose a distinct threat to European security. To eschew a role of either major contributor or leadership in formal alliance in Europe,[28] or contributor to *ad hoc* coalitions outside Europe, and to rely primarily on economic power for influence, risks the neglect of legitimate German interests and the undermining of the very multilateralism Germany values so much. In such circumstances the United States will lose interest as the major security provider for Europe and the security vacuum in East Europe will grow even more dangerous. For the good health of European security it is incumbent upon the present and next generation of German political leaders to undertake a re-education of the German electorate. The people must be alert to the reality that economic prosperity and national security are not cost-free and that, from the unique historical advantage of undisputed German borders, a proactive, outward-looking security policy is essential. To assist good, democratic friends in a serious manner while providing meaningful security assurances to the East is not incompatible with being a peace-loving, liberal democracy.

Notes

1. See Wolfgang F. Schlör, *German Security Policy* (London: IISS, 1993), Adelphi Paper 277, p. 46.
2. See Josef Joffe, 'After bipolarity: Germany and European security', *European Security after the Cold War, Part II* (London: IISS, 1994), Adelphi Paper 285, p. 41.
3. See James H. Wyllie, *European Security in the Nuclear Age* (Oxford: Blackwell, 1986), pp. 112–26.
4. David Calleo, *The German Problem Reconsidered* (Cambridge: Cambridge University Press, 1980), p. 206.
5. See Josef Joffe, 'After bipolarity: Germany and European security', *European Security after the Cold War Part II* (London: IISS, 1994), Adelphi Paper 285, pp. 34–50.
6. Timothy Garton Ash, 'Germany's choice', *Foreign Affairs*, Vol. 73, No. 4, July/August 1994, p. 65.
7. See *The Military Balance 1995–1996* (London: IISS, 1995), p. 48 and p. 92.
8. Franz-Josef Meiers, 'Germany: The Reluctant Power', *Survival*, Vol. 37, No. 3, Autumn 1995, p. 83.

9. See K. J. Holsti, *International Politics. A Framework for Analysis* (London: Prentice Hall International, 2nd Edn, 1974), p. 72.
10. Timothy Garton Ash, 'Germany's choice', *Foreign Affairs*, Vol. 73, No. 4, July/August 1994, p. 73.
11. For a robust commentary on German discovery of national interest, post-Cold War, see Roger Boyes, 'Europe under Germany', *Times*, 11 May 1994, p. 18.
12. See Anne McElvoy, 'Germany talks a good fight', *Times*, 30 August 1995, p. 21.
13. See 'The eagle's embrace', *Economist*, 30 September 1995, p. 21.
14. See Josef Joffe, 'After bipolarity: Germany and European security', *European Security after the Cold War, Part II* (London: IISS, 1994), Adelphi Paper 285, p. 45.
15. 'The Germany that can say No', *Economist*, 3 July 1993, p. 37.
16. Franz-Josef Meiers, 'Germany: The Reluctant Power', *Survival*, Vol. 37, No. 3, Autumn 1995, p. 82.
17. See Wolfgang F. Schlör, *German Security Policy* (London: IISS, 1993), Adelphi Paper 277, pp. 17–19.
18. Franz-Josef Meiers, 'Germany: The Reluctant Power', *Survival*, Vol. 37, No. 3, Autumn 1995, pp. 92–3.
19. T. G. Ash, J. Joffe and W. R. Smyser, 'Dateline, Berlin: Germany's new vision', *Foreign Policy 97*, Winter 1994–1995, pp. 140–58, consider various German foreign and security policy alternatives.
20. See T. G. Ash, J. Joffe and W. R. Smyser, 'Dateline, Berlin: Germany's new vision', *Foreign Policy 97*, Winter 1994–1995, p. 151.
21. See Dominique Moisi, 'The bomb won't go away', *Financial Times*, 26 September 1995, p. 14.
22. See Robin Gedye, 'Bonn reels as party breaks EC ranks', *Sunday Telegraph*, 5 November 1995, p. 30.
23. See T. G. Ash, J. Joffe and W. R. Smyser, 'Dateline, Berlin: Germany's new vision', *Foreign Policy 97*, Winter 1994–1995, p. 146.
24. See 'Germany and its interests', *Economist*, 20 November 1993, p. 19.
25. See Timothy Garton Ash, 'Germany's choice', *Foreign Affairs*, Vol. 73, No. 4, July/August 1994, p. 79.
26. *Ibid.*, p. 77.
27. See Thomas Kielinger and Max Otte, 'Germany: The pressurised power', *Foreign Policy 91*, Summer 1993, p. 52.
28. For discussion of how East Europeans are reassured by German power within a NATO framework, see Gerhard Wettig, 'Controversial Foundations of Security in Europe', *Aussenpolitik*, Vol. 46, No.1, January 1995, pp. 42–3.

Chapter 4

Russia – Quest for Identity, Status and Hegemony

The political concept of a German Reich is no longer ethically acceptable, practically functionable or politically popular in contemporary Germany. The concept of a German nation-state, as a normal actor in the European state system, leading the way in the integration process with other normal West European states, has been the dominant characteristic of German foreign and security policies since 1990.

In Russian politics there is no such dominant, core conviction. Since the disintegration of the Soviet Union in 1991 there have been competing views over the nature and interests of the modern Russian state and what are the most appropriate foreign and security policies. From 1993 the balance of argument has tilted towards a kind of state, with foreign and security policy characteristics, potentially threatening to the West and destabilising for European security. This is not to suggest that Russia poses the same level of threat to West Europe as did the old Soviet Union. Clearly it does not, and even if it was to adopt an overtly hostile, militaristic posture towards the rest of Europe it would take at least a generation before Russia could muster the relative levels of capabilities deployed by the Soviet Union in its long confrontation with the Western democracies. Nonetheless, the markedly more strident, dominant condition of Russia's foreign and security policies in the late 1990s, compared to the first two years after the Soviet collapse, and the obvious desire to be acknowledged as a Great Power in the Eurasian world at least, does make contemporary Russia the most significant force for security instability in relations between European states. Enlargement of NATO to include a raft of East European countries could seriously exacerbate this condition, and heighten the prospect of Russian hostility which the West and many East European states wish to avoid.

The salient characteristics of Russian foreign and security policy have emerged from a difficult, complex and tumultuous period in Russian political history. The current phase may pass and, in the long-term, Russia could come to terms with a future as an ordinary European nation-state. But it is highly unlikely that such a future will materialise because Russia never has been, nor is currently, an ordinary European state like France, Germany or Britain. Its political and social culture, economic condition and geo-strategic position predispose Russia to be an extra-ordinary Eurasian state, not at all comparable to other historic European states.

Since 1991 Russia has been a new country born out of a dramatic, sudden, traumatic experience of imperial collapse. The Spanish, French and British empires collapsed over decades, if not over centuries. The metropolitan societies remained largely intact. In historical terms, the Soviet empire collapsed overnight and not only were vassal states lost but so were territories deemed part of Russia for centuries, for instance the Ukraine and Belarus. When Communism collapsed in 1991 it brought down the Russian empire with it. What was created was not a return to 1917 Tsarist Russia or even nineteenth-century Russia. A new state structure covered much of East Europe, with a new Russia the largest and most powerful local state – but a state which had never existed before.[1] The existing state borders of Russia do not match any earlier, historical Russian borders. What Russia is, or what it should be, are questions which have perplexed the body politic since 1991. For centuries the Russian state and empire were the same thing, and there are serious doubts if a Russian state can be disentangled from a Russian empire – perhaps one cannot exist, or is invalid, without the other? The contiguous nature of much of the Russian empire to the Russian heartland, unlike the West European empires, has compounded the difficulties of state validation for Russians. In December 1991, 450 years of Moscow's rule in central Asia formally came to an end: but where Russia ends and central Asia begins is not clear to many Russians. Borders conforming to the old administrative provinces of the Soviet Union exist, but do not answer the conceptual question about the nature of the Russia which is left or its relationship to contiguous independent states which were integral parts of the old empire since before Peter the Great.

Because of its imperial history, the concept of a Russian nation-state is unfamiliar to most ordinary Russians as well as to the political élite. The term 'Russian nation' is not present in the language. What is available is either 'Russky', meaning an ethnic Russian, or 'Rossysky' meaning a polyethnic community.[2] Twenty per cent of the population of the Russian Federation is ethnically non-Russian but continual concern expressed by Moscow for the conditions of Russians, defined ethnically, in the former Soviet Union undermines the notion of Russia within its current borders as a polyethnic state. It also perpetuates neo-imperial tendencies and longings among the Russian body politic. The definition of a Russian nation-state within the current borders, based upon a polyethnic citizenry, would be the one most conducive to security and stability in the region. European states to the west and the newly independent states to the south would be much happier with the notion that borders rather than ethnicity were the determining factors for Russian nationality. But, to date, Russian foreign policy and the tone of Russian domestic politics give impressions to the contrary.

The persistent uncertainty over the nature of the entity which replaced the Soviet Union has been a marked characteristic of Russian politics since 1991. In the first few years, picking up the trend from the late 1980s, President Yeltsin, Foreign Minister Kozyrev and the new ruling élite looked to the West for a model and a role. The Atlanticist view of Russia as a Western liberal-democratic state-in-waiting was dominant. By 1993 disillusionment and bitterness with the political and economic costs of reform and the absence of tangible benefits engendered domestic pressures for an introspective analysis of Russia's problems. Concentration on the identity of the new Russian state and its national interests – as distinct from an international role – came to the fore. Russia's crises of identity, cohesion and regional position caused a reassessment of basic foreign and security policy assumptions. With no defining ideological adversary, nor a serious security threat from any other Great Power, Russia looked for a role within its capabilities and which addressed its national interests and priorities.

As the twentieth century ends there is a broad spectrum of political opinion in Russia, including the Yeltsin government, intent on establishing Russia's dominant position in Eurasia. There is the perception, from which very few vary, that there is a 'space' where Europe meets Asia in which Russia, by virtue of geo-strategic position, history, culture and even religion is and ought to be the hegemon. This 'space' incorporates not just the Russian Federation but swathes of territory around its long borders to the east, south and west. The 'space' includes not only the newly independent states of the former Soviet Union but also other Slav, Orthodox states. By definition, the concept of Russia's 'space' ordains a leading role for Russia in Europe. It is deemed vital that the Russian Federation, as a new state struggling for cohesion and identity at the same time as attempting to exert Great Power influence to reinforce that brittle identity, should not be isolated outside a *de facto* buffer zone of Central and East European states linked to the Atlantic states via NATO and the EU.

But Russia's aspirations and expectations to be treated as a great European power are deeply incompatible with European security arrangements as they stand, and as the Western powers seem to wish them to develop. Formal NATO membership in the next few years for a selection of former non-Soviet Warsaw Pact states and EU membership for one or two from the same group extends the influence of the major Western powers, most notably the United States and Germany, further east. It also restricts the influence that Russia has historically exercised in this region and acts as a brand of post-Cold War containment. Either European security attitudes held by countries such as the United States, Germany and Britain are modified, and European security institutions radically adapt to accommodate Russian ambitions – most in Moscow would say requirements – to some degree, or Europe will be faced with a suspicious, embittered, anxious and somewhat brittle nuclearweapons state on its easternmost borders. These political and strategic circumstances will also have the potential to create unease and insecurity in many regions peripheral to Europe, but important to the West for economic and political reasons.

Partnership thwarted

The current and likely future relations between Russia and the West are very different from the year or two before December 1991 and the heady days following soon after the dissolution of the Soviet Union. In the late 1980s President Gorbachev extolled the concept of 'mutual security' and common interests between East and West in collaborating in security structures based on cooperation rather than challenge. The notion of concert with the West advanced by Gorbachev in his 'New Thinking' foreign policy was carried over by Yeltsin's Foreign Minister Kozyrev into the core of Russian foreign policy when the new Russian Federation emerged. Even before the collapse of the Soviet Union, Kozyrev, as the Russian Republic's

Foreign Minister, advanced the argument that the major threat to Russia's future was political and economic isolation from the dominant world political and trading system.[3] Close collaboration with the West and rapid integration in the international relations of the advanced industrial liberal democracies were proposed as essential for post-Cold War Russia, and economic and political expectations were raised. Military power and imperial advance were described as redundant policies, and emphasis was to be given to economic efficiency. Resources should be concentrated on internal, civil capabilities such as high-quality education. Multilateral cooperation, including military cooperation, was the route to progress and stability. It was deemed vital that Russia strike up a close relationship with the G7 (the USA, Germany, France, Japan, Britain, Canada and Italy) leading industrial states.[4] In the summer of 1991, even before the Soviet disintegration, Yeltsin was making trips to Strasbourg, Paris, Prague and Washington. The foreign policy of Russia, at that time still theoretically a constituent part of the Soviet Union, was tilted more towards the West than even that of Gorbachev. High political rhetoric from many quarters in the West encouraged the Yeltsin government to pursue such a strategy. Implicit in it was the assumption that the United States would reward the Russian reformers by leading the West in bankrolling economic transformation, and by assisting Russia in the recovery of its Great Power status. This would allow it to act as a global 'strategic partner' to the United States in the new world order. The concept of 'strategic partnership', admittedly nebulous, was one much touted by the Bush White House in its closing stages and in the early years of the Clinton Administration.

Cooperation with the West did produce a rapid thaw in the Cold War. Arms control such as the Conventional Forces in Europe agreement producing real cuts and deployment constraints was accepted in late 1990, and the Strategic Arms Reduction Talks (START) Agreement, reducing US and Soviet strategic nuclear arsenals, was finalised in 1991 to be followed by a Bush–Yeltsin agreement on START II in January 1993. At the United Nations, Moscow was supportive as never before, not least over the Iraqi invasion of Kuwait. In the 2 + 4 talks over the future of Germany, historic agreements were reached which facilitated German unification and the withdrawal of large Soviet military forces from central Europe. These were agreements inconceivable barely two or three years before they happened, and were the consequence of the revolution in Russia's strategic perspective which led to a near-complete surrender of previously entrenched positions. In the excitement of the time there was little effort to define rigorously Russia's real interests, but merely to equate its interests with a close relationship to the West.[5] The old enemy, NATO, was not viewed as a threat; it was viewed as more of an opportunity. Domestic issues were the absolute priority, and NATO provided the stable international environment without which successful domestic reform would not be possible. Only a few voices, such as those supportive of the August 1991 failed coup, warned of NATO as an instrument for the advance of American influence into East Europe, the danger of the containment of Russian power, and the necessity for domestic reforms to be secondary to the assertion of Russian national interests outside the homeland.

The unrealistically high expectations of the Atlanticist reformers were encouraged by some official circles in the West, particularly in Washington.[6] Common strategic interests were identified, such as countering Islamic fundamentalism, stabilising post-Cold War East Europe, bringing Russia and its natural resources into the world trading system, and preventing nuclear proliferation.[7] The issue of nuclear proliferation was one consideration in particular which influenced official Washington policy. Good relations with the Yeltsin administration were deemed essential to see through the START agreements and to gather and disarm much of the old Soviet arsenal spread around the former Soviet Union. Persuading the Ukraine to relinquish its nuclear arsenal and encouraging Russia to adopt a posture towards the Ukraine conducive to fulfilment of American arms-control objectives was a major American motivation. Similarly, Washington was profoundly concerned about the movement, legal or otherwise, of nuclear expertise and material from the Russian civil and military nuclear industries to so-called rogue states such as Libya and Iran. However, while most of these concerns were common interests, they were not of equal interest to both the United States and the Russian Federation. For the West, Russian participation in successful arms control is more important than rapid Russian economic improvement. For the Russian Federation the necessity of having a different set of priorities emerged by 1993.

Rapid economic decline and the relative failure of Western economic aid and Western-inspired economic reforms to address domestic problems produced disillusionment with the Atlanticist, integrationist posture. From late 1992 the Yeltsin government began to apply more pressure on the West to assist Russia, and raised the spectre of a return to ultra-nationalist, anti-Western ways if Western support, assistance and understanding of Russian needs was not forthcoming. One sensational illustration of this was Foreign Minister Kozyrev's address to the CSCE Council of Ministers in Stockholm in December 1992. To astonishment and surprise he made a very hawkish speech, reminiscent of Cold War rhetoric and painting a dire picture of Russian foreign and security policy. He then explained that he made the speech to illustrate the consequences of the failure of Russian reform, and how it was in the West's security interests to prevent such a course of events coming to pass. At the December 1994 CSCE Budapest Summit, President Yeltsin administered another dose of shock treatment when he warned the West of a 'Cold Peace' if Russia's interests were not addressed.[8] By that time the Atlanticist reformers had been driven from the high ground in Russian domestic politics and President Yeltsin's rhetoric was more of a warning to the West that political circumstances inside Russia now demanded a narrower, more traditionally nationalistic appreciation of national interests than that predicated upon the 'New Thinking' philosophy.

Qualms and anxieties in political circles in 1992 about the West-tilting policies expanded into a dominant political force in 1993. Grave disappointment with the benefits Russia enjoyed from the 'strategic partnership' pervaded the Russian body politic and the Yeltsin administration was obliged to readjust its foreign and security policy positions to accommodate the tangible discontent. American unquestioning support for Yeltsin, reluctance to criticise his attitude to the Legislature in early 1993, and his authoritarian constitutional proposals disaffected many in Russian politics. The West's support for market reforms but in the form of harsh, strict IMF models also engendered discontent with Western links. Apparent intentions to push NATO to the east, clear reluctance to accept Russia as a member, and resistance to any reform of NATO to accommodate another great power, created further deep suspicions of a Western strategy to isolate Russia. Talk in Washington about an American role in the Caucasus and Central Asia, and the need to deny Russia a free hand throughout the former Soviet Union, compounded discontent. As early as May 1992 senior figures in Moscow were setting out models of Russia's vital strategic interests at odds with the Yeltsin–Kozyrev perspective. Colonel-General Igor Radionov, Chief of the General Staff Academy, enunciated a set of objectives he saw as vital to Russian interests. These included the neutrality of East European countries, Russian military and economic access to the seaports of the small Baltic republics, no 'third country' forces in the Baltic states, keeping former Soviet republics to the south and the east close to Russia and preventing any buffer being created, and reviving good relations between Russia and important countries in the Middle East and the Far East.[9] Rhetoric to accompany such objectives began to slip back into the lexicon of Russian foreign policy. 'World power', 'pan Slavism', 'defending own interests' and other neo-imperial language was increasingly used towards the end of 1992 and into 1993.[10] A sense that long-standing Russian – as distinct from Communist – interests were being neglected gathered pace and exerted itself politically. Two Yeltsin visits to Japan in 1992 and 1993 respectively were cancelled because of opposition in high defence circles to any prospects of an agreement to return the Kurile Islands. Apparent Western criticism of and pressure on the Serbs in the conflict in ex-Yugoslavia raised anxieties about the exclusion of Russian influence from a region of historic interest, not least because of the Slavic link. And the growing conflicts in the newly independent states to the south, where 25 million Russians still lived, required Russian involvement to protect not only ethnic Russians but also vital strategic and economic interests. No other country was willing to, or practically could, protect such interests. However, when, in February 1993, President Yeltsin asked the United Nations to grant special powers to Russia to keep the peace in states such as Tadjikistan or Georgia, his request was denied.

This brought home to many the reality that core strategic questions about Russia's future had never been properly addressed in the wake of the sudden, surprising collapse of the Soviet Union. The compatibility of Russia's self-perception as a Great Power with efforts to align with the Western multilateral political, security and trading systems was not considered in any depth until Russia found itself facing hard choices in 1993. Nor was any real thought put towards Western reactions to Russian use of force to maintain the integrity of the Federation or to manage stability in surrounding newly independent states. Efforts by foreign policymakers to make Russian behaviour compatible with its new relationship with the Western system came to be seen as humiliating and degrading for a great Eurasian power. In May 1992 Russia's first vote in the UN Security Council was for sanctions against Serbia, a fellow-Slav state. Improved relations with Japan would depend on some resolution of the long-standing dispute over the Kurile Islands in Japan's favour. Foreign ministry efforts to achieve this created despondency in nationalist circles and led to mounting opposition which eventually blocked any deal. Further perceived humiliations included Foreign Ministry support for US sanctions against a Russian firm exporting booster missile engines to India, allegedly against MTCR (Missile Technology Control Regime) rules, and a restrictive arms-sales policy holding back the earning of valuable currency in one of the few business areas where Russia was globally competitive. Perceived neglect of the large Russian minorities in the newly independent states – an area which had become known as the 'Near Abroad' – created further political unhappiness, as did the clear intention of NATO to expand further eastwards. The impetus for NATO to expand east was a condition which Russia's pro-West policies and alignment was supposed to block.[11] Consistent NATO discussion over how best to incorporate East European states into Alliance structures and bring them under NATO security protection was a profound blow to the morale of the Russian security establishment. Many had invested considerable political capital in arguments that a pro-West posture would induce a decline in NATO cohesion, and its growing irrelevance would lead to its relegation and eventual disbandment. CSCE was prescribed as the lead vehicle for European security but, by 1993, it was clear that Western powers were determined to sustain NATO. The North Atlantic Cooperation Council, largely a loose conference between NATO and its former adversaries, was well under way, and concrete proposals for a more structured functional relationship between NATO and some East European states were being considered by late 1993. In 1994 these proposals crystallised as the 'Partnership for Peace' programme. Through Russian eyes, NATO was active and thriving four years after the fall of the Berlin Wall, and the Yeltsin–Kozyrev strategy of debilitating the organisation by removing the reason for its existence seemed to have failed miserably.

Permeating all the anxieties about foreign policy was a deep unease about the very cohesion of the Russian Federation itself. It is a multiethnic state, held together in the past by Marxist–Leninist ideology, party discipline, authoritarian repression or claims of divine legitimacy. Much of the cement has crumbled or worn away. The example of ethnically-based nationalism in many of the newly independent states sets uncomfortable precedents to many of the republics within the Russian Federation. There is a Russian majority in most of the 21 republics which constitute the Federation, but not in all. It is in those other republics, mostly in the Caucasus, where threats to the sovereign integrity of Russia were anticipated and have arisen, most notably in Chechnya. Across the Russian political spectrum, from the reform to the conservative camps, the mood grew throughout 1992 and 1993 that a more assertive and distinct notion of Russian state power and interests was required in the interests of national security. Different factions felt this and expressed it, to different degrees, but there was clearly a general shift in the centre of gravity of Russian foreign and security policies between late 1992 and the end of 1993 towards a consolidation of Russian national interests which did not necessarily align with Western expectations or preferences. An illustration of this reorientation of mood was the unexpected success of the ultra-nationalist Liberal Democratic Party (LDP) and its extrovert leader, Vladimir Zhirinovsky, in the December 1993 parliamentary elections. The LDP won 25 per cent of the vote, though only 14.2 per cent of the seats. In total, neo-imperial, expansionist parties won 39.4 per cent of the vote. The nationalist agenda of historic Russian rights, the reassertion of Russia's great power status, Slavic loyalty, independence from overweening Western influence, and Russian dominance in regions around its borders had a considerable constituency. The Yeltsin Administration flowed with the domestic mood and tuned its posture and behaviour accordingly to present the image of defenders of Russian interests more than enthusiasts for conversion to Western nostrums about correct international behaviour. In the February 1994 State of the Nation address, President Yeltsin caught the new mood:

> Consistent promotion of Russia's national interests is the main task of our foreign policy. Openness and cooperation are prime means for achieving it. But if required to protect the state's legitimate interests, Russia has the right to act firmly and tough when it is really necessary.[12]

By 1994, following wide, vigorous debate, some of the nationalist agenda had been met, though not the extremes. Nonetheless the broad consensus within the body politic places Russian national interests to the fore in foreign policy. There has been a retrenchment of the unbalanced pro-West alignments of 1992 and a large part of 1993, and there is an expectation that the West show due respect to specifically Russian interests. The political cornerstones of contemporary Russian foreign and security policy have been described thus:

1. Russia remains a great power with vital national interests;

2. It is a major actor in the international system and merits comparable status with other Great Powers;

3. Other states, especially newly independent states of the former Soviet Union, must respect and defer to Russian strategic interests; and

4. Given its peculiar geo-strategic position in Eurasia, with instability around its borders, Russian interests are sometimes bound to diverge from those of the West.[13]

Cold peace

Ironically, the robust stand against the Russian parliament by President Yeltsin in October 1993 was the most lucid demonstration, at the time, that central government was changing its attitudes. Any concern over Western feelings about the forceful disbandment of the parliament were discounted by the government, and the interests of strong Russian government were given priority. Concepts of 'mutual security' and 'strategic partnership' and fears of isolation from Western political and economic contact, have been relegated below Russian national interests. This is not to argue that ultra-nationalists are in control in Moscow, but that Russian foreign and security policy has become much more pragmatic. Romantic, reckless adventurism is eschewed, but there is a steady policy of addressing Russia's vital interests first. This tilt towards robust pragmatism was given impetus by the subsequent elections for the new parliament. Not only did Zhirinovsky's LDP poll well, but the reformers polled poorly. The aggregate of the LDP and other Nationalists, Conservatives, Communists and Neo-Fascists comprised a majority over the reformers. The new Russian constitution, very similar to that of the French Fifth Republic, puts foreign and security policy essentially in the hands of the President. But a hostile parliament can attract public attention, set a mood and impede foreign policy.

Unquestionably the philosophy of 'state power' has overtaken the more liberal, Western-oriented political philosophy of the Atlanticist reformers. Russia presents a fluid, complex political picture, but in the late 1990s there are four dominant groups, all of which have moved away from the discredited 'New Thinking' to a greater or lesser extent.[14] There is a democratic, secular, market-oriented grouping which supports authoritarian government and a great power foreign policy, especially in the 'Near Abroad'. Another collection can be categorised as the 'Great Russia' group, which supports a more ethnically defined base and does not accept current borders as final. It attaches priority to protecting the 25 million Russians and 5 million Russophones outside the Russian Federation. A large part of the armed forces, the military–industrial complex, internal security services and collective farms can be put in this group. A third group is the Slavophile group, intent on spiritual rebirth and religious revival. It is isolationist in foreign policy and largely autarkic in economic policy. The final group is the highly authoritarian Red–Brown alliance of Communists and Fascists who see the dismemberment of the Soviet Union as treachery, who wish to regain superpower status and want to resurrect the Russian 'empire'. The LDP would belong to this group. Whatever the differences between these crude groupings – and there is some overlap among them – the mass feeling is that a strong, powerful state is essential to maintain order. Throughout Russian history anxieties over anarchy and instability have been endemic in Russian politics. That remains so today – and these feelings are reflected in broad support for a strong, authoritarian state structure.

This is reflected in the 'Russia first' foreign and security policies. In 1993 the Foreign Ministry, the Defence Ministry, the Ministry of Foreign Economic Relations, the Intelligence Services, the Defence Council and two parliamentary committees (foreign policy and foreign economic relations, and defence and security), reached a consensus expressed in *Basic Principles of the Foreign Policy of the Russian Federation*.[15] The document makes it clear that the defence of the territorial integrity of the Russian Federation is top priority. This is followed by the defence of the integrative processes of the Commonwealth of Independent States (CIS), the loose, multilateral organisation comprising the Russian Federation and most of the republics of the former Soviet Union which Moscow wishes to use as a vehicle to exert influence over lost Soviet territories. There is a bow towards Western liberalism by mention of the need to defend human rights and freedoms, but most of the document is concerned with the question of traditional national security. The requirement for Russia to defend itself against and to manage the resolution of dangerous conflicts in neighbouring countries is declared, as is defence against any weakening or disrupting of the international position of Russia.

Apart from the unremarkable top priority of defence of the homeland, certain core Russian perspectives are discernible from the *Basic Principles*. Relations with the former Soviet Union, and security of the region surrounding the borders of Russia, are deemed to be of crucial importance. After this objective Europe, not the United States, is the next priority. Russia sees itself as a great European power, with a claim to high influence on its own continent where it has some common interests with other European states, not least the question of stability in East Europe.

A range of national political, strategic and economic interests lie at the heart of the 'Russia first' perspective. In the domestic political scene some of the conservative institutions of the old Soviet system have made a comeback in the mid- and late-1990s. The armed forces, the military–industrial complex, the oil and gas lobby, collective agriculture and the KGB have clawed back power and influence on the vehicle of a strong state apparatus. While its name was changed, the basic structure of the KGB emerged almost intact from the disintegration of the Soviet system, and is again a major actor in high politics. The trend of decline for the conservative institutions, from soon after Gorbachev came into power in 1985 until the reform programme in the Russian Federation encountered great difficulties in 1992–1993, has been reversed. In 1992–1993 soaring inflation, high and rising unemployment, ineffective social security and rising crime soured public support for reform. To retain some level of popular legitimacy Yeltsin had to adapt. This allowed the conservative institutions the opportunity to advance their views of the state and to recover considerable power and influence.

NATO is a primary target of the new foreign policy perspective. Foreign Minister Kozyrev made it clear that NATO expansion to the east would be seen as a geo-political challenge to Russia.[16] As NATO ambitions developed from 1993, so despair grew in Russian ruling circles that NATO was not withering away, to be overtaken by CSCE, as anticipated. Through Moscow's eyes the 'Partnership for Peace' programme creates a waiting-room for East European states preparing themselves for formal entry into the Alliance. By the end of 1994, 23 countries had signed up for 'Partnership for Peace', including ten CIS states. In addition to prospective isolation, the security establishment in Russia was concerned that NATO expansion would provide a vehicle for German ascendancy. This concern was clearly expressed in November 1993 in a speech by Yevgevi Primakov, head of Russian external intelligence, at the Foreign Ministry Press Centre in Moscow. He stressed that his interpretation had the support of the Defence Ministry and the Armed Forces General Staff.[17] Mr Primakov, who was President Gorbachev's special envoy to Iraq during the 1990–1991 Gulf crisis, is a strong advocate of concentrated state power and the ascendancy of Russian national interests in foreign and security policy. He is deeply opposed to NATO enlargement while supporting Russia's right to extend protection to the 25 million Russians living outside the Russian Federation. In January 1996 President Yeltsin appointed Primakov Foreign Minister, in succession to Kozyrev. In an effort to exert influence over NATO, in the summer of 1994 Russia decided to join 'Partnership for Peace', and was due to sign the agreed programme of NATO–Russian relations at a Brussels ceremony in December 1994. A dramatic, last-minute retreat by Foreign Minister Kozyrev emphasised Russian determination to carve out a special role for itself in 'Partnership for Peace': a role which would reflect its status as a Great Power. This was not just hubris, but served political functions. Acknowledgement by external sources of Russia's rank as a Great Power is deemed important for purposes of national self-identification. Russia should not be assumed to occupy the same level of political importance in East Europe as Slovakia or Bulgaria. But even more important, Russia wanted to exercise special influence over NATO business in what used to be the Soviet sphere of influence in Europe. If NATO was not going to wither away, then it was in Russia's national interests to exercise as much power as NATO would grant it over NATO's external relations. After six months of lobbying for a special role, Russia finally agreed its relations with NATO in the 'Partnership for Peace' programme in the summer of 1995. Specific details of the programme are not public and are kept confidential to NATO and the Russian government. Foreign policy is a subject of great debate in Moscow, but there is a rare consensus across the political spectrum that NATO should be discouraged from expansion to the east, and that every effort should be made to inhibit it. One argument received favourably is that put forward, in 1994, by Chief of the General Staff, Mikhail Kolesnikov. If NATO expands to the east then the Russian Federation is freed from the constraints and limits of the 1990 CFE treaty, negotiated when the Warsaw Pact existed. There have also been strong hints in security circles that NATO's eastward expansion would jeopardise strategic arms control. With its decline in conventional military power, Russia relies even more on nuclear weapons for status as a great military power. START II aims to eliminate Russia's heavy land-based missile force, which is the core of its strategic nuclear arsenal. To date, the Russian parliament has not yet ratified START II.

General Russian dissatisfaction with CFE is widespread in the security community. There is support for an assertive Russian policy to amend CFE to address the new strategic circumstances. Russian forces returning from East Europe were deployed on the northern flanks, around the Baltic Republics and St Petersburg, and to the south, near the Ukraine and in the northern Caucasus. As the CFE was due to be in effect by late 1995 Russian forces in these areas exceeded agreed ceilings. Technically Russia did breach the treaty, but the 30 nations which engaged in the CFE agreed to redefine the zones within the limits to facilitate Russian deployment of more troops to sensitive areas, in particular the north area of the Caucasus. Moscow was insistent that new conditions in the Caucasus region made it essential for Russia to deploy more forces there than ever anticipated in the very different circumstances of 1990. In 1990 the world had barely heard of a place called Chechnya, and at that time Georgia was a loyal, constituent part of the Soviet Union. One device to overcome these problems was to consider areas previous assigned to the flanks as part of the Russian central zone. US Defence Secretary William Perry and Russian Defence Minister General Pavel Grachev held bilateral discussions to reach an acceptable compromise. In early 1996 this was still to be ratified by all the CFE members, some of whom would be reluctant to establish precedents of treaty amendments to address Great Power strategic advantage. Yet with NATO in support of the compromise, it will be difficult for other countries to resist.

After the coercive disbandment of parliament in October 1993, the following elections returned the reformers with a minority of seats. The Russian people were clearly unhappy with the reform programme, particularly the economic repercussions. Attempts to turn the Russian economy into a model Western free-market system were not delivering on promises. In 1992 and 1993 the collapse in industrial production exceeded that in the United States during the Great Depression. Integration in the world economy was fine rhetoric but it did not actually happen. Germany did provide the largest portions of government-directed aid, but economic links with Germany did not deliver prosperity for most of the population. World private investment was insignificant. Between 1989 and 1995 external private investment in the Soviet Union and Russia totalled nearly $2.7 billion; in 1993 alone in China in reached $15 billion.[19] Western aid conditions came to be deemed humiliating for a great power. In 1992 and 1993 Russia's foreign debt rose to over $80 billion. It was hoped that a swing away from radical, reformist economics could ameliorate the hardship and bring some economic improvement, at least in the short- to medium-term.

Policy and behaviour on Russian arms sales provide an illuminating measure of the change of political mood from 1993. Arms-sales policies convey signals about political, strategic and economic motivations. Modern military equipment is one area where Russia can compete with the advanced economies of the West. At the heart of the large, unwieldy, moribund Russian economy lies an effective, productive micro-economy – the Russian military–industrial complex. Part of the reason for the backwardness of the civilian economy may well be the resources drained from it by the military–industrial complex but, nevertheless, Russia can produce many weapons systems to compete with those of the West. Yet, with the end of the Cold War, the reformers felt reluctant to push Russian arms sales. It was feared that there would be political costs in competing in arms sales with those states from whom massive aid, debt rescheduling and economic advice was requested and whose political and economic systems Russia was hoping to join. There was also strong persuasion that the 'New World Order' called for the strict containment of weapons proliferation to unstable regions. In the 1980s the Soviet Union was the second biggest arms seller in the world, behind the United States. By 1993 it was sixth. Its sales declined from an average of $12 billion a year in the 1980s to $2.5 billion in 1993. As well as a lack of will, some old customers such as Iraq and Libya were under UN boycotts supported by Russia. By 1993 the new political mood persuaded the government to devote efforts to modernise the arms industry and to go out looking for customers, rather than converting or dismembering the military–industrial complex. So vigorous arms campaigns were launched, with sales to China, Iran and Syria among others. Some of Russia's customers were not to the West's tastes – for instance Iran – but Moscow carried on with its sovereign right to sell arms where deemed appropriate in Russian interests. A celebrated cause of disharmony between the United States and Russia in 1995 was the sale of civilian nuclear reactors by Russia to Iran while the United States was pursuing a unilateral economic embargo of Iran. Russia went ahead with the sale. In the previous two years Iran had been a good customer, buying Russian military aircraft and conventional submarines. Russia still has a long way to go until it claws itself up to where it was in the world arms-sales rankings in the 1980s. In 1996 it sold about $3.5 billion in arms. But it is vigorously seeking out markets in Latin America, the Mediterranean area, South East Asia and China. Dealing in commercial terms, with none of the old Soviet political ties hampering business, the Russian military–industrial complex presents formidable competition to the other big arms producers.[20]

The post-1993 focus on Russian national interests and the relegation of the integrationist preference is not to suggest that Russia has no common interests with the West. The peaceful withdrawal of Russian military power after 45 years of domination in Central and East Europe has been remarkable. The creation and sustenance of good relations with the old enemy, Germany, has also been remarkable and is clearly a Russian national as well as a common European interest. German support for Slovenia, Croatia and Bosnia in ex-Yugoslavia was not allowed to jeopardise friendly Bonn–Moscow relations nor, so far, has growing German economic dominance in East Europe. Joint US–Russian efforts to control nuclear proliferation in the former Soviet Union constitutes a common interest where much has been achieved. By mid-1992 all tactical nuclear weapons spread around the former Soviet Union were in Russian hands. In January 1994 the Trilateral Agreement between the US, Russia and the Ukraine agreed to the transfer of the Ukraine's strategic nuclear warheads to Russia. This paves the way for START II to be pursued which, by the year 2003, ought to reduce US strategic warheads to 3500 and Russian strategic warheads to 3000. Nonetheless, when it comes to an overall vision of the structure of European security, the role of the extant institutions, and the power and status of Russia in the European theatre and around its long borders, there are profound differences between the Atlantic Powers and the Russian Federation. Russia is not and does not perceive itself as an ordinary European state. It has unique rights, responsibilities and requirements. It needs to be accepted as a Great Power.[21]

Great Power

The distinguishing feature of Russian foreign and security policy since 1993 has been the determination to establish the Russian Federation as a Great Power. While Great Power aspirations are often expressed through military activity, support for status is as much a civilian enthusiasm as one of the military. The civilian leadership has become as aware as the military that Great Power status induces a sense of national pride and identity. They are also alert to the dangers and challenges surrounding the borders of the new Russian Federation which could threaten the integrity of the state if not addressed. This common perception has created a strong link between the civilian and military establishment. Foreign Minister Kozyrev conveyed this mood in 1994 when he wrote:

> Russia is predestined to be a great power. It remained as such for centuries in spite of repeated internal upheavals. What matters now is whether it is resurrected as a hostile nation under nationalist role or a peaceful and democratic one.[22]

A 'realist' view pervades both elements of the ruling establishment, especially over the strategic importance of the former Soviet Union and the 25 million Russians living there.[23] Instability in the 'Near Abroad' would be detrimental to Russian strategic security, deep economic ties and the physical and social wellbeing of ethnic Russians. Instability might also bring a flood of refugees – potentially hundreds of thousands – which could cause serious problems for the creaky Russian socio-economic infrastructure.

It may be because of, or despite, economic and military decline that nearly every political opinion in Russia wishes to see Russia treated as the Great Power it has historically been. That they fear that it may no longer be, but that they wish to remedy that situation, is evidenced by the repetition of Great Power claims. A salient feature of Russian Great Power behaviour in Tsarist and Soviet times was a central role for the military. Again, after a short hiatus between the late 1980s and 1993, the military is a leading pillar of state power. Of all the major institutions of state the military adapted, in the political sense, most easily to the post-Communist system. Structural change, such as withdrawal from East Europe and downsizing, was painful and unwelcome and seriously affected morale and performance. But there was little problem in changing from a Communist army to a nationalist army. Ideology was discarded with little regret and a realist view of Russia's national security requirements quickly adopted. One of these requirements was the need for a strong, legitimate authority at the centre of the nation-state. The army's role in countering the August 1991 coup attempt and supporting the Yeltsin Administration in the October 1993 confrontation with parliament were crucial in recent Russian political history. It allowed the military to resume a position close to the centre of national power.

Throughout 1992 and 1993 a debate took place in military circles as to how the armed forces could best serve Russian national interests. In May 1992 the Russian Ministry of Defence published a draft *Military Doctrine* for the new Russian Federation. Unsurprisingly, so soon after the demise of the Soviet Union, it carried distinct echoes of the Cold War. Its sentiment was anti-NATO and robustly in favour of defending Russians in the 'Near Abroad'. The focus of the draft doctrine was on large-scale traditional war. This draft was much criticised and acknowledged to be inappropriate for the new circumstances. The new, finalised military doctrine was produced in November 1993.[24] It was approved by President Yeltsin, ratified by the Security Council, given the status of law and granted a place in the new constitution. Most, but not all, of the doctrine's 23 pages have been published. Certain key features of the doctrine illustrate the military perception of Russia's foreign and security role in the future. What is described as 'local war' is seen as the major threat to stability and must be suppressed before it can escalate into general war. There is heavy emphasis on defending the 'rights, freedoms and legitimate interests' of Russians outside the Russian Federation. Threats to the Russians diaspora in the former Soviet Union are seen not just as a security issue for Russia, but as a threat to Russian security itself. The security aspect of Russia's relations with the 'Near Abroad' are clearly central to Russian security policy. The doctrine is not specific on potential threats in the 'Near Abroad', but the breadth of the Russian commitment is conveyed. CIS peacekeeping is claimed as one of the highest missions for the Russian military, and the doctrine states that Russia has the right to 'terminate any unlawful violence' within the CIS. The doctrine talks of 'creating the conditions' for peace as distinct from enforcing or facilitating a peace once it has been agreed by local belligerents.

The November 1993 *Military Doctrine* illustrates Russia's view of a Great-Power, neo-imperial role for itself throughout the territories of the former Soviet Union. Many of these territories are in Europe and some are contiguous with NATO powers or with former non-Soviet Warsaw Pact members which aspire to NATO and EU membership. If, for instance, Russia is playing a Great-Power, hegemonic role in Georgia, then Turkish security is affected; if Russia is hegemonic in Belarus, then Polish security is affected. Furthermore, the Russian security focus on the 'Near Abroad' also precludes any meaningful role for other external states in that area. So any attempt by the United States or a major West European power to construct a security relationship with the Ukraine, or the Baltic republics, or any central

Asian state would, by definition, be viewed as a direct threat to Russian security interests.

Other secondary but important features include the adoption of a Western style concept of deterrence. As distinct from the 1992 draft, the United States and NATO are no longer seen as major military threats, but the 'no first use' of nuclear weapons doctrine of Soviet days is abandoned. To compensate for wider conventional weakness Russia reserves the right to strike with nuclear weapons first, even in response to a conventional attack or an attack by a conventionally armed state allied with a nuclear-weapons state. The Russian definition of 'attack' is very wide. It includes not only Russian Federation territory but also CIS territory, which raises interesting notions of how the Russian military and the ruling political establishment which support the doctrine really define Russian territory. Following the November 1993 Doctrine, Chief of the Russian General Staff Kolesnikov announced, in March 1994, that Moscow was seeking bilateral agreements to establish 30 military bases throughout the CIS. Every newly independent state was involved except the Ukraine and the Baltic republics.[25] Within the political establishment the main opposition to the rise of the military came from the economic reformers and some of the Atlanticist elements in the Foreign Ministry. The ascendancy of the economic consolidators, the rout of the reformers since 1993, the redirection of the Foreign Ministry towards a more nationalist posture, and the replacement of Kozyrev with Primakov in 1996 demonstrate the congruence of Russian foreign and military policy.

Inter alia, Russian anxiety over stability and security in the former Soviet Union is linked to concern about the territorial integrity of the Russian Federation itself. There is the view that a strong Russian military presence throughout the CIS, helping to sustain the integrity of the newly independent states, influences the behaviour of the constituent parts of the Russian Federation, especially those without an ethnic Russian majority. Tumultuous events in Chechnya in 1995 and 1996 vindicate such anxieties. Alone among the 89 Federal components, only Chechnya asserted full independence and organised heavily armed forces. This challenge to sovereign Russian authority, and the example being set to other federal components, was unacceptable to President Yeltsin's government.[26] Eventually the military instrument was deployed in an extremely coercive, if not always highly efficient, manner to destroy the independent Chechnyn state structure. Such a policy was commensurate with a Great Power. Russia could hardly expect to exercise dominant military influence throughout most of the former Soviet Union if small federal elements of the state were allowed to go their own way. The determination of the Yeltsin government, after some years of attempting to persuade the Dudayev regime to comply, to bring down the illegal administration, and the manner in which this was accomplished, illustrated a national security policy putting national interests high above any concern for Western liberal opinion. It also illustrated the dominance of the executive in foreign and security policy issues over the parliament, where many objections were raised to the sweeping exercise of Presidential power. In the contest of geo-political interests versus human rights, executive power versus legislative power, and large countries versus small countries, Russian Great Power interests won every contest.

As well as the question of Russian territorial integrity and regional influence, other vital strategic matters were at stake. In Chechnya most of the population is Islamic. A successful bid for independence would be unsettling for other Islamic groups in the Russian Federation. Chechnya is also an oil producer, and is part of the route for a vital pipeline from the Tenzig oilfields in Kazakhstan to the Russian port of Novorossisk on the Black Sea. Chechnya has been a testing internal problem for the Russian Federation, and has given signals about the Russian proclivity to use blunt military force when deemed necessary. But even louder and clearer signals about how Russia views national security come from its policies and behaviour in the 'Near Abroad' in recent years.

The 'Blizhnee Zarubezhe' ('Near Abroad') is considered to be a very special area of exclusively Russian geopolitical 'space'. No other external powers should meddle in political matters in the newly independent states which used to be part of the Soviet Union or the 1917 Tsarist empire. Some Russian commentators draw parallels between the special American strategic interest in Central America and the Caribbean and Russian interests in the 'Near Abroad'. The 'Near Abroad' concept envelops the loose multilateral CIS which includes 12 of the 15 former republics of the Soviet Union which have become independent. The small Baltic republics, with their avowedly Western orientation, have declined to join. In total, Russians make up half of the CIS population, and the Russian economy constitutes 60 per cent of the gross national product of the CIS. In late 1991 and early 1992 there was a short period of uncertainty and indecision about the role of the Russian Federation to-wards the newly independent states. The prevarication was largely among the political and foreign policy élite rather than the military. A major reason was the prevailing enthusiasm for looking West and concentrating on fitting Russia into the non-communist world system. Another reason was the inexperience and the bureaucratic problems of the Foreign Ministry in managing relations with the states which used to be part of the domestic structure. It took most of 1992 for the Russian Foreign Ministry to bring itself to deal with the newly independent states.[27] There remains the feeling that countries such as Georgia and Uzbekistan are not really 'foreign', and relations with such states fall between domestic politics and foreign policy. There are distinct echoes of Soviet relations with the Warsaw Pact satellites. It soon became obvious that many of the newly independent states faced a range of economic, political and security problems common to new, fledgling states through-out the world. It also became clear that European institutions such as NATO, the CSCE, the WEU and the EU, for reasons of limited jurisdiction, restricted capabilities and resources, and lack of will, could not address most of the problems – problems which are often of crucial strategic importance to the Russian Federation.

The Yeltsin government found itself with a range of model relationships with the 'Near Abroad' from which to choose.[28] A return to the Soviet model, with reincorporation of most or part of the former Soviet Union, which would stretch Russian capabilities and resources and create deep animosity in the CIS and in the West, was one unattractive model. Another costly model – the Warsaw Pact model – was that of nominal independence for the newly independent states, but political and economic domination by Moscow. Less unattractive was the model of Russian control over security forces but political autonomy for the new states, or the model of

Russian training and logistical support but political independence. This latter model has been dubbed the 'Nixonov' model after the Nixon Doctrine of the 1970s for American relations with vulnerable, anti-Communist regimes in the Third World. The final model was extensive Russian influence over security but political and economic independence (Finland Cold War model).

In the past few years, elements of all the models except the first have been followed, in a pragmatic manner, by Moscow in its relations with most of the newly independent states. For instance, the Warsaw Pact model applies to Tadjikistan and the 'Nixonov' model to Uzbekistan. And it is not always a case of Russia forcing its will upon reluctant client states. Russia does have deep interests at stake, but there is also a vast network of personal, economic, political and military ties built up over decades which declarations of national independence cannot undo. For instance, in 1996 the presidents of Georgia, Kazakhstan and Uzbekistan were all former members of the Soviet Politburo. It is hardly surprising that Moscow argues that the 'Near Abroad' is a separate security and international system in which Russia ought to have a special role. In February 1993 President Yeltsin announced that he wished the UN to grant the Russian Federation special powers as guarantor of peace and stability in the region of the former Soviet Union. By 1994 the Foreign Ministry and Defence Ministry were as one on the importance of the 'Near Abroad'. At a January 1994 conference of high Foreign Ministry and Defence Ministry officials, Foreign Minister Kozyrev spoke of the need for a Russian presence in 'regions which have been the sphere of Russian interests for centuries' and of the importance of preventing a 'security vacuum' in the 'Near Abroad'.[29] For some time Defence Minister General Grachev argued the necessity for a defensive zone to the south, particularly as a buffer against the Islamic threat. On other occasions, Foreign Minister Kozyrev requested the West's understanding of Russia's special problems with the 'Near Abroad', suggesting that Russian activities are preventing more 'Yugoslavia's'. He also suggested that close CIS relationships are not unlike those between West European states in the EU. Where there have been security problems, parallels have been implicity drawn with Western behaviour such as the US policies in Somalia – but Russia cannot withdraw so easily because the territories are contiguous with the Russian Federation. A human rights angle is also played upon, with Russian expectations of normal citizenship rights, not special privileges, for Russians in the 'Near Abroad'.[30] There is a consensus across the Russian body politic that Russia has legitimate and ethical rights to exercise enlightened hegemonic powers in the Eurasian geo-political space which was the former Soviet Union.

In a southern arch, sweeping from the Black Sea to Afghanistan, Russia has a range of interests at stake. In the Caucasus there is anxiety about Turkish and Iranian influence replacing the Russian. While there is concern over politicised Islam, there are also considerable economic interests at stake. There are substantial oil and gas deposits in the Caspian Sea and strategic pipelines from Azerbaijan to the Black Sea will cross the Caucasus to Russian ports. Russian textile factories use Uzbek cotton, Russian cars get tyres from Armenia, Russian oil-industry equipment comes from Azerbaijan. These are just some of the economic links criss-crossing the former Soviet Union. Towards the end of the Soviet Union, most republics 'exported' at least half of net material product to other fellow Soviet republics. In central Asia there is the feeling that if Russian influence waned, then Chinese, Iranian and Turkish influence would reach out towards the borders of the Russian Federation. There is the general policy in the region of supporting authoritarian governments with Russian military aid or troops. In Tadjikistan, Russian forces have been supporting the government against Islamicist rebels for some time.[31] The 201st Motorised Rifle Division has been patrolling Tadjikistan's borders with Afghanistan to prevent Islamicist infiltration since 1992. Russian forces fulfil a border-protection role not just for Tadjikistan but also for Uzbekistan and Turkmenistan. More than 175 000 Russian troops – 8 per cent of the army – are deployed in newly independent states in the south. To the west is the Ukraine, formerly part of Russia since the seventeenth century. After many false starts, denuclearisation of the Ukraine is proceeding, largely with American assistance. But other sensitive issues persist. The division of the Black Sea fleet, the position of the Crimea in the Ukraine or Russia, and the discontent of the large Russian minority in eastern Ukraine continue to keep relations cool. Early in 1992, Russian plans for a joint CIS armed services, naturally under Russian command, were checked by the Ukraine taking the initiative in creating its own armed forces. The Baltics are the newly independent states least under Russian military influence since troop withdrawals were eventually completed in 1994. Yet their geographical position makes them of the utmost strategic importance to Moscow. Lithuania straddles the supply route to the Russian Baltic enclave of Kaliningrad. If the Baltics were to join a hostile alliance, then enemy power could be brought to the heart of Russia. Russian policy towards the Baltics is based on a mixture of concession and pressure, with the threat of economic sanctions ever-present and the prospect of military intervention probable if Baltic behaviour was perceived to be seriously against Russian strategic interests. As in some other newly independent states, there are large Russian minorities, the condition of which Russia uses to legitimise close interest in the political and economic affairs of the small, vulnerable republics.

Apart from the Baltic republics and the Ukraine, Russian military influence is considerable in all the forces of the other newly independent states. And Russian forces have been active within most of these countries. As mentioned above, Russian forces sustain the secular Tadjikistan government. They play a major role in supplying and training Uzbek forces, which in turn support the government in Tadjikistan, not wishing militant Islam to succeed in that neighbouring country. The Uzbek Commander-in-Chief is an ethnic Russian, as are most of the officers. Since 1991 the Russian 14th army has virtually ruled in the so-called Trans-Dneister republic, a Russian-ethnic breakaway from the newly independent state of Moldova. General Alexander Lebed, controversial national security adviser to President Yeltsin from June to October 1996 and his special envoy to Chechnya, was the charismatic but autocratic commander of the 14th army. His army of 8000 troops collected its own taxes and seemed to function as a virtual government. The question of ethnic Russians, their security and their rights, is an issue which looms large in Moscow's relations with all the newly independent states. In some states the numbers constitute a large proportion of the population; the result of decades and even centuries of colonisation and settlement. Ethnic Russians often constitute the technocratic and professional backbone of the host societies, yet there have been problems of civil rights and political and linguistic discrimination. As Table 4.1 demonstrates, the ethnic Russian issue is not one contrived for political reasons: it is a real, practical problem. The Russian diaspora in the newly independent states is larger than the population of many European nation-states. If discontented, many may wish to return to a Russia they do not really know and understand or, worse, become involved in civil conflict within the newly independent states.

Table 4.1   Ethnic Russians outside Russia

	Million	*% of local population*
Ukraine	11.4	22
Kazakhstan	6.4	38
Uzbekistan	1.7	8
Belarus	1.4	13
Latvia	1.0	34
Kyrgyzstan	1.0	22
Moldova	0.6	13
Estonia	0.5	30
Turkmenistan	0.4	10
Tajikistan	0.4	8
Azerbaijan	0.4	6
Lithuania	0.3	9
Georgia	0.3	6
Armenia	0.1	2

The concept of the CIS is close to Moscow's heart as a vehicle to address many of these issues, not least the question of ethnic Russians. Naturally not all newly independent states were keen to place themselves in a neo-imperial organisation so soon after achieving independence. But Moscow was determined to have as many in the CIS as possible, and to use the organisation for political, economic and security cooperation and some degree of reintegration. Where newly independent states were reluctant, Russian pressure has been brought to bear. Initially Azerbaijan was determined not to joint the CIS. Russian support for Armenia in its war against Azerbaijan over the disputed Ngorno-Karabah enclave caused a change of government in Baku, and the new regime of President Aliev joined the CIS.[32] In Georgia, President Shevardnadze was determined that Georgian independence should be more secure outside the CIS. Russian support for the Abkhazian rebels allowed the small Muslim minority to pose such a threat to the Georgian government that Shevardnadze had to call for Russian assistance, in late 1993, to sustain the political integrity of the country. Part of the price paid was Georgian membership of the CIS and what looks like the permanent presence of Russian forces. Russian behaviour in Georgia was the worst case of covert intervention, destabilisation and the ruthless manipulation of civil conflict in order to address Moscow's strategic objectives. Russian forces now patrol Georgia's border with Turkey.

Throughout the CIS Russian military influence and presence is pervasive. In addition to the above activities, Russian soldiers guard the border of Kyrgyzstan with China and the border of Turkmenistan with Iran. In February 1995, Russia and Belarus signed an agreement allowing Russian troops to guard the Belarus–Polish border. Also in February, Russia and Kazakhstan agreed to partially integrate their armed forces. In March 1995, nine CIS members agreed to construct a common air defence, managed by Russia. Given that it has the air-defence resources and is by far the largest participant, Russia will dominate the system. According to the founding articles of the CIS in 1991, it was to be an organisation of equals with headquarters in the Belarussian capital of Minsk. That remains so, but the real power is in Moscow. The CIS Council of Defence Ministers is based in the old Warsaw Pact headquarters in Moscow, and President Yeltsin is chairman of the Council. Early in 1995 the CIS agreed to the establishment of a Commission of Economic Relations, to be based in Moscow. Under the CIS 1992 Collective Security Pact (Tashkent Treaty), to which nine members were signatories in 1996, each state is responsible for helping to defend the others. Since 1992, Moscow has insisted that the CIS has a common external border, which Russia has the right and duty to defend. Konstantin Zatulin, head of the CIS Affairs Committee of the Lower House of the Russian parliament, is recorded in 1995 stating that 'the centre of CIS activities is definitely the Kremlin' and that the borders between the CIS members 'were never intended to be real borders'.[33]

Russian forces are undergoing reform, with 'Near Abroad' operations in mind. By the end of the 1990s, total armed forces should be down to 1.9 million. In 1992 the total was 3 million. Conscripts will be reduced to only half the armed forces. Rapid deployment forces will be developed, with two motorised rifle divisions equipped and trained specifically for 'peacekeeping' roles. Heavily armed border guards, who are distinct from the army but are often ex-army, will be strengthened. But whatever Russian strategic ambitions and military plans may be, there are constraints on action. There is what is known as the 'Afghan syndrome' and some inkling of a so-called 'Tbilisi syndrome' as well.[34] While intervention is relatively easy, the subsequent propping-up of a regime or countering insurgency over the long-term is dispiriting and often costly. The cost of Russian policies in the 'Near Abroad' is expensive. There are efforts to get the newly independent states to contribute. Part of the reason for Yeltsin attempting to get UN or OSCE authorisation for special Russian 'peacekeeping' in Eurasia is to get access to external funding. And there are domestic political restraints. If operations go wrong or costs escalate, domestic political forces in Moscow use the problems to criticise the executive.

There is also the constraint applied by the potential criticism and condemnation of the wider international system, in particular the Western liberal democracies. However, the record here is of muted concern and only discreet diplomacy. Behind any occasional rhetorical flourishes there is a realistic appreciation in the foreign departments of most Western states that the 'Near Abroad', especially in the Caucasus and Central Asia, is unstable and insecure. There is the fear that potential disorder could spill over into the Russian Federation, and that it is not in the interests of the West to risk fragmented, civil conflict in the world's second, most powerful nuclear-weapons state. In 1996 the West had still not acceded to Russian requests for UN or OSCE mandates to operate as a 'peacekeeper' in the former Soviet Union. Concern over neo-imperial objectives and behaviour inhibited international approval for Russia's unique practice of peacekeeping. But is this posture by the West wise and realistic? After all, the West has no intention of dispatching forces to patrol the Tadjikistan–Afghanistan border or to impose order in Georgia. Perhaps it would be best for the West tacitly to accept a brand of 'Finlandisation' for the southern arch of the 'Near Abroad'?[35] On the other hand, there is the genuine concern that to endorse proto-imperialism to the south of the Russian Federation will, at some point, induce such behaviour in Russia's old sphere of influence in East Europe, so recently lost to the West.

The Western flank

In grand strategic terms, Russia's centre of gravity lies towards the West. Securing borders and influence to the south is crucial to the security of the Russian Federation, but to recover Great Power status the rehabilitation of Russian influence in Europe is essential. In the quest for Great Power influence, the exercise of hegemonic power over Dushanbe does not compensate for the steep decline of Russian influence over Warsaw, Prague and Berlin. Only a leading role in European security arrangements can recover for Moscow the status previously enjoyed by many Tsars and CPSU General-Secretaries.

To achieve this goal Russia has pursued a multifaceted, interrelated strategy. The salient facet is to transform NATO. NATO defeated the Soviet Union. It is the world's, and modern history's, foremost military Alliance. It is an alliance which projects American military and political power over Europe, well beyond the Alliance's formal treaty limits, to those countries which seek out American protection. It is also the Alliance which nurtured West Germany and protects Germany, perhaps from itself, but most certainly from others. Under the NATO umbrella, more so than under any other institution, Germany has prospered and become the dominant European political and economic actor in Central and East Europe. While NATO persists as a cohesive security institution with limited members and led by the United States, Russia cannot overcome its influence. Indeed, the more robustly Russia behaves towards NATO, the more NATO cohesion and sense of purpose are reinforced. If Moscow cannot overcome NATO, it must change it.

Through Russian eyes the 'Partnership for Peace' programme is a device to ease Central and East European states into NATO, leading to a new era of containment of Russia. At the Budapest 1994 December CSCE Summit, President Yeltsin described NATO as a Cold War product whose legitimacy had gone. He described the challenges posed by NATO to Russia's place in Europe as a threat to democracy inside Russia. There is not the same depth of Russian antipathy towards the EU or the WEU. Moscow does not have the same antagonism towards Central and East European states joining the EU and the WEU.[36] These institutions do not have an American presence; they are all-European. The WEU seems destined to become an agency of the EU and, if there is ever real agreement, an implement for a European common foreign and security policy. If such circumstances ever come to pass, the WEU would be subservient to a collective, multipurpose EU which would seek to replace NATO in the defence field. Security would only be one function of a future

EU and the United States would be absent. The security decision-making process would be much less decisive and there would be plenty of opportunity for greater Russian influence. Indeed, in the long-term, Russia could even become the largest member of an extended EU.

In the short- to medium-term, probably for the next five to ten years, the WEU and the EU do not pose real competition to NATO in the field of European security. Therefore Russia's preferred option is to emasculate the American-led military alliance. Foreign Minister Kozyrev, six months before he left office to assume a seat in the Russian parliament, made it clear that Russia expected a reform of NATO to allow pan-European involvement. The simple expansion of NATO was not welcome. He insisted that some form of partnership with Russia was required. After a short period of Russian–NATO cooperation, NATO should transform itself into a pan-European organisation with a Permanent Consultative Body, of which Russia would be a leading member. Foreign Minister Kozyrev suggested that the focus of such an organisation would move from inter-state security threats to ethnic threats, terrorism, the proliferation of weapons of mass destruction, drug-trafficking and other transnational issues. It is self-evident that Foreign Minister Kozyrev was advocating the transformation of NATO into a multipurpose collective security organisation with a leading role for Russia.[37] As a consequence, the role of the US in European security would be much diminished, to Russia's advantage.

A related Russian strategy, which has been active since 1993, is to elevate the role of the OSCE and to lobby for the incorporation of NATO into the OSCE structure as an instrument of the OSCE. Moscow's investment in CSCE (later OSCE) as an instrument to extend influence throughout Europe harks back to Communist days. In the early 1970s Leonid Brezhnev supported CSCE in the belief that he had found a device to project Soviet power over the whole continent. When he and 34 other government leaders signed the Helsinki Final Act in 1975, Brezhnev was delighted that the Soviet Union was at the heart of a collective organisation alongside Britain, France and other historic European powers. That the US and Canada were present was a drawback, but at least the Soviet Union could compete on equal terms in the CSCE as it could not from outside the North Atlantic Alliance. As it turned out, the net effect of the CSCE during the Cold War was to agitate the human rights issue inside the Soviet bloc rather than reinforce the Soviet Union's position as an all-European power. But the Cold War and related human rights issues have gone and the Soviet successor state, the Russian Federation, wishes to use the OSCE to regain lost status. Russia pressurised fellow CSCE members at Budapest to turn the Conference into a bureaucratic, institutionalised organisation with established, functional duties. In this Russia was successful. But it was not successful in other proposals which further illustrate how Russia would like to elevate the OSCE above NATO in European security arrangements.[38] The Russians proposed the creation of an OSCE Security Council in which it would have one of the few permanent seats. It also proposed a system by which limited groups of states would handle issues of direct concern to them. As a Great Power, Russia would be a member of all groups. Moscow also proposed that CIS be accorded the same status as NATO and the EU, and that the OSCE financially support and validate Russian 'peacekeeping' in the CIS area. In 1994 Foreign Minister Kozyrev wrote that:

It was the democratic principles of the 56-member CSCE that won the Cold War – not the NATO military machine. The CSCE should have the central role in transforming the post-confrontational system of Euro-Atlantic cooperation into a truly stable, democratic regime.[39]

Russian ambitions for the OSCE are clear. The OSCE, in which Russia has a veto like all other members, should become the most authoritative security body in Europe. Russia should have a special role in the OSCE. The OSCE should legitimise Russian policy in the 'Near Abroad', but not meddle itself. If all this was achieved then, together with Russia's special relations with NATO via its later membership of 'Partnership for Peace', Russia could find itself exercising wide, deep influence right across the whole of Europe.

Another facet of this strategy is to maintain pressure on the Baltic republics and the Ukraine, and to court Belarus. Any further move of the Baltics from under Moscow's influence would be a serious geo-strategic loss. The cutting of energy supplies and the possible return of Russian military forces, after their slow withdrawal, are frequently brandished when any of the Baltic republics indicate a proclivity to move closer to the West. The Ukraine has also been subject to Russian economic pressure to adopt a more comfortable relationship with Moscow in general and to create movement over particular issues such as denuclearisation. A strongly pro-West Ukraine would act as a serious balance to the Russian Federation in East Europe. Fortunately for Russian ambitions, the Ukraine is one of the least reformed of the CIS economies and its economic and financial plight is profoundly serious. Unless economic conditions improve, the political fragmentation of the Ukraine, with a large portion of the Russian-speaking east hiving off to join the Russian Federation, is likely. Russia's close relationship with Belarus has created expectations of a reunification of these two parts of the former Soviet Union. Political, economic and military relations are exceptionally close but, in the short-term, the economic costs of reintegration are inhibiting the resumption of Russian sovereignty. Nonetheless, to bolster its European security objectives, the Russian Federation is projecting tangible power right to the Polish border.

The Russian goals of domination in European security arrangements and exclusive political, economic and security rights throughout the former Soviet Union are opposed by the United States and the West European democracies. But there is an inherent political and geo-strategic incompatibility between an active, viable, reformed, democratic Russian state as currently configured, and NATO expansion into East Europe with military and constitutional characteristics largely unchanged. These realities pose dilemmas for the West. Should the West accede to Moscow's wishes that former Warsaw Pact East European countries remain out of NATO and stay neutral? To do so may encourage Russian Great Power ambitions – but not to do so will undermine the pragmatists in the Russian government to the advantage of the authoritarian nationalists. There is the argument that, since 1993, the 'Russia first' nationalists have been in the ascendancy anyway and that NATO must not appease them by abandoning long-term plans to bring countries like Poland and the Czech Republic into NATO. However, to drive on may vindicate the conservative, nationalist position, deepen the 'Cold Peace', and create instability. Given Russia's residual power, stability inside the country may be the most practical and realistic objective for the West rather than accelerated economic reform and democratisation.[40] It has been the cost of these reforms which have disaffected the population with the reformist, Atlanticist platform. The West may need to accept Russian hegemony in the 'Near Abroad' and dominant influence over the Ukraine, Belarus and the Baltics as the price of stability. So accommodation with the latent power of Russia may have to be the West's priority, above the legitimate granting of NATO membership to a clutch of Central and East European states. Incorporation of some East European states could wait until ultra-nationalist, imperial behaviour towards East Europe became extant. In the meantime Russia will work away at politically undermining the West's premier security institution and supporting the cause of rival institutions from which Russia would derive most advantage.

The parliamentary elections of December 1995 were catastrophic to the prospects of any revival of Atlanticist foreign and security policies. In the foreign policy arena majority public support went to the Nationalists and Neo-Imperialists. The Communist Party led by Gennady Zyuganov made a remarkable comeback to win 22 per cent of the vote and more than twice the seats of any other faction. This gave the Communist Party more than one-third of the seats in the Lower House. Zhironovsky's LDP won 11 per cent of the vote. No other organised party won a higher percentage of the vote.[41] Among other foreign policy repercussions, the new balance of power in the Russian parliament makes it very unlikely that the long-waited ratification of the 1993 START II Treaty will go ahead. In 1993 President Yeltsin took his cue from foreign and security policy for the swing towards state-centric power and the priority of Russian national interests over multilateral relationships. When he faced the electorate in June 1996 there was every incentive to stick to and to burnish the nationalist character of his foreign and security policies. His definition of the Chechnya policy as a national security interest illustrates the character of high Russian politics in the late 1990s. The second half of the 1990s has witnessed a distinct cooling in US–Russian relations. Nearly all the pro-Western reformers from President Yeltsin's inner circle were removed by 1996. No one of real influence remained. Reference to a US–Russian 'strategic partnership' ceased. Currently, Russian foreign and security policy is not a threat to prevailing European security arrangements; it is more of a challenge. But it is a challenge which, if mismanaged, could reconstitute itself as a serious threat. The outcome of the Russian challenge depends, crucially, upon the attitudes and policies of the United States towards post-Cold War European security.

Notes

1. See Bruce D. Porter and Carol R. Saivetz, 'Once and future empire: Russia and the "Near Abroad" ', *Washington Quarterly*, Vol. 17, No. 3, Summer 1994, p. 75.
2. See Gerhard Wettig, 'Controversial foundations of security in Europe', *Aussenpolitik*, Vol. 46, No. 1, 1995, p. 44.
3. See James H. Brusstar, 'Russian vital interests and Western security', *Orbis*, Vol. 38, No. 4, Fall 1994, pp. 607–8.
4. For discussion of the character of 'New Thinking' see Hannes Adomeit, 'Russia as a "great power" in world affairs: image and reality', *International Affairs*, Vol. 71, No. 1, January 1995, pp. 42–5.

5.   See Leszek Buszynski, 'Russia and the West: Towards renewed geopolitical rivalry', *Survival*, Vol. 37, No. 3, Autumn 1995, p. 104.

6.   See Zbigniew Brzezinski, 'The premature partnership', *Foreign Affairs*, Vol. 73, No. 2, March/April 1994, for a critical appraisal of official American policy towards Russia.

7.   For detailed discussion of how such common interests were viewed, see Hannes Adomeit, 'Russia: Partner or risk factor', in *European Security after the Cold War, Part II* (London: IISS, 1994), Adelphi Paper 285, pp. 25–9.

8.   See Andrei Kozyrev, 'Partnership or cold peace', *Foreign Policy 39*, Summer 1995, pp. 3–4.

9.   See James H. Brusstar, 'Russian vital interests and Western security', *Orbis*, Vol. 38, No. 4, Fall 1994, p. 609.

10. See Hannes Adomeit, 'Russia as a "great power" in world affairs: image and reality', *International Affairs*, Vol. 71, No. 1, January 1995, p. 45.

11. See Leszek Buszynski, 'Russia and the West: Towards renewed geopolitical rivalry', *Survival*, Vol. 37, No. 3, Autumn 1995, pp. 107–8.

12. See James H. Brusstar, 'Russian vital interests and Western security', *Orbis*, Vol. 38, No. 4, Fall 1994, p. 610.

13. See Renée De Nevers, *Russia's Strategic Renovation* (London: IISS, 1994), Adelphi Paper 289, p. 5.

14. See Hannes Adomeit, 'Russia as a "great power" in world affairs: image and reality', *International Affairs*, Vol. 71, No. 1, January 1995, pp. 50–2.

15. Cited and discussed in Hannes Adomeit, 'Russia: Partner or risk factor', in *European Security after the Cold War, Part II* (London: IISS, 1994), Adelphi Paper 285, pp. 24–5.

16. See Andrei Kozyrev, 'Partnership or cold peace', *Foreign Policy 39*, Summer 1995, p. 4.

17. See Leszek Buszynski, 'Russia and the West: Towards renewed geopolitical rivalry', *Survival*, Vol. 37, No. 3, Autumn 1995, p. 110.

18. See Peter Felstead, 'Flanking manoeuvres leave CFE on hold', *Jane's Intelligence Review POINTER*, December 1995, p. 8; and 'Tanks and flanks', *Economist*, 18 November 1995, pp. 52–5.

19. See Hannes Adomeit, 'Russia as a "great power" in world affairs: image and reality', *International Affairs*, Vol. 71, No. 1, January 1995, p. 57.

20. See 'Firing back', *Economist*, 2 December 1995, pp. 102–7; and Jonathan Eyal, 'The Bear looks to a new Yalta', *Times*, 7 April 1995, p. 18.

21. For discussion of the Russian national psyche and the argument that authoritarian nationalism fills the psychological vacuum created by the sudden collapse of Soviet power, see Rodric Braithwaite, 'Russian realities and Western policy', *Survival*, Vol. 76, No. 3, Autumn 1994, pp. 11–15.

22. Andrei Kozyrev, 'The lagging partnership', *Foreign Affairs*, Vol. 73, No. 3, May/June 1994, p. 62.

23. See John W. R. Lepingwell, 'The Russian military and security policy in the "Near Abroad" ', *Survival*, Vol. 36, No. 3, Autumn 1994, pp. 70–3.

24. For detailed, illuminating analysis of the November 1993 Russian military doctrine, see Charles Dick, 'The military doctrine of the Russian Federation', *Jane's Intelligence Review Special Report No. 1*, January 1994, p. 12; and James Sherr, 'The Russian Army's New Charter', *Wall Street Journal Europe*, 9 December 1993, p. 6.

25. See Bruce D. Porter and Carol R. Saivetz, 'Once and future empire: Russia and the "Near Abroad" ', *Washington Quarterly*, Vol. 17, No. 3, Summer 1994, p. 87.

26. See Leszek Buszynski, 'Russia and the West: Towards renewed geopolitical rivalry', *Survival*, Vol. 37, No. 3, Autumn 1995, pp. 114–18, for background and details of Russian Chechnya policy.

27. See Renée De Nevers, *Russia's Strategic Renovation* (London: IISS, 1994), Adelphi Paper 289, p. 19.

28. See James H. Brusstar, 'Russian vital interests and Western security', *Orbis*, Vol. 38, No. 4, Fall 1994, p. 611.

29. Cited in John W. R. Lepingwell, 'The Russian military and security policy in the "Near Abroad" ', *Survival*, Vol. 36, No. 3, Autumn 1994, p. 74.

30. See Andrei Kozyrev, 'The lagging partnership', *Foreign Affairs*, Vol. 73, No. 3, May/June 1994, pp. 67–70.

31. For more details on Russian military behaviour in the south of the 'Near Abroad', see Alvin Rubinstein, 'The geopolitical pull on Russia', *Orbis*, Vol. 38, No. 4, Fall 1994, pp. 571–6; John W. R. Lepingwell, 'The Russian military and security policy in the "Near Abroad" ', *Survival*, Vol. 36, No. 3, Autumn 1994, pp. 75–8; Bruce D. Porter and Carol R. Saivetz, 'Once and future empire: Russia and the "Near Abroad" ', *Washington Quarterly*, Vol. 17, No. 3, Summer 1994, pp. 84–8; and Maxim Shashenkov, 'Russian peacekeeping in the "Near Abroad" '; *Survival*, Vol. 36, No. 3, Autumn 1994, pp. 46–69.

32. See James Wyllie, 'Turkey's eastern crisis', *Jane's Intelligence Review*, Vol. 5, No. 11, November 1993, pp. 506–7.

33. Cited in Claudia Rosett, 'New states are finding Russian embrace tough to resist', *Wall Street Journal Europe*, 2 March 1995, p. 9. For another bleak view of Russian 'proto-imperial' ascendancy in the former Soviet Union, see Zbigniew Brzezinski, 'The premature partnership', *Foreign Affairs*, Vol. 73, No. 2, March/April 1994, pp. 73–5.

34. See John W. R. Lepingwell, 'The Russian military and security policy in the "Near Abroad" ', *Survival*, Vol. 36, No. 3, Autumn 1994, p. 88.

35. See Maxim Shashenkov, 'Russian peacekeeping in the "Near Abroad" '; *Survival*, Vol. 36, No. 3, Autumn 1994, pp. 63–4 and John W. R. Lepingwell, 'The Russian military and security policy in the "Near Abroad" ', *Survival*, Vol. 36, No. 3, Autumn 1994, pp. 87–8 for discussion on how the West may respond to Russian policy in the south.

36. See Gerhard Wettig, 'Controversial foundations of security in Europe', *Aussenpolitik*, Vol. 46, No. 1, 1995, p. 49.

37. See Andrei Kozyrev, 'Partnership or cold peace', *Foreign Policy 39*, Summer 1995, pp. 11–13.

38. See John J. Maresca, 'Russia's emerging European policy', *Wall Street Journal Europe*, 6 September 1994, p. 8.

39. Andrei Kozyrev, 'The lagging partnership', *Foreign Affairs*, Vol. 73, No. 3, May/June 1994, p. 65.

40. For discussion of some of these dilemmas see James H. Brusstar, 'Russian vital interests and Western security', *Orbis*, Vol. 38, No. 4, Fall 1994, pp. 614–18; Renée De Nevers, *Russia's Strategic Renovation* (London: IISS, 1994), Adelphi Paper 289, pp. 6–7; and 'Getting Russia right', *Economist*, 14 January 1995, pp. 15–16. Zbigniew Brzezinski, 'The premature partnership', *Foreign Affairs*, Vol. 73, No. 2, March/April 1994, pp. 79–82, proposes a radical strategy of 'geopolitical pluralism' – active Western involvement in the newly independent states to block Russian proto-imperialism and direct Russian energies towards domestic democratic and economic reform.

41. See Richard Beeston, 'Communists set their sights on key jobs', *Times*, 27 December 1995, p. 11.

Chapter 5

The United States and European Security – Pragmatism and Sharing

During the Cold War the security of West Europe was the top regional priority for United States foreign and security policy. Other regions, such as North-East Asia, were deemed vital but Europe was the locale where American and Soviet power met on the ground. If West Europe fell to Communist power, the Cold War was lost. The importance of Europe in American Cold War strategy was of a different order from that of any other part of the world. For much of the Cold War era there was a convenient coincidence of economic, political and cultural affinities between the United States and West Europe which no other region enjoyed. These affinities underpinned common security interests and produced a long period of international stability for the region. At the heart of this security arrangement, conducive to remarkable economic development, was an unprecedented American political and military presence. The past 50 years of European international relations has been most notable for this American commitment, which provided the bedrock for the European security regime which prevented international war in the region during a period of intense ideological rivalry between two halves of the continent.[1] During this era the United States and West Europe shared many interests, but the most profound was opposition to Soviet Communism. It is difficult to exaggerate the extent to which countering the Soviet military threat, especially in Europe, obsessed American defence planning in every way from tactics and weapons' design to budgets. The same can be said for most of NATO Europe, particularly after the demise of the old West European empires in the 1960s. Even though the Cold War is now over, the security culture derived from that shared experience over many decades plays a major part in sustaining the current United States–West European security relationship. But as the Soviet threat recedes into history, the institutional memories fade and the culture is diluted.

Today, as the threat in Europe has steeply declined, greater threats and real competitive interests have grown in other regions. America's closest allies may still be in West Europe, but the greater dangers challenging American strategic interests are in the Middle East and East Asia. President Clinton's first Defence Secretary, Les Aspin, identified four salient new dangers in the post-Cold War world, all of which lay outside the North Atlantic area: regional conflict, the proliferation of nuclear and other weapons of mass destruction, threats to economic well-being and the failure of democratic reform in the former Soviet Union.[2] American strategic concern over Iraqi or Iranian behaviour in the Gulf and Chinese policy towards Taiwan take clear priority over West European security. A declining profile and presence in West Europe does not indicate an American retreat from world politics at the historic moment when it finds itself the world's only superpower, but other regions have overtaken Europe in the hierarchy of American strategic interests. Official pronouncements have made this change of perspective clear. Since 1993 American defence-planning has been predicated on the priority to deter and fight two major regional conflicts almost simultaneously and unilaterally if needs be.[3]

The regions of concern do not include Europe. The 'ready-to-fight two wars' American military machine is focused on East Asia and the Middle East. Apropos East Asia, the Clinton Administration declared in 1994 that nowhere was 'the need for continued United States engagement more evident'.[4] In the defence intellectual community in the United States, East Asia is the focus, with European affairs now clearly of secondary importance.[5] Japan and the People's Republic of China are seen as potential superpower competitors for the United States in the future, operating in a regional environment with characteristics prone to conflict: high economic growth; rapid social transformation; deep, historic animosities and suspicions; and no multilateral security framework. On the Middle East it has been asserted that the United States has 'enduring interests', which include 'assuring the security of Israel and our Arab friends, and maintaining the free flow of oil at reasonable prices'.[6] A range of crises in recent years does seem to have vindicated the two dominant major-regional-conflict perspective of US foreign and security policy. In October 1994, at the same time as sensitive negotiations between the United States and North Korea over its nuclear weapons programme, Iraq was seen to move large military forces towards the Kuwait border. Within 72 hours the United States had heavy ground forces in Kuwait with a further 150 000 troops poised to deploy if necessary. In March 1996, at the same time as the Arab–Israeli peace process was in deep crisis over militant Islamicist terrorist outrages inside Israel, two US carrier battle groups were moved to Taiwanese waters to counter extremely belligerent behaviour by mainland China.

Undoubtedly, through most of the 1990s, the greatest efforts of high US foreign and security policy have been expended outside traditional Euro–Atlantic relations and these efforts have demonstrated the core priorities. Non-proliferation pressures on North Korea, Iraq, Iran and the Ukraine, and the renewal of the Non-Proliferation Treaty in 1995, have yielded some successes. The Mexican loan guarantee, the North American Free Trade Agreement (NAFTA), the completion of the Uruguay Round of GATT, the formation of the World Trade Organisation and the implementation of robust trade policies with Japan show the central role world trade occupies in contemporary American foreign policy. Global trade figures bear out this reorientation of Washington's foreign policy priorities. In 1960 Japan and East Asia accounted for 4 per cent of world GNP, and the EEC for 25 per cent. In 1995 the EU accounts for about 25 per cent, as now does Japan and East Asia, and also NAFTA, but growth is much higher in East Asia. Since the late-1970s, US trade with Japan and East Asia has exceeded that with West Europe. In 1992, US exports to Asia exceeded that to Europe by 33 per cent to 26 per cent. In the mid-1990s, US trade with East Asia was about $350 billion; with the EU it was $220 billion and with Latin America $232 billion.[7] Sponsorship of the Arab–Israeli peace process and the unprecedented, simultaneous dual containment of Iran and Iraq, have also absorbed much of US foreign policy-making energy. European security issues, including the Balkan crisis, have taken a secondary position behind East Asian, Middle Eastern and global trade matters in post-Cold War US foreign and security policy.

American interests in and policy towards Europe is now just an element of Washington's global policy. It is fair to argue that for 50 years Europe was the central focus of American policy overseas; as the twenty-first century beckons Europe is but one prop supporting the edifice of global US policy. When United States policy-makers scan the world it is clear that the remnants of Communism no longer pose a real threat. The threat from China is not ideological: it is a traditional geo-strategic challenge. But while the fear of monolithic Communist advance has disappeared, it has been replaced by fear of chaos. George Bush's idealistic vision of a New World Order where states behaved according to international law and on the basis of justice has not come to pass. Instead, Washington sees potential for profound disorder, particularly in East Asia and the Middle East where vital American national interests are at stake. There is also the anxiety that democratic reform in the former Soviet Union could go into reverse and, in the longer-term, a Russian military threat could be reconstituted. American forces and strategy need to address these contingencies. Forces capable of addressing the two major-regional-conflicts scenario provide a hedge against a major hegemonic challenge in the longer-term, but such provision is expensive and politically fraught at home as well as overseas. Europe's primary value to the United States in the contemporary world is to provide moral and practical support to United States global policy. In the event of a major regional conflict, as in Desert Storm, the United States will look to its close West European allies for a collective, multilateral effort. If assistance is not forthcoming, the United States will act unilaterally – but West Europe would then be further diminished in Washington's eyes, regardless of who occupies the White House into the next century. American policy-makers see the United States as the 'sheriff of the posse'.[8] No other country can fulfil the deterrent role in the world's most volatile regions. To neglect the Middle East and East Asia is to make war more likely. If conflict does break out, it is very damaging to the whole developed world. It is in the interests of West Europe, Washington would argue, to support the United States.

The United States does not wish to cold-shoulder West Europe. In aggregate terms – political, economic and strategic – Europe will always be a leading interest of US foreign policy, but it is not a top-security concern. Matters in East Asia and the Middle East are more pressing and look set to be so for some time. While US force levels in Europe have declined considerably, they are increasing in the Gulf. Europe is quiescent. Viewed from North America, conflict in the Balkans, Georgia and Chechnya are brushfire wars not of central strategic concern. Given the policies pursued and the timeframe followed, the same may be said of the perspectives of these conflicts from many West European capitals. Compared to the Middle East and East Asia, Europe is a sea of calm with no core security problems, only a few peripheral nuisances. The framework of interlocking international institutions provides a web inhibiting serious interstate crises and war in the short- to medium-term. This is why, between 1990 and 1997, US forces in Europe could be reduced from 300 000 to 100 000; two out of three US military installations could be closed; the US Air Force could cut its combat aircraft from 666 to 168; and nuclear forces in Europe could be reduced by 80 per cent.[9]

The end of the Cold War has eased but not removed American hard choices. More American soldiers on the ground look set to stay in Europe – 65 000 – than in both the Middle East and East Asia combined. Yet the characteristics and circumstances of these two regions are more volatile and threatening than Europe. With US power in inevitable relative, but not absolute, decline, there is the mood that the United States should not and cannot bear too many burdens alone. Domestic demands saw the US defence budget decrease by 23 per cent in real terms between 1990 and 1994.[10] Defence Secretary Aspin's 'Bottom–Up Review' of US defence produced another $20 billion of reductions each year between 1995 and 1999. Nonetheless, as a percentage of GDP, US defence-spending will still be higher than most West European states and in absolute terms will exceed the whole of NATO Europe. To cover the range of global contingencies, the flexibility and adaptability of US forces will be the order of the day. West Europe's strategic value is and will continue to be, as a vehicle for the strategic flexibility and adaptability of US forces which have a global role addressing American national interests – which may often, coincidentally, also be West European national interests. But there may be occasions where interests do not coincide. Currently, the utility of West Europe as a staging post, reinforcement and resupply base for the Middle East largely sustains the relatively high level of US military presence on the continent. Rapid deployment to the Gulf in 1990 was made much easier by the presence of large standing forces in Europe and the use of NATO infrastructure. US European Command area of responsibility includes not only Europe, but Africa and the Middle East littoral. The pace of US military operations in Europe in the late 1990s is largely driven by humanitarian requirements and out-of-area security needs.[11] Essentially, the US security commitment to Europe is not valued for its own sake, but for what it can do for US global strategic policy.

New realism

This robust geo-strategic perspective took hold of the Clinton Administration in the period 1994–1995. Plummeting opinion poll ratings for the President and stunning electoral setbacks for the Democratic Party in the November 1994 Congressional elections changed the White House attitude towards foreign and security policy in two ways. First, the President shifted his focus from domestic affairs to foreign policy in search of a platform which would allow a greater exercise of presidential power and, hopefully, provide more tangible success than domestic matters. Second, with the new focus on foreign policy came the change of theme, in practice if not always in rhetoric. In the first 18 months or so of the Administration, practice had tried to match rhetoric and failed. In the Presidential campaign of 1992, candidate Clinton accepted the New World Order rhetoric of 'ideals and justice' with vigour. When in the White House, he chose to direct US foreign policy on the bases of American perspectives of principle and morality rather than tightly-defined national interest.

Moralistic but peripheral concerns such as domestic conditions in Bosnia, Somalia, Haiti and China took precedence over the strategic management of relations with other Great Powers which had a more direct influence on US national interests. Early in the Administration, Anthony Lake, National Security Adviser to the President, defined the role of United States foreign policy as 'helping the helpless'.[12] The idealism of these years not only neglected these relations with larger powers, it often hampered them as well. For two-and-a-half years United States–West European relations were severely hurt by disagreements over Bosnia. The United States would not back the West European support for the Vance–Owen, Owen–Stoltenberg and 1994 Contact Group peace plans. The Clinton Administration perceived the complex conflict not as a Yugoslavian civil war but as Serbian aggression against Bosnia and argued that justice was not served by any of the peace plans. It was a 'realpolitik' approach in 1995, driven by domestic political weakness, which produced the Dayton Agreement and a respite to the conflict. The 'abandonment of justice' as a guiding principle, and the political and military sponsorship of a Croat–Bosnian Federation, transformed the balance of forces on the ground and obliged the Bosnian Serbs to move towards some degree of compromise.

The conduct of all the external powers in ex-Yugoslavia is culpable, but the ethos of American foreign policy in 1993 and 1994 hindered a realistic compromise and severely damaged trans-Atlantic relations. Even where relations with large, regional powers were addressed, disproportionate influence was often exercised by domestic interest groups, for instance, trade issues being allowed to damage strategic relations with Japan and human rights issues jeopardising working relations with China. Of special importance to US–West European relations and US–Russian relations is the thorny issue of NATO expansion to the East. Much of the official American enthusiasm for expansion is driven by Central and East European ethnic groups inside the United States and by human rights lobbies anxious to anchor democracy in the brittle post-collectivist societies. But given the declaratory platform on which high US foreign policy was based, it was difficult for the Executive not to be seen to address its own principles of promoting American values rather than pursuing American national interests.

In his 1996 *Foreign Affairs* article, Michael Mandelbaum argued that the United States has definable national interests which the Clinton Administration neglected in its early years – and in the process damaged relations with allies.[13] Sustaining the American military presence in Europe and the Asia–Pacific region is attached priority. The Cold War is over, but vital allies need to be assured that there will be no rapid change in security circumstances. He argues that this is particularly important for the two economic Great Powers of the developed world: Germany and Japan. On the issue of the proliferation of weapons of mass destruction, no other country can lead like the United States and on this issue it is legitimate for American foreign and security policy to look to the periphery. Free trade is important and can play a role in economic reform in authoritarian societies, but is not so vital as geo-strategic stability. Such a distinct categorisation of US national interests was lost in the Clinton grand strategy of 'Engagement and Enlargement' with which the Administration replaced Containment. But the principles and moral attraction of engaging old enemies and enlarging democracy proved to be 'hardly stirring, vital or lucid'.[14] Abroad, some antagonism has been created among normally friendly states, such as Singapore, over the suggestion that societies which do not conform to American liberal social and political values are somehow wanting. US foreign policy also lays itself open to accusations of hypocrisy when it pressurises some regimes to democratise, yet turns a blind eye to authoritarian regimes such as Saudi Arabia. But the core weakness of 'Engagement and Enlargement' is the marked reluctance of the American public to support it. The American public has made it clear that it does not support the policy of nation-building in peripheral parts of the world when the deaths of young American soldiers is high among the costs it has to pay.

Given the natural, declining public interest in foreign and security policy consequent to the end of the Cold War, such disaffection with the American world role is alarming for America's allies, not least the prosperous West Europeans. The November 1994 mid-term elections were a turning point for the practice of American foreign policy, but the new realism is now faced by a new generation of legislators with a different world view from many of those they replaced. The US domestic agenda is now more pressing than foreign affairs and it is reflected in the dominant political ethos of the Congress. But when foreign policy is on the agenda, Congress is less willing than at any time since the interwar years to accept the direction of the Executive. The process of the reassertion of the Legislature began in the early 1970s as a consequence of the Vietnam War and the Watergate political scandal. It has proceeded gradually, without remission, until today. November 1994 gave the balance of power in foreign policy between Executive and Legislature an extra large push in favour of the Congress. George Will, the noted commentator, has described the Presidency as now 'miniaturised'.[15] It is ironic that Presidential authority in foreign and security policy is at its lowest for more than 50 years at the very time when, throughout the world, American power capabilities have little real competition. Yet foreign and security policy priorities and choices are at their most complex for more than 50 years. At the very moment when the United States needs an agile, imaginative, clearly focused foreign policy with a lucid appreciation of what are the interests of the United States, and what kinds of relationships with key allies are required, the chief organ of foreign policy-making is at its weakest.

The years 1992–1994 saw the largest influx of new members of Congress since 1946–1948. In the 1940s new members had to pay heed to foreign policy. The Cold War was beginning. Stalin had huge armies at the heart of Europe and those parts of the continent liberated by the Red Army were being forcibly Communised. In Asia, Civil War was raging in China, with the Communists gaining the upper hand. The global strategic situation today is very different: young congressmen, most with no military or world travel experience unlike their predecessors in the 1940s, feel they have no need to pay disproportionate attention to foreign policy. In Washington in the late 1990s foreign policy has become a sideshow. Domestic, economic and particularly budgetary matters are the concerns that exercise most legislators. It is when foreign and security policy interfaces with budgetary issues that the world outside receives most attention. In 1992, 110 new members joined the Lower House and 12 new members the Senate. In the Republican landslide of 1994, a further 86 freshmen joined the House and 12 new members the Senate.[16] Over 50 per cent of the Lower House and nearly 25 per cent of the Senate have been elected since the collapse of the Soviet Union. They do not have the Cold War habit of bipartisanship on national security matters; nor do they automatically assign high foreign-policy matters, such as NATO, high ranking on the government's agenda. Given that an inexperienced Administration came into office in 1993 committed to focus on the domestic economy 'like a laser beam' it is not surprising that no clear definition of firm US foreign policy interests was articulated towards a mass of equally inexperienced, unaware legislators. Whenever interest in foreign policy is demonstrated, a crude, unsophisticated general billet of foreign-policy perspectives may be discerned, some of which may coincide with the Democratic Administration but some of which clearly do not.

There is a visceral distrust of Russia regardless of who occupies the Kremlin. The Clinton Administration has invested a lot of political capital in supporting President Yeltsin, despite some distinct changes in the political mood and behaviour of the Russian government since 1993. Defeat for President Yeltsin in the June 1996 presidential elections could have been a major blow to American foreign policy. Many US legislators are enthusiastic for a rapid expansion of NATO into East Europe. They see it as a cost-effective way to check Russia: yet the prospect of such action undermines President Yeltsin and drives him towards the nationalists. The early Clinton Administration enthusiasm for NATO expansion has receded, but it is politically difficult to retreat now from the extravagant positions taken in 1994. Protecting American employment from perceived 'unfair' foreign competition is a leading concern of the Congress. It has also been a declared priority for President Clinton, but it creates difficulties in security relationships with leading trading partners such as West Europe and Japan. Preventing the spread of weapons of mass destruction to regimes unstable and hostile towards the United States was common to the Executive and the Legislature. But when the Executive faces a sensitive dilemma over policy towards a government it wishes to support but which is engaged in exporting nuclear material to a rogue state, the Executive cannot assume bipartisan support. For instance, in 1995 the Legislature showed much less sensitivity over President Yeltsin's predicament when the US asked him to desist from earning vital foreign currency by exporting nuclear reactors to Iran. Protecting sources of imported oil is another clear national interest where Executive and Congress are as one, except that to do so obliges the executive to compromise its own idealistic rhetoric about promoting American values abroad and persuading authoritarian states towards democratic political reform. Indeed, deep hostility by Congress towards the proclivity of the Clinton Administration to undertake moral crusades in strategically non-vital parts of the world, was a major cause of the readjustment of American foreign policy towards traditional national interests rather than values in 1994–1995. The misadventure in Somalia and the imagery of dead American soldiers displayed before the world's media was a 'pivotal event'.[17] The behaviour of an administration apparently lurching from crisis to crisis contributed to the election loss in 1994, the advent of a legislature suspicious of a world role and doubtful of the contributions of allies, and the enforced refocusing of high US foreign and security policy on traditional geo-strategic issues. The continuing weakness of American foreign policy is that the Legislature, so critical of much of the Executive behaviour, has little coherence in its own view of the wider world. Whether a Republican president can remedy this situation is open to doubt: as Robert Dole is a Cold-War veteran with foreign-policy perspectives derived from that era.

Today, in practice, US national interests – traditionally defined as those issues which could directly affect American lives – are to the fore rather than the global projection of American values or the pursuit of indirect strategies of support for American allies and distant protectorates. The shrinking of real resources for foreign and security policy demonstrate this mood. On foreign aid, at less than 0.3 per cent of GDP, the US now ranks at the bottom of the OECD per capita ranking. Nor is the public prepared to spend more on the military. While there remains some tolerance for high-technology weaponry to keep the United States forces the best in the world, there is little patience for ground operations in faraway places which risk casualties unless there is a clear and vital interest. In 1986, US defence-spending was 6.5 per cent of GDP; under current plans it will approximate 2.9 per cent in 1999, the lowest proportion of GDP since before the Second World War. Debate between moral duty and national interest in American foreign policy has raged since the early days of the Republic. At the end of the twentieth century, narrow, traditional interest is in the ascendant over nebulous notions of moral duty.

Much of the 'Engagement and Enlargment' rhetoric persists;[18] but it cloaks the more robust, self-interested approach which the Executive is now obliged to adopt. US *Presidential Review Document 13* illustrates the new realism. It acts as a guide to the White House over when to commit US forces overseas. A unilateral US response is to take place only when there is a direct threat to US security, such as an attack on a NATO country or the procurement of nuclear weapons by a hostile, unstable regime. Such contingencies constitute a Level One crisis. Building a coalition, imposing pressure or sending some but limited US troops as part of a peacekeeping force would be the response to a Level Two crisis, when there is trouble in a region where US allies have direct interests or Washington has important secondary interests. The Bosnian conflict fits this category. Humanitarian concerns in faraway countries have been relegated to Level Three contingencies. There may be calls for intervention, but the US should restrict itself to funds and not send troops.[19]

Without a Cold War type of threat, it is difficult for any kind of state to construct a coherent, overarching strategy. In the face of the Soviet threat, Containment was such a grand strategy. Containment has not returned, but the new realism has spawned a discerning, pragmatic variation of the venerable Cold War grand strategy. A series of mini-containments is being put into practice by the United States in an effort to protect geo-strategic interests in parts of the world deemed vital to US national interest.[20] Since 1994, as Russian foreign and security policy has swung towards a more authoritarian proto-imperial posture, a distinct coolness has entered Russian–US relations. Against clear Russian objections, the United States has sponsored 'Partnership for Peace' and rejected any notions of a Russian veto over NATO behaviour in East Europe. In Bosnia, American policy from early 1995 has been to contain Serbian power by sponsoring Croat–Bosnian Muslim power. In the Gulf, the 'dual containment' of Iran and Iraq is underway. There is a recent history of American Containment of one or other of these states. Following British military withdrawal from the Gulf in the early 1970s, the United States assumed the role of protector. Washington adopted a 'twin pillar' strategy of arming Saudi Arabia and Iran and encouraging an *entente* between the respective Sunni and Shia monarchies. This brought order to the Gulf and contained the Soviet client state of Iraq. The fall of the Shah of Iran in 1979 undermined this strategy, but the subsequent Iran–Iraq War absorbed the energy of two states hostile to Western interests. With the prospect of Iranian victory in 1987, Western assistance was given to those Gulf monarchies supporting Saddam Hussein. After the cessation of the Iran–Iraq War in 1988, Iran became the focus of US strategy in the Gulf, but the Iraqi invasion of Kuwait in 1990 presented the United States with two large hostile states in the region. No longer able to balance one against the other, 'dual containment' is the strategy forced upon the United States. Washington policy is to wage economic sanctions against Iraq via the UN embargo and against Iran with its own unilateral economic embargo. Underpinning the economic instrument of containment is the demonstrable military firepower of US Central Command, for which the Gulf region forms the core strategic focus.

The 'Atlantic' perspective

With American strategic attention drawn primarily to the Middle East and North East Asia, questions are raised as to the place of West Europe in Washington's strategic affections in the late 1990s. Writing in 1992, General Colin Powell, Chairman of the Joint Chiefs-of-Staff, argued that the American engagement in Europe is 'guaranteed', and talked about an 'Atlantic force conceptual package'.[21] The term 'Atlantic' was chosen carefully and the perspective he conveyed in 1992 has gathered pace and established itself firmly in the American national security community. 'Atlantic' means 'forces across the Atlantic', on the European side of the ocean but not exclusively for use in Europe. 'Across the Atlantic' incorporates Europe and the Middle East and South-West Asia. Powell saw heavy, well-trained and equipped, mobile American forces addressing not merely NATO European functions but, very importantly, national security missions in the Middle East and South-West Asia. He implied that European acceptance of such an extra-European role for US forces and European tolerance of the training required for it, was crucial to American Congressional and public acceptance of expensive US military forces in Europe after the collapse of the Soviet threat. West European maintenance of its own force levels was also important to sustain the American will to deploy 'across the Atlantic', which included Europe.

The 'Atlantic' concept does not mean that Europe, of itself, is no longer important to the United States. Troop levels have been drastically reduced in recent years. United States' forces are down from the final days of the Cold War. In 1989 US European Command deployed an all-service figure of 326 400 personnel. In 1995 the figure had declined to 139 200. But the figure still exceeds the total of US forces deployed in Japan and South Korea: 50 000 and 43 200 respectively.[22] There continues to be profound American political and economic interests in Europe which the end of the Cold War has not brought to an end, but in some cases enhanced. Trans-Pacific trade may exceed trans-Atlantic, but trans-Atlantic investment exceeds trans-Pacific. Inward investment from Europe to the United States is 60 per cent of the total; 25 per cent of the total comes from Asia. The gap is larger when manufacturing investment alone is considered: 71 per cent against 14 per cent.[23] On trade, it is correct that US–European trade is less than US–Asian trade, but it is much better balanced, with considerably smaller deficits. In 1993 the United States had a $7 billion deficit on trade with Europe; with Asia it was $115 billion. Fifty per cent of US direct investment abroad is in Europe and, in 1993, Europe was the US's second largest customer, receiving 31 per cent of American goods and services exports. Asia took 33 per cent. Three million Americans are employed by European firms in the United States; 1.5 million are employed by American exports to Europe.[24] Moreover, such economic activity, while lagging behind the high Asian growth rates, is taking place in a region of relative democratic stability. The political risk factor associated with business in the European Union is considerably less than that in China, Thailand or the Philippines. Political links with Europe, along with North America the world's most democratic region, remain of high priority. NATO is the world's most successful alliance and America's most entangling security commitment. To break or shun that link after 50 years would be a loud signal to the world of an American retreat from world power. To stop being a NATO member or to lead the argument for dissolution would be more traumatic for the United States body politic than was creating the Alliance in 1949. Such political attachments are reinforced by cultural links. The United States was founded by West Europeans and, in the 1990 census, 56.9 per cent of the 249 million population claimed European descent.

Nonetheless, Secretary of State Warren Christopher has spoken openly of the 'primacy of Asia', and has criticised 'Eurocentric' attitudes.[25] Trade with Asia is outstripping that with Europe, and will continue to do so even as the Asian economies mature and growth rates decline. East Asia is insecure: it demands strategic attention in a way that West Europe no longer requires. Objectively, Europe remains a major interest of US foreign policy, but to sustain the American commitment inherent continental interests must be compounded by other strategic benefits for the United States. Europe does provide the United States with friends and allies which can help to balance Russian power should it ever revive as a major threat. But, most important of all, in the contemporary world Europe can act as a base for American trans-Atlantic strategic interests and as a repository of dependable allies who will share the responsibility for the international security from which they also benefit. If NATO Europe hinders and inhibits the American use of forces and facilities for 'trans-Atlantic' purposes outside NATO Europe and shirks 'responsibility sharing', then a major prop to a continuing US security commitment to Europe will be destroyed.

For the American body politic 'responsibility sharing' is no mere slogan. It is taken very seriously. The end of the Cold War left the United States as the world's only superpower. No other state or coalition can challenge its range of 'hard' and 'soft' powers, but it is not so powerful that it can manage all of global security alone. The United States sees a role for itself 'enabling' and 'mobilising' coalitions. A leading Clinton official has described the US pivotal role in 'leading shifting coalitions of friends and allies to address shared security concerns'.[26] To make such coalitions effective, interoperability of equipment, common rules of engagement and burden-sharing arrangements need to be agreed. The old concept of burden-sharing (associated with host-nation support for forward-deployed US forces during the Cold War) is only one element of 'responsibility sharing'.[27] Other elements include alliance support, foreign aid, peacekeeping and anti-proliferation measures. The 1994 CJTF initiative, allowing the WEU the opportunity to use NATO assets for West European tasks, is cited by the Clinton Administration as an example of encouraging 'responsibility sharing'. NATO Europe, where there is a long, practised history of defence cooperation and integration, is attractive as a staging post to the Middle East. Much of the American heavy equipment used in the Gulf War came from West Europe, an ocean closer to the Middle East than North America. American peacetime deployments in Europe are seen as useful leverage over West Europe in the event of any objection to American use of the facilities for out-of-area operations.

Consistent NATO European objections to the American use of NATO infrastructure for non-NATO purposes would seriously upset the US Congress and put into jeopardy the American commitment to Europe. But NATO Europe is only partly valued as convenient real estate. The higher value is that it furnishes Washington's favoured candidates for coalition operations outside Europe. The two major-regional-conflicts strategy bears heavily on a US defence budget which is shrinking, yet will remain, by any measure, greater than that of NATO Europe. But as American forces get smaller, the premium increases on effective interoperability with NATO European forces in extra-European operations. The way in which the British armoured division worked effectively with US forces in the Gulf War of 1991 stands as a model. Defence Secretary Aspin saw Allied cooperation on global security issues as critical and advocated that NATO must focus on out-of-area to keep itself relevant to the United States.[28] Given that the US spends about 37 per cent of total global defence spending and its Allies about 30 per cent, effective cooperation can contribute great advantage to the Western democracies. Russia, China and the rogue states, such as Iran and Syria, combined spend about $103 billion on defence annually, which is about 15 per cent of the world total.[29]

NATO is Washington's preferred vehicle for 'responsibility sharing'. In its European security policy collective defence, as distinct from collective security, a dominant voice for the United States and the premier institutional role of NATO, are Washington's clear priorities. Exerting influence over Russian behaviour and pragmatic intervention in peripheral crises such as the Balkans, are important but secondary objectives linked to the top priorities. Since 1949 the United States has been the leader of NATO and is determined to remain so. NATO is the only trans-Atlantic institutional link binding the states of North America with West Europe alone. It is the most direct route for American influence in West Europe and has proved its worth over decades. The collective defence nature of the organisation has sustained its cohesion. No government in Washington has any intention of allowing NATO to be superseded either by a solely West European defence organisation or an all-European collective security organisation. In the case of the former, the vital American link to Europe would be broken. For reasons of 'responsibility sharing' a European defence identity is encouraged, but Washington is intolerant of any notion that NATO take a back seat to the WEU. In the short- to medium-term a lack of political will and agreement among the West European states and the absence of appropriate capabilities and infrastructure means that the WEU poses no real political threat to NATO. If it ever does, that is a recipe for American withdrawal from European security. The political threat from collective security comes from the OSCE. The institutionalisation of the CSCE into the OSCE, with various functional offices spread throughout Europe, for example, National Minorities in the Hague and Conflict Resolution in Vienna, does pose a challenge to NATO influence. The OSCE is not a military alliance and does not have military capabilities, but Russia has been pressing since 1994 for the elevation of OSCE as a Europe-wide security forum above NATO. Moscow wishes OSCE to become the paramount arbiter of acceptable norms of state behaviour in Europe, with special roles assigned to the Great Powers. As Chapter 4 makes clear, Moscow's objective is to dilute America's influence over European security by diminishing the role of NATO and relegating it to an agency of the OSCE. Washington is utterly opposed to such a vision. It is determined to sustain the centrality of NATO, and as a consequence the United States, to European security arrangements.

The political necessity to keep NATO vibrant, apparently relevant and to deflect accusations of atrophy, played a major role in American support for the North Atlantic Cooperation Council and the 'Partnership for Peace' initiatives. The political imperative was more compelling than any threat assessment or grand strategic manoeuvre. So was Washington's consideration of the formal expansion of NATO to the East to incorporate, at some unspecified date, some carefully selected East European states. No matter who occupies the White House, it is an article of faith that all the elements that constitute trans-Atlantic security demand the sustenance of NATO as Europe's premier security institution. Aside from the political imperatives, NATO still fulfils traditional military functions by insuring against atavistic developments in the former Soviet Union and by reassuring Europe, and the Germans themselves, about German military intentions and capabilities. The Cold War may have been over for nearly a decade but many security uncertainties persist in Europe. Within Europe NATO presents an unrivalled 'zone of stability' where, in international security matters, assumptions may be made about benign state behaviour that cannot be made anywhere else in the world apart from North America.

The United States has no intention of allowing Russia to join NATO, as is often suggested by Moscow. To do so would be to open the membership door to the rest of East Europe. An alliance of more than 25 states would require new constitutional arrangements: NATO would be transformed into a collective security organisation where the United States would find its influence challenged by Russia. In the event of aggression or intimidation, NATO would be unable to act against a member unless all agreed. Yet while Russia is denied NATO membership, Washington does not want to exclude Moscow from the concert of democratic states. To shun the new Russia is to feed resentment and to fuel nationalist paranoia. Despite its weakened state, Russia still has the potential to do considerable harm to American interests in Asia as well as Europe. So the construction of a set of relationships with Russia is seen as a way to entangle Russia into the democratic international system without damaging the institutions, particularly NATO, which contributed to the historic transformation of East–West relations.[30] Encouraging Russian membership of 'Partnership for Peace', which is a bilateral relationship with NATO, while acknowledging a parallel relationship between the United States and Russia as two Great Powers, addresses the policy of gradually admitting Russia to the democratic international system. Russian membership of the Contact Group on ex-Yugoslavia and its special role as an adjunct to the NATO Implementation Force in 1996 provide further illustration of the strategy of entanglement without formal incorporation. Promoting Russian good behaviour in Europe is a leading American objective, but protection of NATO's integrity and Washington's pre-eminent position within the organisation are attached clear priority.

Pragmatic self-interests

It is generally accepted in Washington, including the new Congress, that to 'lose' Europe after winning the Cold War would be an historic foreign policy disaster. But the well-being of Europe now takes second place to domestic issues, trade interests and global strategy. In Secretary of State Christopher's evidence to the Senate Foreign Relations Committee on 14 February 1995, he placed open trade and exports at the top of his list of foreign policy priorities:

> First, we must sustain the momentum we have generated towards the increasingly open global and regional trading system that is vital to American exports and American jobs. A core premise of our domestic and foreign policy is that our economic strength at home and abroad are mutually reinforcing.[31]

A few months later Under-Secretary of Commerce Jeffrey Garten reinforced the Christopher message. 'The days when we will subordinate our economic interests to political and security alliances – unless we are directly threatened militarily – are over.'[32] There is an acceptance that there is no cast-iron formula or neat blueprint for US–West European relations. The intellectual and strategic vacuum left by the demise of the Cold War has made it difficult to construct a grand strategy. This conceptual problem has been exacerbated by the decline in the authority of the presidency and the incumbency of the first post-Cold War presidency by a politician poorly qualified to fill the post. In office, the Clinton foreign policy learning curve has been very steep and very deep. Fighting the Cold War was a great US–West European project; now there is no great project. On the big issues such as managing reform in Russia, global trade and global security there is not the clear unanimity of purpose that was present in the resistance to Soviet Communism.[33] Indeed, to force the pace on these issues in order to construct a great project will produce deep fissures in a US–West European security relationship which is still in fairly good repair. But in this 'pick and choose' strategic environment the United States will be reluctant to assume responsibility for security issues unless they are vital to American national interests, whether in Europe or anywhere else.

In global security, the strategic priorities for NATO Europe are in Central and East Europe and the Mediterranean littoral, particularly North Africa. For the United States the strategic priorities are the Middle East and Gulf, East Asia and Russia. There is some overlap but there is also considerable divergence. Currently, there is little agreement beyond rhetoric on prioritising and constructing a strategy to counter terrorism, to contain rogue states, to inhibit the proliferation of weapons of mass destruction and to pacify militant Islam. Leaving the United States to act unilaterally outside Europe, while expecting it to act as the patron of multilateral action in the NATO area whenever there is a problem, is no longer politically realistic. Regardless of old ties and allegiances, the national interest ethic is now pervasive in American foreign policy circles.[34] The future good health of the US–West European relationship depends upon the West Europeans making it evident to Washington, especially the Congress, that it is in the strategic self-interest of the United States to sustain NATO. Valuable as NATO's contribution to the protection of American political and economic interests on the European continent may be, it is the threats to American interests outside Europe that capture the attention of US policy-makers in trans-Atlantic relations. If West Europe retreats from a meaningful role in supporting American strategic policy in the Middle East, any residual, sentimental affection for NATO in Washington will be reassessed.

The leading West European military powers – Britain, France, Germany, Spain and Italy – need to address this matter urgently. To expect total compliance of West Europe with American strategic priorities and policies would be to put unbearable strain upon NATO and to break the very link that requires protection. But prudent, expedient actions by West Europe can conform to the American model of trans-Atlantic security and bolster the US commitment to Europe. These actions can be political and military and of such a nature that they convey a clear signal that the West European democracies appreciate US strategic interests and problems and wish to support their major ally. On the political front, EU foreign ministers could abandon the 'critical dialogue' they have pursued with Iran and support the American economic embargo and political isolation of a regime which supports terrorist activity throughout the Middle East and leads the Rejectionist Front against the Arab–Israeli peace process. It is a source of growing resentment in Washington that West Europe appears to place economic links with the militant regime in Iran above American efforts to pacify the Gulf, support the Arab–Israeli peace process and inhibit state-sponsored terrorism.[35] On military matters West Europe should divert more resources from continental defence towards power-projection capabilities and flexibility. High-quality West European forces able to deploy quickly, with considerable fire-power and sustainability, need to be procured in strength over and above the small packages present in British and French forces. Areas of operation should not be confined to South East Europe or the southern shores of the Mediterranean. Contingency planning should be seen to conform to the geographical area of US Central Command. An out-of-area strategy ought to be codified into NATO doctrine. None of these developments need oblige all of NATO Europe to provide multilateral support to all US initiatives in the Middle East and South-West Asia. But it does enable some West European states, in some contingencies, to ease the burden on the United States. It does enhance NATO's relevance to American trans-Atlantic security interests. This is particularly important in the light of the increasing emphasis on 'flexibility' in US military doctrine.[36]

Globally, US military responsibilities are divided into five commands in regions outside continental USA: European Command, Central Command, Atlantic Command, Pacific Command and Southern Command. These commands require various combinations of general purpose forces, but the aggregate requirements of all the commands exceed the forces available. So flexibility is essential. This is acceptable because it is not expected that all five theatres will require forces at the same time. Such a strategic approach is of significance for Europe because arguments are circulating at the highest levels that deploying large, heavy forces in Europe inhibits flexibility. Flexibility is increased by having most forces home-based.[37] US-based forces can train without restrictions and are available for deployment to the Middle East, or Asia, or South America. Based in West Europe, alternative deployments are more limited. When it comes to speed of deployment, sea-lift for heavy equipment is only marginally longer to the Middle East from the east coast of the United States than from Germany. In the deployment of personnel by air, the time differences are even less significant. Political flexibility is also enhanced with more home-based forces. There are no problems with host governments perhaps objecting to the departure of American troops or the use of local infrastructure. There are persuasive arguments that flexible American strategic power-projection is better served by maintaining only a very token presence, rather than a large deployment, of US forces in West Europe, and that West Europe's value as a base and staging-post to the Middle East is much exaggerated. As the perceived value of West Europe to US global strategic needs declines, West Europe needs to work all the harder to convince Washington of its advantages in maintaining a strong military commitment on the continent. In the meantime, the United States is determined to continue its leadership in European security. This is not to be surrendered to the European Union, France or Russia. In the short- to medium-term the United States will attempt to persuade the leading West European powers to view their strategic interests from a global perspective and to take serious rather than symbolic action. Washington has made it clear that it will not and cannot assume every European security task, in or out-of-area, and will rely more on local powers exerting influence in their own areas. The United States believes that there is a US–West European security relationship worth preserving, in the strategic interests of both sides of the Atlantic, but as the strategic environment has changed so must West European strategic perspectives. In this regard the attitudes and policies of Britain and France, America's traditional allies on the West European Atlantic seaboard, are crucial. These are regional powers with an historic, global outlook which, particularly in the case of Britain, may have considerable empathy with the 'transatlantic' security model.

Notes

1. See Gregory Treverton, 'America's stakes and choices in Europe', *Survival*, Vol. 34, No. 3, Autumn 1992, pp. 119–21 for analysis of how European security became an in-tegral part of the American 'foreign policy landscape' during the Cold War.
2. See Les Aspin, 'Forces and alliances for a new era', in *European Security after the Cold War Part II* (London: IISS, 1994), Adelphi Paper 285, p. 72.
3. See *A National Security Strategy of Engagement and Enlargement* (Washington: White House, July 1994), p. 7.
4. *Ibid.*, p. 23.

5. See Harold Brown, 'Transatlantic security in the Pacific century', *Washington Quarterly*, Vol. 18, No. 4, Autumn 1995, p. 77. Also, see 'America's Chinese puzzle', *Economist*, 25 May 1996, pp. 79–85 for analysis of Washington's preoccupation with East Asia.

6. *A National Security Strategy of Engagement and Enlargment* (Washington: White House, July 1994), p. 25.

7. See Philip H. Gordon, 'Recasting the Atlantic Alliance', *Survival*, Vol. 38, No. 1, Spring 1996, p. 38.

8. Joseph S. Nye, 'Conflicts after the Cold War', *Washington Quarterly*, Vol. 19, No. 1, Winter 1996, p. 6.

9. *United States Security Strategy for Europe and NATO* (Washington: Department of Defense, Office of International Security Affairs, June 1995), p. 29.

10. See 'The price of staying secure', *Economist*, 14 January 1995, pp. 46–9.

11. *United States Security Strategy for NATO and Europe*, pp. 27–8.

12. Cited in Michael Mandelbaum, 'Foreign policy as social work', *Foreign Affairs*, Vol. 75, No. 1, 1996, p. 29. This article presents a severe critique of first-term Clinton foreign policy. On the same theme, see Henry Kissinger, 'Foreign policy is more than social engineering', *International Herald Tribune*, 13 May 1996, p. 9.

13. *Ibid.*, p. 28.

14. Richard Ullman, 'A late recovery', *Foreign Policy 101*, Winter 1995–96, p. 77.

15. Cited in William G. Hyland, 'A mediocre record', *Foreign Policy 101*, Winter 1995–96, p. 74.

16. See Robert Greenberger, 'Dateline: Capitol Hill: The new majority's foreign policy', *Foreign Policy 101*, Winter 1995–96, p. 160.

17. *Ibid.*, p. 163.

18. See foreword by Defence Secretary William Perry in *United States Security Strategy for Europe and NATO* (Washington: Department of Defense, Office of International Security Affairs, June 1995).

19. See 'The Clinton Doctrine', *Newsweek*, 28 March 1994, p. 3.

20. See 'Introducing neo-containment', *Economist*, 6 May 1995, p. 57.

21. See Colin L. Powell, 'The American commitment to European security', *Survival*, Vol. 34, No. 2, Summer 1992, p. 7.

22. See *The Military Balance 1989/90* and *1995/96* (London: IISS, 1989 and 1995).

23. See Harold Brown, 'Transatlantic security in the Pacific century', *Washington Quarterly*, Vol. 18, No. 4, Autumn 1995, p. 77.

24. See *United States Security Strategy for Europe and NATO* (Washington: Department of Defense, Office of International Security Affairs, June 1995), pp. 3–4.

25. Cited in Philip H. Gordon, 'Recasting the Atlantic Alliance', *Survival*, Vol. 38, No. 1, Spring 1996, p. 39.

26. Joseph S. Nye, 'Conflicts after the Cold War', *Washington Quarterly*, Vol. 19, No. 1, Winter 1996, p. 20.

27. See *United States Security Strategy for Europe and NATO* (Washington: Department of Defense, Office of International Security Affairs, June 1995), pp. 31–2.

28. See Les Aspin, 'Forces and alliances for a new era', in *European Security after the Cold War Part II* (London: IISS, 1994), Adelphi Paper 285, pp. 74–6.

29. See Stephen Rosenfeld, 'When it comes to defense, America lacks a coherent strategy', *International Herald Tribune*, 20 November 1995, p. 8.

30. See Philip Zelikow, 'The masque of institutions', *Survival*, Vol. 38, No. 1, pp. 15–16.

31. 'Christopher: Bipartisan foreign policy will be sustained' (Text: statement to Senate Foreign Relations panel), *USIS European Wireless File*, 15 February 1995, p. 5.

32. Cited in Philip H. Gordon, 'Recasting the Atlantic Alliance', *Survival*, Vol. 38, No. 1, Spring 1996, p. 35.

33. See Gregory Treverton, 'America's stakes and choices in Europe', *Survival*, Vol. 34, No. 3, Autumn 1992, pp. 127–8.

34. See Jonathan Clarke, 'Leaders and followers', *Foreign Policy 101*, Winter 1995–96, p. 42.

35. See Toby Helm, 'EU resists move to punish Iran', *Daily Telegraph*, 11 March 1996, p. 12; and 'Christopher assails Europe for dialogue with Iran', *International Herald Tribune*, 22 May 1996, p. 10.

36. See Paul R. S. Gehhard, *The United States and European Security* (London: IISS, 1994), Adelphi Paper 286, pp. 32–9 for a lucid exposition of these arguments.

37. See *ibid.*, pp. 45–50, for detailed examination of strategic flexibility. For discussion of broad-based political, economic and military flexibility linked to clearly defined US national interests, see David M. Abshire, 'US global policy: Toward an agile strategy', *Washington Quarterly*, Vol. 19, No. 2, Spring 1996, pp. 41–61.

Chapter 6

France and Britain – Competing Visions

France: continental manoeuvres

On the general issue of continental European security, within the remit of Article 5 of the North Atlantic Treaty, France appears very supportive of NATO and Washington's leadership of the Alliance. In the short- to medium-term, this looks likely to continue. Indeed, given the record of French national security policy from the foundation of the Fifth Republic in 1958 until the end of the Cold War, and then the first two years of the post-Cold War era, the degree of commitment and support shown to NATO by France since 1993 seems remarkable.

For about 30 years, from the presidency of Charles de Gaulle until midway through the second term of President Mitterand, French security policy had certain consistent, core characteristics. High foreign policy was emphatically independent in objectives and management, being seen to address what were deemed to be French national interests. This foreign policy was supported by a defence policy, heavily reliant on French procured and commanded strategic and tactical nuclear weapons, which was as autonomous as France could afford. It was deemed a contradiction of French sovereignty for the control of French capital weapons and conventional forces to be under the command and control of foreign generals and the influence of foreign governments. From an ultra-realist position, successive French governments insisted that it was inconceivable that another country's generals and leaders would ever put France's strategic interests ahead of their own, especially in time of war. Hence French sovereignty and national interests, as well as self-esteem, required that French leaders control French national security policy.[1] Where this required France working with NATO Allies it would do so, but it would not subordinate French interests to collective NATO command and control under the dominant direction of the United States, assisted by Britain. Hence, in 1963 the Franco–German bilateral treaty heralded a long-term strategy of French courtship of West Germany as a balance to Anglo–American dominance in European security matters, and in 1966 France announced its withdrawal from the NATO integrated military structure. This did not mean that France withdrew from NATO. Contrary to much popular belief, it did not. France remained a member of the North Atlantic Treaty and retained its seat on the North Atlantic Council. But it absented itself from formal membership of those bodies where integrative planning and decision-making took place, such as the Defence Planning Committee (DPC), the Military Committee (MC), and Supreme Headquarters Allied Powers Europe (SHAPE). Throughout the remainder of the Cold War various agreements were reached between SHAPE and French governments about how France would work with other NATO allies in the event of war. During this period it stretched the strategic imagination to envisage how France could choose not to fight with NATO allies, not least West Germany, should a major East–West conflict break out in Europe. Nonetheless French governments insisted that their forces should not fall under command of the Supreme Allied Commander Europe (SACEUR) and that France retain the choice of where and when to act. French strategic doctrine, particularly the 'Tous-azimuths' (all-horizons), multi-directional, proportionate deterrence nuclear strategy declared to the world French independence in foreign and security policy, and fulfilled an important psychological and domestic political function for a society and body politic which had experienced so many traumas in the twentieth century. But rebuilding French national pride and sense of nationhood after calamitous wars and loss of empire were not the sole motivation. As ever, Germany loomed large in French foreign policy. As the Federal Republic gathered its economic strength and won some political rehabilitation, France needed its independent foreign policy and military might both to balance German strength and to entice Germany into an entangling relationship which, at the political level at least, France hoped to dominate.

For a short spell at the end of the Cold War, the unification of Germany and the collapse of the superpower bipolar security regime intensified France's commitment to an independent foreign policy and the entanglement of Germany in a French-dominated European system of security. Deeper West European integration became the hallmark of French foreign policy from 1990. Integration within the European Community, with France as the dominant force, was acceptable and desirable, while integration in a US-dominated NATO was unacceptable. The surprising unification of Germany, and the prospect of living with a local superpower, provided a great impetus to French plans for a common European defence policy. In Paris there were distinct fears of a major American military retreat from Europe before German strength could be anchored in a European security organisation. The Franco–German brigade of 1989 was transformed into the Eurocorps in 1991 just before the Maastricht summit, and other West European Union (WEU) members were invited to contribute. Belgium and Spain subsequently did so. France looked to the WEU as the vehicle for a concrete European security and defence identity (ESDI). In the period 1990–1992, France was very hostile to the prospect of NATO reform, seeing a revamped alliance providing an obstacle to French objectives of European defence integration via the WEU which Paris intended to develop into an agency of the post-Maastricht European Union.[2] Yet, while pushing for an ESDI, France remained critical of NATO's integrated military structure and gave clear signals that it wished to remain as distant as ever from the Alliance. Paris argued that the end of the Cold War reduced the need for an integrated military structure, and that all that was required were capabilities for joint planning, common procedures for interoperability and some occasional joint exercises. It argued that there was no need for complicated, institutionalised, multinational commands, and that NATO ought to return to its original condition of 1949 as a diplomatic guarantee pact.[3]

The early post-Cold War US initiative to push NATO towards non-Article 5 out-of-area activities was resisted by France, and the evolution of the Franco–German brigade to the Eurocorps was one manifestation of French attitudes. Another was the establishment, in July 1992, of separate WEU and NATO naval task forces in the Adriatic to police the UN arms embargo of ex-Yugoslavia. At the highest political levels, Paris–Washington relations remained cordial over European security. France was careful not to aggravate the US too much. Throughout the Fifth Republic France has always wished to limit American influence in Europe but it has never desired complete American withdrawal. The United States was the vital balance to the Soviet Union, and was and is welcome as an additional constraint on German behaviour. So, with little enthusiasm, France participated in the 1990–1991 NATO Strategy Review, joined the Western coalition to the Gulf, agreed (with clear reservations) to the New Strategic Concept, and went along with the June 1992 NATO Foreign Ministers acceptance of the possibility of non-Article 5 missions for the Alliance. But, at high bureaucratic level, competition between Americans and French views was said to be intense.[4] This period of rivalry, coupled with the residue of frustration derived from French Gaullist policies during the Cold War, has created a culture of suspicion and distrust among a generation of senior American foreign policy-makers when working with French officials.[5] French sponsorship of the WEU as a rival to, and potential replacement for, NATO particularly upset the sensibilities of American officials who have spent much of their careers dealing with Europe. Until very recently, many American government servants in the foreign and security policy fields spent most of their careers dealing with European affairs. European interests and expertise were deemed the primary career path to advancement to senior levels. That may now be changing with the relative promotion of the Middle East and East Asia over continental Europe in American foreign-policy concerns – but such changes will take some time to work their way through the foreign and security policy bureaucracy of the United States.

However, since 1992, the change in French behaviour in some important aspects of France's relationship has been marked. The years between the fall of the Berlin Wall and NATO's adoption of a non-Article 5 role brought signs of France's growing isolation and potential irrelevance to European security arrangements rather than the contrary. In May 1991, despite pressures from Paris, the NATO DPC, of which France was not a member, agreed to a NATO multinational Rapid Reaction Force. This undercut France's efforts to propagate a purely West European defence organisation and reinforced NATO's superior position above other European security institutions. At the same time, France's unique role between the two blocs was no longer apposite when both the Warsaw Pact and then the Soviet Union disintegrated in 1991. Yet while France argued for a scaled-down NATO but a more integrative European defence system, its foreign-policy record trumpeted Gaullist shibboleths of independence and national sovereignty. On the ground, the contribution France was able to make to the coalition forces in the 1990–1991 Gulf conflict revealed serious deficiencies in conventional forces. Shortcomings in modern command, control and intelligence, air and sea lift, and rapidly deployable, large forces illustrated French inability to assume a serious, unilateral, world role. At home, the unification of Germany and the liberation of East Europe rendered the intermediate and tactical nuclear arsenal redundant and converted those missiles into potential political liabilities rather than reasons to listen to what Paris had to say. Nor was the ESDI concept gathering momentum. Maastricht ratification was experiencing great difficulties in many EC countries, including France where it scraped home in the 1992 referendum. Apart from France, defence spending was in sharp decline throughout West Europe. There was clearly not the political will in West Europe to invest in a French-inspired, self-sustaining ESDI. In order to retain influence, it was clear that France would need to realign its foreign and security policy to a large extent, and to work with prevailing strategic and political realities.[6]

From 1993 France has worked more closely with NATO, and has readapted itself to NATO procedures while retaining some elements of traditional Gaullism in its foreign and security policy posture. Ironically, as France has pursued this pragmatic course, the reasons for doing so have gathered strength. This is not to say that President Chirac, elected in 1995, has abandoned the European foreign and security policy objectives of his predecessor. He has not. On some vital NATO issues there is clear evidence that the ESDI objectives of Paris survive and that the 1990s rapprochement with NATO is a tactical phase in longer-term French security ambitions. As one noted French commentator has stated, 'In order to be more European tomorrow it is necessary to be more Atlanticist today.'[7]

January 1993 brought the initial salvo of France's charm offensive towards NATO. French, German and NATO discussions agreed that the Eurocorps would be placed under NATO operational command at times of crisis and war. In other words, France's 1st Armoured Division, its contribution to the Eurocorps, would fall under SACEUR command in the event of a threat or attack against NATO. This still left the vast bulk of French forces outside NATO command, but it was a gesture which ran contrary to French security policy of the previous 30 years. Notions of France following the 'Spanish model' of limited involvement in the integrated military structure and the need for Paris to exert influence over decision-making in the Alliance began to circulate.[8] Already, in December 1992, President Mitterand had allowed French participation in NATO staff work on Bosnia. Indeed, the self-evident difficulties of the EU to manage the resolution of the conflict in ex-Yugoslavia and the inexorable slow march towards NATO intervention at a range of levels reinforced the argument that France should not be isolated from NATO initiatives and decisions.[9]

Since 1966 the French mission to the NATO Military Committee had only a 'consultative voice' and observer status. From April 1993, Head of Mission General Jean-Paul Pelisson joined meetings which considered peacekeeping. Two months later the NATO and WEU naval task forces in the Adriatic combined under NATO command. Also in 1993, Paris stated that Washington, as the lead power in NATO, should be consulted first in the event of crisis, and only if the US did not wish to become involved could Europe then consider going ahead alone. At first sight this seems to be recognition of United States primacy in European security – but it could also be interpreted as an astute response to the advent of the new Clinton Administration. Paris was aware that President Clinton wished to cut defence expenditure, encourage allies to bear more of the burden, and devote most of his attention to American domestic and political economic matters. Benign American neglect of European security would facilitate France's encouragement of the ESDI. The landslide election of a conservative coalition in the French National Assembly in early 1993 fuelled moves towards a closer relationship with NATO. President Mitterand, already moving slowly down that route, had a new government more supportive of that realistic policy than the previous one. Another indication at this time of a French reconsideration of defence posture was a move towards Britain on nuclear matters, though without jeopardising French nuclear independence. Paris evinced an interest in close, bilateral, nuclear consultations. In July the French–British summit agreed to establish the Joint Commission on Nuclear Policy and Doctrine, agreed at the 1992 NATO Gleneagles Summit as a temporary measure, as a permanent institution. In 1993–1994 new French military missions were assigned to the three major SACEUR subordinate commands. French links with SHAPE were expanded and, at the landmark January 1994 Brussels summit, France took the lead with the United States as co-chairman of the NATO counter-proliferation initiative. As NATO became more deeply involved in ex-Yugoslavia, and there was the prospect of on-the-ground intervention, if for no other reason than to rescue the retreating UN forces, France moved closer to the crisis-management bodies.

In September 1994 Defence Minister François Leotard attended an informal gathering of defence ministers at Seville. This was the first time since 1966 that a French defence minister had attended a NATO meeting. It was a clear signal that France had decided to work inside NATO to change NATO in the direction of greater military independence for Europe. In the context of the Leotard attendance at the Seville meeting, one French policy-maker is noted as stating, 'If you want European defence, you discover that NATO has most of the bricks, and you want to get your hands on them.'[10] A year later, in September 1995, 60 aircraft and 1000 personnel from seven countries conducted the first NATO exercise on French soil since 1966. In October the Defence Minister Charles Millon attended another informal defence ministers meeting – discussions but no decisions taken. The French Chief-of-Staff, General Jean-Philippe Douin, attended the NATO Military Committee, the first time a French general had attended since 1966. In December 1995 Foreign Minister Hervé de Charette declared France's full participation in the Military Committee and 'regular' attendance by French defence ministers at NATO meetings. With major French involvement in the NATO IFOR deployment in ex-Yugoslavia in January 1996 to implement the Dayton Agreement, French forces came under NATO command for the first time in 30 years. France's new alignment with NATO has been further underscored by French participation in the NATO Defence College in Rome, the SHAPE school at Oberammergau, and the round-the-clock crisis management NATO Situation Centre in Brussels.

By the mid-1990s, the conservative French presidency and government seemed to have acknowledged the primacy of NATO in European security and the premier role of the United States. In February 1996 President Chirac made the first state visit by a French president to the United States in 12 years. In his address to the US Congress he stated that, 'Today, as yesterday, the world needs the United States … [Your] political commitment to Europe and military presence on European soil remain an essential factor in the stability and security of the continent.' However, in the same address, President Chirac made it clear that reform of NATO was required, that change should bring a greater role to the European allies and that 'France is ready to take part fully in this process of renovation'.[11] The European use of NATO facilities even when the United States did not wish to become engaged was advocated.[12]

In 1994 the new French Defence Law, the first for 22 years, illustrated salient elements of the new conservative defence thinking. Due respect was given to the Gaullist heritage by a continuing insistence on French control of national security. The projected expenditure emphasised the importance attached to military power as a political instrument. An extra-European, world role for France was still envisaged in 1994, with plans for air and sea lift capabilities for 130 000 men and their equipment to overseas crisis spots, supported by a navy which would not be allowed to fall below 100 ships. Contrary to most other West European states, France was not seeking a real peace dividend, but looked ahead to steady and increasing defence expenditure into the next century.[13] But the realities of the complex, post-Cold War world did oblige the government to speak of 'strategic autonomy' rather than independence. The Defence Law also adopted a constructive attitude towards NATO. However, France's European ambitions lay at the heart of the law, and a bargain seemed to be on offer to NATO. France would work more closely with NATO if the European dimension of NATO would prosper. It was declared that the European defence project required sacrifices and that there would need to be 'mutualisation of power'.[14] French defence policy would be governed, at its core, by the 'common defence' objectives laid out by the Maastricht Treaty. One feature of this was the ambition for greater arms procurement with EU partners, and proposals for a Franco–German joint arms procurement agency.

Given France's European defence aspirations, the January 1994 NATO Summit in Brussels was very encouraging. In French eyes it marked the creation of a great opportunity for France's European defence objectives and made the resumption of serious involvement in NATO inner circles imperative. The three core pronouncements of the Summit seemed to set NATO's course for the remainder of the decade and France had a major interest in each core issue. Eventual enlargement of the Alliance towards the East was endorsed by the creation of the 'Partnership for Peace' programme. France sees enlargement, albeit all very gradual, as an impediment to the deepening of West European defence integration. In particular, a possible NATO enlargement policy encompassing Poland, the Czech Republic and Hungary would be a severe distraction for Germany, not least if enlargement provoked an unfriendly Russian response. Since 1994, France has not been pressing, unlike Germany at times, for decisive NATO responses towards East Europe. The NATO decision in December 1995 not to announce a membership timetable and to adopt a more gradual approach was welcomed by Paris.

A second core issue was NATO's counter-proliferation measures against the spread of nuclear, chemical and biological weapons and material. France was very supportive of this initiative, which is a matter to which Washington attaches the highest priority. But it was the third core issue to emerge from the summit which France found most attractive, and believes is conducive to its ESDI objectives. The Combined Joint Task Force (CJTF) proposals have been seen by successive French administrations as seriously addressing French aspirations towards a stronger European pillar within NATO and the longer-term fulfilment of an ESDI. The CJTF concept has been acceptable to the Clinton Administration because it serves the American European security policy of the 1990s. This does not mean that Washington policy-makers are unaware of the reasons for French enthusiasm for the CJTF. There is a strong lobby in the United States which perceives France as positioning itself within NATO for a longer-term challenge to American leadership from the basis of a cohesive European pillar within the Alliance, which may become detachable from NATO some day. French officials, while admitting that they wish to reform NATO's internal workings, deny any subversive intentions. Yet there is persistent insistence on the renovation of Alliance structures to accommodate Europe's rightful place in Western security.[15]

Such uneasy suspicions of French intentions have been exacerbated by the wrangle between Washington and Paris over command and control procedures for the CJTF. Central to the CJTF is the notion of 'separable but not separate' forces. NATO Europeans are granted access to NATO equipment, logistics and communications for operations in which the United States feels it does not wish or has no need to become involved. Nonetheless the US must be consulted and its agreement gained and, to date, command and control of the CJTF is to operate primarily through NATO structures, though command and control may be granted to the WEU for peacekeeping and humanitarian operations where overt conflict is very low or absent. Since 1994, France has been campaigning for a separate command structure for CJTF. Paris argues – as it has done since 1966 – that NATO's integrated military structure gives too much authority to SACEUR and too little to political authorities in Member States in Europe. The reason for France's problematic relationship with NATO's DPC is its managerial control of the integrated military structure which France sees as the prerogative of national capitals. Hence France's current posture is to work on an *ad hoc* basis with the DPC but not to participate in decision-making within the DPC. France accepts that the integrated military structure may be suitable for other NATO countries in situations of total war, and for automatic Article 5 type scenarios, but it insists that non-Article 5 out-of-area situations will be highly political, limited-war or crisis-management, *ad hoc* problems. The strategic straitjacket imposed by the integrative military structure and SACEUR would be inappropriate, especially if the United States is not involved in the operation on the ground. So, while Washington wishes to keep SACEUR in a central role for CJTF operations, France wishes to dilute the influence of SHAPE.[16] But while Paris has been calling for the CJTF to operate outside SHAPE, Washington argues that CJTF missions may affect NATO territory and command and control should normally work through the tried and tested integrated military structure. Paris wants a CJTF outside NATO command and within a WEU structure; Washington wants CJTF headquarters within NATO command. Even though reliant on NATO/SHAPE assets, Paris wants to avoid a WEU/CJTF subject to an American general at SHAPE. Clearly France sees its ideal vision of ESDI compatible only with a separate command structure for CJTF. If, over the longer term, France does not achieve much of what it wants over CJTF, then its rediscovered enthusiasm for cooperation with NATO may lose some *élan*.

Within NATO France has a clear reformist agenda.[17] It wishes to assert greater political control over the military structure by downgrading the DPC and major

NATO commands, and elevating the North Atlantic Council. It supports the attendance of Defence Ministers as well as Foreign Ministers at the North Atlantic Council. It also wishes to use a revamped NATO as a major plank in its construction of an ESDI. A European bloc within NATO to bargain with the United States would advance the ESDI cause. Setbacks on the CJTF would be a major blow to the French agenda and self-esteem.

It is NATO's post-Cold War policy of considering non-Article 5, out-of-area peacekeeping and related mission which most clearly elucidates the differences between Anglo–American and French views over NATO's future organisation and direction. In February 1996 it was announced that, just two years after its introduction, the 1994 French Defence Law was to be scrapped.[18] Under new plans, defence spending was to be cut by 18 per cent between 1997 and 2002. Conscription is to be abandoned and the armed forces cut by one-third. Professionalism on the British model is to be introduced, with an all-professional armed forces by 2002. In the restructuring of the armed forces, emphasis will be given to flexibility and rapid deployment. There is the objective of a Rapid Deployment force of 50 000–60 000 men anywhere in the world by 2002. France's determination to continue to play a global role was clearly stated. But France sees global security policy as essentially a political matter, not amenable to mechanistic command and control procedures determined by committee at SHAPE, and under the control of an American general who owes loyalty primarily to the President of the United States.

Washington welcomes the French willingness to 'responsibility share' for trans-Atlantic security issues outside the confines of NATO's Article 5. But harmony is disrupted by French insistence on a command and control structure separate from normal NATO systems even when France and other European nation-states are using NATO assets. French insistence that NATO/CJTF be at the disposal of the WEU, that staff be representative of those countries whose forces are committed, and that there be a specially defined relationship between the CJTF and the political–military community has seriously obstructed the smooth process of the CJTF concept.[19] The heart of the conflict is that France sees the CJTF as a mechanism that allows Europeans to act militarily outside American control; the United States and some other NATO allies see the CJTF as a device for sustaining the relevance of NATO's integrated military structure to new tasks in a complex world, while avoiding the creation of wasteful rival structures.[20]

A central consideration for French policy in this whole debate is relations with Germany. For many years France used its independent nuclear arsenal as a vehicle for prestige *vis-à-vis* an economically superior West Germany. Now Germany is unified and even more dominant economically. But unification has also brought a new confidence and assertiveness to German politics in Europe at the very time when the political utility of French nuclear weapons is in decline. Paris now looks to France's peacekeeping and out-of-area roles as a political substitute for nuclear weapons in the effort to keep France superior to Germany in European and wider security arrangements. France's membership of the UN Security Council provides a strong platform for such a posture. This policy perspective largely explains French support for the Oslo North Atlantic Council decision in June 1992 empowering NATO to put forces at the disposal of the CSCE and the UN for peacekeeping. Once that was agreed, France felt the need to sit on the NATO bodies which would manage peacekeeping activities. Hence, the politics of France's security relations with Germany, as well as related ESDI objectives, drove France back towards NATO.

But if political independence in non-Article 5 missions is lost to the NATO integrated military structure, France loses its superiority to Germany and the power Paris would expect to derive from being, probably, the leading contributor to the CJTF. Outside West Europe there are distinct elements of political and economic competition rather than cooperation between the United States and France. The Middle East is a region where the views of France and the United States do not always coincide. On the issue of militant Islam in Algeria, France has adopted a robust line towards the activities of the Islamic Salvation Front (FIS), provided French economic aid for the struggling government of President Zeroual, and urged EU support for North African secular governments. The United States, fearful of creating another Iranian-type state hostile to the US but very close geographically to West Europe, has adopted a much more conciliatory approach. In April 1994, US Presidential National Security Adviser Anthony Lake stated that 'Islam is not the issue ... our foe is oppression and extremism, whether in religious or secular guise. We also reject the notion that a renewed emphasis on traditional values in the Islamic world must inevitably conflict with the West or with democratic principles.'[21] On Algeria, French statements and actions take the opposite view.

Across the Middle East, French foreign policy is much more centred towards the Arab states than is that of the United States.[22] French sympathy for Israel is markedly less than that of the US, as was clearly illustrated by the French initiative to bring to an end the Israeli offensive against Hezbollah in Lebanon in April 1996. This move was ahead of, and separate from, any American policy. Another instance of American and French divergence on the Middle East has been the subject of the economic embargo on Iraq, in place since 1990. France, along with Russia and China, takes a more relaxed view of the conditions necessary to lift sanctions than do the two other permanent members of the UN Security Council, Britain and the United States. There are strong economic motives for France wishing to have access again to an Iraqi market which, in the recent past, has been attractive to French business, not least for arms sales. Throughout the global arms market France and the United States are major rivals. In 1994 France overtook the US in arms sales to the developing world. Its sales totalled $11.4 billion, up from $3.8 billion in 1991 ($1994). Between 1993 and 1994, US arms sales to the developing world fell from just over $15 billion to about $6 billion.[23]

The increasingly intense arms-sales competition between France and the United States adds an edge to divergent political interests and policies in the extra-European world. It also strengthens France's commitment to an ESDI with as much autonomy as possible and in which Paris is in the driving seat. France's aspirations to be the dominant military power in West Europe are signalled by its nuclear-weapons policy. Nuclear weapons may no longer have the same salience in the internal politics of European security arrangements as during the Cold War, but they have not altogether lost their utility as tools of communication. The nuclear arsenal is being scaled back, but there is a long-term commitment to a core, modern, sea-based strategic missile deterrent force under independent French command and control. In late 1995 this force was offered, not for the first time, as a European deterrent force extending protection over NATO Europe – but, naturally, outside the control of NATO's Nuclear Planning Group. The message to the European allies was not to worry about the United States withdrawing its nuclear commitment to Europe some day because France can assume that role.

On continental, Article 5, NATO business, French–NATO relations have reached a level of cooperation not witnessed for more than 30 years. Post-Cold War strategic changes obliged France, after two years hesitation, to move closer to NATO while still retaining elements of the traditional Gaullist defence posture. France's motives, however, are reformist. Some NATO traditionalists might even accuse France of subversive motives. Between 1990 and 1992 it became clear that France could not achieve the cherished ESDI, with France in the premier position, outside NATO. Since 1992 France has followed the strategy of working within NATO rather than against it. NATO adoption of non-Article 5 missions, the vagaries of the conflict in ex-Yugoslavia, and the harsh realisation that meaningful power projection required collective NATO assets all compelled and attracted France back towards the NATO fold. But within NATO France has waged a political offensive to create a cohesive, powerful European pillar, in particular by pressing for command and control structures for CJTF separate from the American-dominated integrated military structure. To date, the intra-NATO tensions this approach have created have been manageable, but French behaviour has fed the suspicions of some American policy-makers that France is committed, as soon as possible, to promote a European pillar of NATO into a competitive security institution.

This is not the kind of 'responsibility sharing' which endears senior American security officials to France's rediscovery of the virtues of NATO. French reliability on non-Article 5 missions is suspect in Washington, and contributes to a degree of persistent discomfort in United States–French relations on European security issues. The June 1996 Berlin meeting of NATO foreign ministers attempted to give the impression that a workable compromise had been reached. It was accepted that the WEU could, occasionally, take the lead with NATO assets, but the United States and Britain insisted that the WEU mission was restricted to humanitarian assistance, helping refugees and giving aid to civil powers. The French delegation made it clear that they did not agree with that restrictive interpretation of the outcome. The official communiqué made no mention of ESDI.

Britain: the 'trans-Atlantic' preference

In February 1996 the British Chief of the Defence Staff, Field Marshal Sir Peter Inge, declared that NATO 'remains absolutely pivotal to the security of this country.'[24] Three months later, in May, the 1996 Defence White Paper demonstrated the value Britain placed in NATO over other international security organisations. The first of the Departmental Standing Objectives of the Ministry of Defence was stated as:

> To contribute to the formulation of the Government's security policy and to develop and adopt the defence strategy and policy which best safeguards our national interests, taking into account changing strategic trends. To this end, to work to sustain the effectiveness of the North Atlantic Alliance.[25]

The commitment to the primacy of NATO at the heart of British national security policy is clear and steadfast, and runs through the foreign and defence policy-making establishment.[26] NATO has been a central feature of British national security since Britain promoted the concept of a formal North American–West European security pact in 1948–1949. For 20 years, NATO provided an attractive, cost-effective mechanism for Britain to make its contribution to continental West European defence while continuing a major military role outside Europe. Through the 1970s and 1980s, as Britain's world security role and relative power declined, the relative importance of NATO to British security policy increased. This was a reflection not only of Britain's reorientation towards a closer political and economic relationship with West Europe, but also of the increased and improved military capabilities of the Warsaw Pact in the 20 years preceding its political collapse. The British attachment to NATO has survived the collapse of the Cold War and, in the face of perceived contemporary challenges from West European supranationalism and US isolationism, has probably deepened. Given the tenor of regular Ministry of Defence and Foreign and Commonwealth Office pronouncements, it is arguable that in many quarters of the British foreign and security policy establishment membership of NATO is deemed more important than membership of any other international organisation, including the United Nations and the EU.

NATO serves British strategic interests in a number of ways.[27] The status and influence Britain exercises in NATO, and also at the UN, may be seen as greater than that deserved by an ex-imperial power which no longer ranks as a world power and whose GNP is about fifth or sixth on the G7 league table. Within NATO, Britain has a disproportionate share of high-command posts and NATO International Staff appointments. In the NATO-centred security structure, Britain is not regularly isolated in the way it often is within the EU. In the history of intra-alliance disputes, London normally finds supporters from among other West European states or from North America. Britain often enjoys being the bridge between American and continental West European perspectives on contentious issues. If a European foreign and security policy was to replace or relegate NATO there would be two serious consequences: Britain's relative isolation on West European political and economic issues could stretch to envelop security issues, and a common European foreign and security policy could bring moves for a single EU seat on the UN Security Council replacing those of Britain and France. If for no other reason, NATO is valued by Britain as a vehicle for the Anglo–American Special Relationship. The North Atlantic Treaty is the mechanism which legitimises the US military presence in West Europe and Britain has played a crucial role in facilitating the American military deployment. Anglo–American relations within NATO are habitually close, and NATO business reinforces the uniquely close link between London and Washington which successive British governments since 1940 have worked hard to perpetuate. Throughout the Cold War and since, Britain has attempted to sustain both special security links with the United States and a place in the development of closer West European security cooperation. The danger is that too close West European foreign and security policy cooperation could result in bilateral West European–US defence links displacing Anglo–American links.

It remains a core, possibly pre-eminent, British strategic interest to keep the US engaged in European security as it has been for the past 50 years.[28] Britain's contributions to collective defence – which account for at least 90 per cent of the defence budget – are largely based on what is required to keep the United States in Europe and to prop up British influence in NATO. A major American security presence is the constant reminder to a united Germany that there is countervailing power available should the need ever arise. It is an historic British national security objective to deny any single continental power dominance of the West European coastline opposite south eastern and southern England. Twice in the twentieth century, Britain required the assistance of the United States to prevent or overturn that danger. American military personnel in Europe may have been reduced to 100 000 from the Cold War figure of 300 000 but Britain deems such a figure enough to reassure London and many other capitals. It is the American commitment above everything else which attracts Poland, the Czech Republic and many other East European states towards NATO before any other European security organisations. A distant, reconstituted Russian military threat is not the primary anxiety of many NATO aspirants. Nevertheless, while a revived, resentful, expansionist Russia intent on recovering its premier position in East Europe is unlikely in the short-term, it may occur in the longer-term. In such a scenario there is, again, no substitute for American power. Neither a strident Germany nor a revanchist Russia is in Britain's interest, so the American commitment is carefully nurtured.

Most important of all, the American military presence in Europe both sustains and manifests the Anglo–American Special Relationship. For British decision-makers the Special Relationship is a mix of strategic necessity and a canon of faith.[29] Sceptics over the existence of such a relationship, or even its desirability, abound, particularly at times when Anglo–American relations go through a bad patch. However, since 1940, the record shows a culture of close cooperation on matters at the heart of sovereign government which, between two states, has 'no parallel in modern times'.[30] On intelligence matters no states are closer. Each has astounding access to the intelligence apparatus of the other; much of the intelligence gathered is shared with no other state; and there is an Anglo–American intelligence framework which stands apart and distinct from that of NATO.[31] Nuclear military matters parallel intelligence as a central pillar of the Special Relationship. Over the past 50 years, on matters of nuclear research and development, weapons procurement and strategic planning, no other two states have come anywhere near the degree of cooperation between the United States and Britain. The level of access each has to secrets about the capital weapons' systems of the other is unprecedented in international history – and is indeed 'special'.

Other features reinforce the defence and intelligence links.[32] Britain's embassy in Washington is the biggest of any it has in the world. Every year there are about 16 000 official US visits to Britain. There are at least 50 high-level visits from Britain to the US every year, and the British Foreign Minister and US Secretary of State normally meet about eight times a year. Each country is the leading investor in the other. Britain is ahead of Japan as an investor in the United States and vice versa. And still, for the policy-making élites in both societies, history, culture, language and geography – each is a maritime power far away from central Europe – remain important common features.[33] Despite some efforts to relegate it, for example

Prime Minister Edward Heath's determination to rename it the 'natural relationship', and despite occasional deep fissures, for instance the Suez crisis of 1956, the Special Relationship bounces back. Indeed, the deep culture of mutual support and understanding over more than 50 years has allowed the two countries to 'ride out'[34] rare spats over issues such as British reluctance to support American policy in the 1973 Arab–Israeli War or the surprise American invasion of the Commonwealth country of Grenada in 1983. When two heads of government are compatible, such as Prime Minister Macmillan and President Kennedy or Prime Minister Callaghan and President Carter, or Prime Minister Thatcher and President Reagan, the Special Relationship sparkles as an international political fact. In recent times, American support for Britain during the Falklands War of 1982, British deployment in support of the American intervention in Beirut in 1982–1983, American use of British airfields in 1986 to bomb Libya in reprisal for international terrorism while other West European allies denied such use, and British naval deployments to the Gulf during the 'Tanker War' phase of the 1980–1988 Iran–Iraq War, provided vivid illustration of the Special Relationship at work. That it survives uncomfortable relations between heads of government, such as between Prime Minister Wilson and President Johnson, and Prime Minister Heath and President Nixon, testifies to its durability.

The Special Relationship was central to British strategy during the Cold War. British governments worked on certain assumptions.[35] It was assumed that no serious international objective could be realised without American support and that Britain must organise its defence planning in such a way as to maximise influence over the United States. There were also the assumptions that Washington required constant persuasion and that no impression of not wanting the US involved in European security should be given, especially from ambitious, collective West European defence efforts. The Cold War is over but the Special Relationship is not. The many pronouncements in 1990 of its death were premature. The swift despatch of a Tornado squadron to Saudi Arabia, followed closely by the 7th Armoured Brigade, within three weeks of Saddam Hussein's invasion of Kuwait in August 1990 put the Special Relationship into splendid shape just when Germany was expected to replace Britain as Washington's leading Atlantic partner.[36] From the earliest days of the Gulf crisis the US received the clearest, most unambiguous support from the British government, regardless of a change of Prime Minister in November 1990 from Thatcher to Major. The promotion of the Armoured Brigade to a full armoured division, a dashing, brave display by the RAF, close coordination of the Royal Navy with the US Navy, and the provision of British bases for B-52 bombers starkly and firmly reminded the Americans who they could most rely on in a crisis. In sharp contrast to German and Japanese prevarication, prompt, large-scale British action also declared that London did not feel it was correct to expect Washington to struggle alone to maintain world order. By February 1991 43 000 British military personnel were deployed in the Gulf, more than any other American ally.[37]

Throughout the 1990s British national security policy has continued to work on the assumptions of the Cold War – and the Special Relationship has survived. On the ground and in the committee rooms there are ample manifestations of its continued life. In the wake of the Gulf War, Anglo–American initiatives set up the 'safe havens' for up to 2 million Iraqi–Kurdish refugees escaping the wrath of Saddam

Hussein after the failed rebellion. Living conditions on the mountains on the Turkish–Iraqi border were appalling and Turkey, with its own Turkish insurgency under way since 1984, was hostile to a large influx of new, distraught Kurds. Prime Minister Major persuaded President Bush of the benefits of a safe haven, based on Anglo–American air power, in north Iraq for these refugees. Also on Iraq, the US receives strong support from Britain when Russia, China and France press for the UN Security Council to lift the economic sanctions against Iraq. By 1995, these three permanent Security Council members were growing impatient to reopen trading links with the Iraqi regime, but Washington and London have stood together against lifting most of the sanctions until the final letter of all the conditions have been realised. A slight exception was the Anglo–American agreement, in May 1996, to limited Iraqi oil sales linked to the purchase of humanitarian supplies and the provision of some reparations to Kuwait. With evident reluctance and no enthusiasm, Britain is locked into the EU's so-called 'critical dialogue' with Iran, but moral support from London for the US political and economic containment of Iran is evident. As ever, defence and intelligence continue as the central pillars of the Special Relationship but, in the late 1990s, a new dimension is emerging. Britain and the United States, as world trading powers, have a common interest in thwarting protectionist trading blocs. Within the EU Britain fights for an open, competitive trading policy against many protectionist impulses from continental partners. Britain is also the West European state closest to Japan, the major ally and trading partner of the US in the Pacific region. And, of crucial importance to the future of European security arrangements, there is substantial coincidence of Anglo–American views on the future character of NATO.

Nonetheless, Britain still has to pursue a balancing act between the Special Relationship and West Europe.[38] Working with its West European partners is unavoidable – and desirable in a number of ways. If NATO and the American link were to disintegrate, a West European defence arrangement is a strategic fallback position. But to sustain NATO cohesion and the American commitment, the West European allies must be seen to be active and committed. So in the past 20 years Britain has played an active role in promoting the Eurogroup within NATO, and in joint West European procurement projects such as Jaguar, Tornado and the European Fighter Aircraft. However, this is a delicate political business because too much cooperation leading to integration could lead to competition for NATO and disaffection by the United States. The WEU experience demonstrates this conundrum for the British. In the mid-1980s, Britain supported its revival as a ready-made forum for West European discussion of defence matters, but not as a vehicle for defence integration. Yet by the early 1990s, many continental NATO allies were advancing the WEU as the defence agency of the EU, serving a future common foreign and security policy. John Baylis, writing in 1989, was prescient, when he stated:

> The evidence suggests that the dilemma between European cooperation and the 'special relationship' remains an important one for defence planners in the late 1980s and may well become sharper over the next decade.[39]

A component of the British West European defence link has been a working partnership with France on a number of selective issues. There has been some joint procurement and defence research and development, and there is a joint Anglo–French air command. There is also an agreement on discussing aspects of nuclear deterrence strategies.[40] The shared experience of humanitarian intervention and participation in IFOR in Bosnia has firmed up a spirit of *de facto* cooperation between the British and French defence establishments. Britain has a clear preference for an Anglo–French cooperative defence axis at the core of West European defence efforts rather than a Franco–German axis with a distinct bias towards integration and an EU foreign and security policy. But regardless of the change from Mitterand to Chirac in 1995, French policy distinctly favours an integrative defence relationship with Germany over the cooperative model advanced by Britain. The French strategy of enmeshing German power in integrative European institutions is more than 30 years old. It is not to be abandoned in favour of a West European cooperative arrangement which best suits Britain's unique relationship with the United States.

Without the United States NATO will collapse. As NATO best addresses British strategic interests, Britain does its best to address the US concept of post-Cold War NATO. London is alert to the Washington conception of NATO – illustrated by the January 1994 Brussels summit – as an institution with a major contribution to make to wider, trans-Atlantic security issues. From the early 1990s, British defence policy has moved towards adapting to this new strategic environment.[41] Between 1975 and 1990 there were four roles and a fifth secondary role for British defence policy. UK homeland defence, the nuclear-deterrent role, NATO West European continental land and air defence, and NATO North Atlantic and Channel maritime defence were the four main roles. A subsidiary, residual out-of-area role constituted the fifth. The 1992 Defence White Paper reduced all these roles to three: the protection and security of the UK and dependent territories even when there is no major threat; insurance against any major external threat to the UK and its allies; and a contribution to the promotion of the UK's wider security interests through maintenance of international peace and stability. By 1992 it was clear that the new conceptual framework for British defence policy was erasing the distinction between NATO area defence and out-of-area. The 1993 Defence White Paper made a clear declaration that:

> The old distinction between 'in-' and 'out-of-area' is no longer relevant for defence planning. Indeed the criteria will be the depth of British and Allied interests involved and the implications of the crisis for international peace and stability, while recognising our continued commitment to collective defence through NATO.[42]

A practical illustration of the erasing between 'in-' and 'out-of-area' is the equipment of the new British Trident nuclear missile-firing submarine with a single warheaded missile. This 'sub-strategic' system is intended to deter 'rogue state' nuclear or other weapons of mass destruction threats to Britain or to NATO without the prospect of a disproportionate response. There is growing anxiety in the British Ministry of Defence over the medium- to longer-term threat from militarily ambitious but politically unstable and unpredictable less-developed states. Libya, Iran, Iraq and possibly Algeria in the event of a militant Islamicist government, are often cited as states with programmes underway or planned to procure relatively simple missiles and nuclear, biological or chemical warheads which could pose serious threats to West European cities. As well as limited deterrence, a ballistic missile defence system capable of countering unsophisticated offensive systems is under serious consideration in the Ministry of Defence, in cooperation with the United States.[43]

From the late-1960s the emphasis of British defence policy was on NATO European defence and sustenance of the Special Relationship. These two objectives were compatible so long as the European pillar of the Alliance remained a cooperative venture and did not challenge the integrity of NATO. British policy worked hard to maintain that balance. Throughout the 1970s and 1980s, Britain's out-of-area role trailed the core NATO commitments. Now that NATO strategic perspectives have expanded to incorporate out-of-area concerns, British defence policy is moving down that path, but without abandoning influence at the heart of traditional, NATO Article 5 business.

Until the European security landscape is clear, British governments, despite fiscal pressures, have resisted abandoning capabilities. Incorporating versatility and flexibility has become the creed. So British defence expenditure has shrunk from nearly 5 per cent of GDP in 1986 to 3 per cent in 1996 – but no major role has been sacrificed. To retain influence in NATO Article 5 business, Britain inspired the creation of the Allied Rapid Reaction Corps (ARRC) as NATO's military response to the disappearance of the Central Front and the redundancy of the classic flexible response strategy. ARRC is a multinational ten-division force available to SACEUR for rapid reaction to any threats to Article 5 NATO interests. Britain has positioned itself as 'the framework nation'[44] for ARRC, and is at the heart of the organisation. A British general is the Commander in Chief, and 60 per cent of headquarters and of Corps level combat support and combat service units staff are British. Fifty-five thousand British troops are assigned to ARRC, the One (UK) Armoured Division in Germany, and Three (UK) Mechanised Division in Britain. Two of the ten divisions available to ARRC are British. The flexibility of this force has been demonstrated by its deployment of IFOR, with the French and some non-NATO forces under its wings, in Bosnia in 1996–1997. The use of ARRC in this operation outside NATO territory was a clear demonstration of the real obsolescence of the 'in-' and 'out-of-area' distinctions by the mid-1990s.

To address this reality and to conform with American 'trans-Atlantic' security prescriptions, Britain has undertaken policy initiatives for non-Article 5 business. On 1 April 1996 the Permanent Joint Forces Head Quarters (PJHQ) came into operation at Northwood on the outskirts of west London. Its role is to mastermind British involvement in every type of conflict. Planning, training, policy and doctrine for all joint operations from Bosnia to Middle East contingencies are the PJHQ's responsibility. The *ad hoc* joint command structures which responded to the Falklands War and the Gulf War were deemed no longer adequate to the new strategic environment.[45] The PJHQ has more than 300 staff, previously spread through the Ministry of Defence and the single services. Altogether, the ability to respond quickly to crises is enhanced. Within the PJHQ is the core of a deployable headquarters. To address the third defence role for British forces outlined in the 1993 Defence White Paper and the practical demise of the Article 5 constraint, a new Joint Rapid Deployment Force (JRDF) was also established in August 1996. Together with the PJHQ it is a recognition that low-intensity, joint operations and coalitions are likely roles for British forces in the future.[46] The JRDF has been based on a combination of elements of two of the British army's most flexible units: Five Airborne Brigade and Three Commando Brigade. Two large roll-on roll-off ferries have been procured specifically for JRDF use to enhance rapid deployment with armoured and mechanised elements. In large-scale crises JRDF will be supplemented by national contingency forces. Worldwide, flexible communication capabilities have been devoted to JRDF.

The Anglo–American Exercise Purple Star, the largest of its kind held since the Second World War, was a dramatic illustration of British determination to be seen to support American strategic concepts and to be prepared for new-style NATO tasks. In April and May 1996, on the eastern seaboard of the United States, a combined force of 45 000 American and 12 000 British military personnel from all three services practised amphibious and airborne assaults.[47] The scenario envisaged a CJTF (under UN mandate) going to the assistance of a small country suffering attack. There was integration of US and British headquarters staff and the placing of elements of US and British forces under each other's control. The exercise allowed Britain to test the PJHQ and key units assigned to the new JRDF, due to be fully operational by August 1996. The British forces had support from a Royal Navy aircraft-carrier group and RAF frontline aircraft and support units. Exercise Purple Star was also of significance as it was a test for the rapid deployment of a task force outside NATO Europe. In the summer of 1996 the British government announced the placing of contracts for two new amphibious assault ships to replace the ageing HMS *Intrepid* and HMS *Fearless*, which played such crucial roles in the Falklands War. This is another indication of the new strategic framework within which British defence policy has been operating since 1993. In the late 1980s there was serious debate about the worth of sustaining amphibious forces and replacing the expensive amphibious assault ships. Today, they form a key component of the new JRDF, to which the two Royal Navy aircraft-carrier groups are earmarked for support.

Britain has carried on with a range of capabilities which allows it to perpetuate a 'second-in-command' role in NATO, at the centre of ARRC but also with the capabilities and will to support the United States in non-article 5 missions, whether under NATO auspices or not. This strategic posture allows Britain to set an example to other West European states and entice them into 'responsibility sharing'. Alert to American sensitivities on this matter, Britain sees it as important for the US commitment to European security that West European NATO members give more heed to trans-Atlantic security interests outside Europe.

In May 1996 the Permanent Representatives of the North Atlantic Council formally approved the CJTF concept proposed at the January 1994 NATO summit. In June the Berlin NATO foreign ministers' meeting officially endorsed that decision, but fudged the command-and-control question. But, as of the summer of 1996, there was still no definite agreement where the CJTF should have its headquarters or who should command it. In the debate over command and control of CJTF, underway since the concept was proposed in 1994, Britain has supported the American view that NATO structures ought to be used for missions where conflict is likely or war will certainly be waged. The Anglo–American view is that WEU structures, using NATO assets, may be possible in operations such as disaster relief or peacekeeping, but that NATO's comprehensive and sophisticated systems would be essential for conflict. In this dilemma between European cooperation and the Special Relationship, foreseen by Baylis in 1989, Britain clearly favours the American connection. In British eyes, 'strong defence is founded not on institutional arrangements but on practical and credible defence capabilities'.[48] Britain's position is that NATO provides the 'practical and credible defence capabilities', and CJTF deployable headquarters must come from within existing NATO fixed headquarters.[49]

To comply with French arguments and provide a headquarters and command-and-control structure for CJTF separate from NATO and within the WEU would ratchet up the WEU as an alternative to NATO. In turn this would enhance the WEU as a vehicle for a common foreign and security policy within the EU. British policy is deeply opposed to such developments. In May 1996, prior to a WEU Defence Ministers conference in Birmingham, Secretary for Defence Michael Portillo stated support for the WEU as a vehicle to coordinate West European efforts to increase contributions to NATO, but he opposed notions of the WEU as part of the EU. He foresaw a role for the WEU undertaking 'lower level tasks' such as peacekeeping and humanitarian duties but, while the WEU and the EU should have close relations, they should be kept separate.[50] In the late 1990s, as earlier in the decade at the time of the Maastricht negotiations, London is against any military responsibilities for the EU. France and Germany have taken an opposite view, lobbying for WEU political dependence on the EU Council which would establish general directives.[51] Britain cannot accept the WEU working within the common policies of the EU, and any Franco–German attempt to force the issue in the future could bring a major crisis in intra-EU relations. Some members of the EU, such as Sweden, who is neither a member of NATO nor the WEU, or Denmark who is in NATO but not the WEU, are against the EU assuming defence responsibilities. Indeed, there is no uniform pattern of security among members of the EU. Two are nuclear powers, the rest are not. Not all European members of NATO are in the WEU, nor vice versa.[52] The assumption by the EU of defence responsibilities would create an exceedingly complex structure of political and strategic management which would mitigate against effective, flexible action. Nor would it have the quality of command, control and communication systems enjoyed by NATO.

The end of the Cold War has allowed Britain to rediscover the world after a twenty-year concentration on West Europe. A world view never completely deserted Britain but, faced by the Soviet bloc and with large markets outside Europe limited by the East–West conflict, British policy-makers felt it made strategic sense to work much more closely with West Europe. The end of the Cold War has transformed the geo-strategic situation. Large parts of East Europe, the Middle East and Africa are now once again open to British trade.[53] The overarching Communist military threat is gone. In September 1995 Foreign Secretary Malcolm Rifkind described promoting British national interests as a 'global business. Not just because of our history, but because of our security needs and our international trade.'[54] Part of Rifkind's vision is an Atlantic Community of Europe and North America, with free trade and common security interests at its core. Resisting protectionism and recruiting West Europe to international security tasks strikes a chord in Washington, and reinforces the value of the Special Relationship to the United States. Britain's increasingly vocal support for Japanese membership of the UN Security Council, and the enticement of Japan towards a wider international role, also addresses American concerns over 'responsibility sharing'.

While British Conservatives are in office the mutually supportive characteristics of the primacy of NATO, the American link, and a wider, extra-European role will distinguish British defence policy. To a greater or lesser extent, depending upon the vagaries of the global strategic environment, these have been the constant features of British defence policy over the past 50 years. Even if the party in power changes, the salient features are so deeply embedded in British strategic culture it is hard to imagine a radical change in the short-term. British political history over the past 50 years suggests that, once in power, new governments discover the virtues of some of the conservative elements of British national security policy, particularly in matters regarding British links with the United States and the hallowed place of NATO in British foreign and security policy.

Within European security arrangements, a tension between French and British interests and objectives will persist for some time to come. France wants a reformed, reduced NATO, in which American influence is diluted. Paris looks forward to a strong, French-led European security and defence identity within NATO, which may blossom into a separate European security organisation some day in loose diplomatic association with the United States. The struggle over command and control of the CJTF was an early campaign in the French offensive. Britain adopts a conservative view of NATO. For London, NATO protects and sustains British influence in the wider international system as well as within Europe. Britain welcomes American leadership of NATO and dominance of European security arrangements. This both facilitates and reinforces Britain's Special Relationship with the United States. Britain supports the US position on the CJTF, and is eager to 'responsibility share' international security obligations with the United States.

But both Britain and France need to have alternatives in the event of the unexpected, such as American withdrawal or German abandonment of the axis with France. One alternative is each other. Limited, cordial Anglo–French defence cooperation over some sharing of nuclear plans, collaboration on UN peacekeeping or peace-enforcement business and some air-defence coordination take the hard edge off competing French and British visions of future European security arrangements. But in fundamental aspirations for European security there is a gulf between Paris and London.

Notes

1. For detailed analysis of this period of French foreign and security policy, see J. Howorth and P. Chilton, *Defence and Dissent in Contemporary France* (London: Croom Helm, 1984); D. Yost, *France's Deterrent Posture and Security in Europe, Parts I and II* (London: IISS, 1985), Adelphi Papers 194 and 195; and R. Aldrich and J. Connell (Eds), *France in World Politics* (London: Routledge, 1989).
2. See Anand Menon, 'From independence to cooperation: France, NATO and European security', *International Affairs*, Vol. 71, No. 1, January 1995, pp. 22–4.
3. See Robert P. Grant, 'France's new relationship with NATO', *Survival*, Vol. 78, No. 1, Spring 1996, p. 59.
4. *Ibid.*, p. 60.

5. Confidential discussions with a range of senior US officials and officers at NATO and SHAPE.

6. See 'France's changing view of the world', *Economist*, 10 February 1996, p. 37.

7. Jean-Claude Casanova, *L'Express*, 28 September 1995, p. 26, cited in Robert P. Grant, 'France's new relationship with NATO', *Survival*, Vol. 78, No. 1, Spring 1996, p. 63.

8. See Anand Menon, 'From independence to cooperation: France, NATO and European security', *International Affairs*, Vol. 71, No. 1, January 1995, p. 26.

9. For a record of French revival of cooperation with NATO between 1993 and 1996, see Robert P. Grant, 'France's new relationship with NATO', *Survival*, Vol. 78, No. 1, Spring 1996, pp. 61–3.

10. Cited in Joseph Fitchett, 'France to resume seat at NATO military talks', *International Herald Tribune*, 3 September 1994, p. 1.

11. Cited in 'France's changing view of the world', *Economist*, 10 February 1996, p. 37; also, see Mark Yost, 'Why France wants back into NATO', *Wall Street Journal Europe*, 24 January 1996, p. 6, for a robust appraisal of the French short-term interests but long-term objectives of its NATO policy.

12. See Tom Rhodes, 'Chirac calls for reform of NATO's military role', *Times*, 2 February 1996, p. 13.

13. See David Buchan, 'France maps out military strategy into the next century', *Financial Times*, 24 February 1994, p. 2.

14. Cited in Anand Menon, 'From independence to cooperation: France, NATO and European security', *International Affairs*, Vol. 71, No. 1, January 1995, p. 28.

15. See Bruce Clark, 'France aims to apply oil to NATO's squeaky wheels', *Financial Times*, 6 December 1995, p. 2.

16. See 'France may have hidden agenda in retaking seat at NATO table', *Jane's Defence Weekly*, 17 January 1996, p. 17.

17. See Robert P. Grant, 'France's new relationship with NATO', *Survival*, Vol. 78, No. 1, Spring 1996, pp. 70–1.

18. See Ben MacIntyre, 'Chirac's pledges to scrap land-based nuclear missiles', *Times*, 23 February 1996, p. 11; Julian Nundy, 'Chirac cuts back on defence,' *Daily Telegraph*, 23 February 1996, p. 12; and 'A French projection', *Economist*, 2 March 1996, p. 41.

19. See Robert P. Grant, 'France's new relationship with NATO', *Survival*, Vol. 78, No. 1, Spring 1996, pp. 68–9.

20. See 'Stepping into the breach. France's global role: Interview with Admiral Jacques Lanxade, French Chief of the Armed Forces Staff', *International Defence Review*, 4/95, p. 25. Also, see Nicole Gnesotto, 'Common defence and transatlantic relations', *Survival*, Vol. 38, No. 1, Spring 1996, pp. 26–7 on the fundamental clash between French and US conceptions of the CJTF.

21. Cited in James Wyllie, 'Islamic revivalism,' *The World in Conflict 1994/95* (Coulsdon: Jane's Information Group, 1995), p. 15. For further details of the differences within NATO and the EU on policy towards militant Islam, see James Wyllie, 'Militant Islam and the West – dangers and dilemmas', *Jane's Intelligence Review*, Vol. 7, No. 5, May 1995, pp. 217–18.

22. See Barry James, 'Strong ties to Arab nations are key to French foreign policy, Chirac says', *International Herald Tribune*, 9 April 1996, p. 5.

23. See Christopher Dickey and Gregory Vistica, 'We arm the world', *Newsweek*, 21 August 1995, p. 12.

24. Field Marshal Sir Peter Inge, 'The roles and challenges of the British armed forces', *Journal of the Royal United Services Institute for Defence Studies* (RUSIJ), Vol. 141, No. 1, February 1996, p. 1.

25. *Statement on Defence Estimates 1996* (SDE) (London: HMSO, 1996), Cmmd 3223, p. 4, Table 1.

26. See Alyson Bailes, 'Britain's security policy agenda', *RUSIJ*, Vol. 140, No. 1, February 1995, pp. 14–15.

27. See Philip Sabin, *British Strategic Priorities in the 1990s* (London: IISS, 1990), Adelphi Paper 254, pp. 37–8.

28. See Sherard Cowper-Coles, 'From defence to security: British policy in transition', *Survival*, Vol. 36, No. 1, Spring 1994, p. 145.
29. See C. J. Bartlett, *The 'Special Relationship': A Political History of Anglo-American Relations since 1945* (London: Longman, 1992), p. 179.
30. B. Vivekanandan, 'Washington must rely on London, not Bonn', *ORBIS*, Vol. 35, No. 3, Summer 1991, p. 414.
31. See C. J. Bartlett, *The 'Special Relationship': A Political History of Anglo-American Relations since 1945* (London: Longman, 1992), p. 179.
32. See B. Vivekanandan, 'Washington must rely on London, not Bonn', *ORBIS*, Vol. 35, No. 3, Summer 1991, p. 413.
33. See Lawrence Freedman, 'Alliance and the British way in warfare', *Review of International Studies*, Vol. 21, No. 2, April 1995, p. 147.
34. B. Vivekanandan, 'Washington must rely on London, not Bonn', *ORBIS*, Vol. 35, No. 3, Summer 1991, p. 414.
35. See Lawrence Freedman, 'Alliance and the British way in warfare', *Review of International Studies*, Vol. 21, No. 2, April 1995, p. 150.
36. See Martin Walker, 'Rich wimps whipped into line', *Guardian*, 17 September 1990, p. 23.
37. See C. J. Bartlett, *The 'Special Relationship': A Political History of Anglo-American Relations since 1945* (London: Longman, 1992), p. 175.
38. See John Baylis, *British Defence Policy: Striking the Right Balance* (London: Macmillan, 1989), pp. 47–9.
39. *Ibid.*, p. 49.
40. See David Fairhall and Martin Walker, 'Secret deal allows French N-boats to use British ports', *Guardian*, 22 September 1995, p. 12; David Buchan, John Ridding and Bruce Clark, 'Anglo-French air force unit agreed', *Financial Times*, 30 October 1995, p. 9.
41. See Sherard Cowper-Coles, 'From defence to security: British policy in transition', *Survival*, Vol. 36, No. 1, Spring 1994, p. 147.
42. *Defending Our Future: Statement on Defence Estimates 1993* (London: HMSO, 1993) Cmnd 2270, p. 10, cited in Eric Grove, *The Army and British Security After the Cold War: Defence Planning for a New Era* (Camberley: Strategic and Combat Studies Institute, 1996), Occasional Paper 20, p. 11.
43. See Michael Evans, 'Britain "has only 10 years" to protect itself from missiles', *Times*, 12 June 1995, p. 7; Andrew Gilligan, 'Trident fleet has "Club Mad" in its sights', *Sunday Telegraph*, 14 January 1996, p. 11.
44. See *Statement on Defence Estimates 1996* (SDE) (London: HMSO, 1996), p. 36.
45. See Peter Ahmoud, 'Military role for roll-on ferries', *Daily Telegraph*, 27 March 1996, p. 7; and *Statement on Defence Estimates 1996* (SDE) (London: HMSO, 1996), p. 20.
46. See Eric Grove, *The Army and British Security After the Cold War: Defence Planning for a New Era* (Camberley: Strategic and Combat Studies Institute, 1996), Occasional Paper 20, pp. 19–20.
47. See *Statement on Defence Estimates 1996* (SDE) (London: HMSO, 1996), p. 34.
48. *Ibid.*, p. 10, para. 127.
49. See *ibid.*, p. 9, para.116. Also, see Field Marshal Sir Peter Inge, 'The roles and challenges of the British armed forces', *Journal of the Royal United Services Institute for Defence Studies* (RUSIJ), Vol. 141, No. 1, February 1996, pp. 1–2.
50. BBC Radio 4 *Today* interview with Defence Secretary Michael Portillo, 7 May 1996. Also, see *Statement on Defence Estimates 1996* (SDE) (London: HMSO, 1996), p. 13, para. 134.
51. See *Gnesotto*, p. 21; Christopher Bellamy, 'Defence memo outlines UK's Euro-strategy.' *Independent*, 2 March 1995, p. 6; Christopher Lockwood, 'Rifkind resists move to change defence force', *Daily Telegraph*, 15 November 1995, p. 15.
52. See Alyson Bailes, 'European defence and security: The British approach', *RUSIJ*, Vol. 140, No. 6, December 1995, pp. 7–8.
53. See David Howell, 'The shifting winds of British foreign policy', *Wall Street Journal Europe*, 8 February 1995, p. 10.
54. Malcolm Rifkind, 'Interest against influence', *Times*, 21 September 1995, p. 18.

Chapter 7

Prospects

Five salient, interrelated conditions look set to determine the character of European security arrangements over the medium-term, well into the first decade of the next century. These conditions are present and active in European security today, and there is little reason to expect their importance to diminish. Indeed, as detailed throughout this book, there are many reasons to expect the influence of these conditions to increase during the next few years.

First, it is reasonable to assume that the post-Cold War condition of relative uncertainty will continue. In the Euro–Atlantic arena there is no prospect, in the medium-term, of the rise of a countervailing superpower to balance and challenge the United States. In the absence of a global ideological and strategic threat, American foreign and defence policy will remain much more pragmatic, flexible and prone to domestic politics than during the Cold War, and there is little incentive for most West European states to fall in behind American leadership. With the absence of a European superpower – in ideological and military terms as well as economic – there is no vehicle for discipline and hegemony over large parts of East Europe. European high international politics over the next decade or so will be more complex and much riskier than during the Cold War because Europe is now a multipower system rather than a bipolar system. Grand strategic foreign-policy decisions have to take into account the reaction of many other power centres, some of which are or could be of questionable stability. The reactions of some of these power centres may be incompatible and there could be collisions.[1]

Crisis management is made much more difficult when the behaviour of many decision-makers have to be taken into account. Uncertainty is also exacerbated by the increased range of issues over which conflict could occur. Crisis avoidance must now take into account trade and economic issues, ethnic and religious questions, refugee problems, territorial disputes and other traditional, pre-Cold War international-conflict problems to a degree not experienced in the European theatre for more than 50 years. But the uncertainty derives not just from the European theatre, but from regions contiguous to Europe but from which Europe cannot remain immune. In 1994 West Europe consumed 652.5 million tonnes of oil, but produced only 286.7 million tonnes.[2] About 60 per cent of the shortfall in oil was imported from North Africa and the Middle East. In 1994 the United States imported about 25 per cent of its oil from the same region. For economic reasons alone, security and stability in North Africa and the Middle East is important for the United States, but it is vital for West Europe. The region is notorious as the locale of conflict, unpredictability and uncertainty. Conflicts between militant Islam and secular modernism, between Peace Process states and the Rejectionist Front, between rich oil states and poorer, overpopulated states look set to continue and develop. All these issues, and many others, have economic, political and strategic repercussions for European security and all contribute to deep uncertainty.

A second condition which will continue for some time is the determination of most states in the Euro–Atlantic theatre, particularly the Great Powers, to keep questions of national security as the preserve of sovereign governments. Command of the state's military forces is the fundamental symbol and practice of independence and statehood. Unless it is clearly agreed that it serves the perceived national interest, most Western states will not proceed beyond the level of quasi-integration achieved by the end of the Cold War. In carefully selected areas, and for selective contingencies, close cooperation will continue among and between certain states, for instance among Eurogroup members and between the United States and Britain. But the disintegration of the Soviet threat removed the necessity for Western states to pool national security authority in order to protect individual statehood. More than 40 years of steady Western defence cooperation and quasi-integration was not undertaken in pursuit of some worthy, abstract political notion of a single Western or West European state. It was done out of perceived necessity, as the best way to protect the security of the individual states in the face of the Soviet threat. Now that the threat has gone there is no current necessity to continue the derogation of national security authority. Indeed, to carry on doing so out of habit or in obedience to a redundant strategic necessity actively threatens the very statehood it was supposed to protect during the Cold War. Henry Kissinger describes this condition thus:

> The absence of both an overriding ideological or strategic threat frees nations to pursue foreign policies based increasingly on their immediate national interest. In an international system characterised by perhaps five or six major powers and a multiplicity of smaller states, order will have to emerge as it did in past centuries from a reconciliation and balancing of competing national interests.[3]

The fate of the international security institutions spawned by the Cold War will hinge on how effectively they address the competing national interests of the members. To date, NATO is the most successful and robust of these institutions, but even it has been obliged to exercise caution in its development and direction throughout the 1990s. Great care will still be required if it is still to retain its value to key members as an effective collective defence institution. Arguments surrounding the wisdom, pace and scale of any enlargement demonstrate how carefully NATO needs to tread.[4] Enlargement will require political, managerial and doctrinal reform of the Alliance, which could transform it from the entity which members value into an institution which they do not value so much. The CJTF initiative is another development which may render the Alliance less attractive to members than it has been. The assumption is that the CJTF is a mechanism to allow West Europeans to act alone, using NATO assets, without the United States. However, the CJTF could also be construed as allowing the United States, with limited or no West European support, to use NATO assets based in Europe for business outside Article 5 limits which many West European members do not support. Wrangles over the spirit and letter of the CJTF agreements have the potential to cause many serious intra-Alliance disputes. Institutional momentum by the WEU or the OSCE to pressurise individual states' national security policies into supranational integrative modes or unrealistic and prescriptive collective security restrictions risk the rupture of these institutions. The tragedy of ex-Yugoslavia stands as brutal evidence of the practical limits to action of all the international institutions and to the immense degree of compromise required among interested states before collective action can be brought to bear.

Paradoxically, most of the dangers and threats – as distinct from the greatest threats – to international security in Europe will come from dysfunctional states unable to govern themselves. Such states, which stand in stark contrast to those stable states which protect their national security authority, constitute the third condition likely to affect European security arrangements. Apart from ex-Yugoslavia, there are other states in Europe which appear susceptible to ethnic conflict, civil war and disruption. Since the end of the Cold War there have been about 30 significant conflicts – and most of these have been within states rather than between states. The Cold War trapped many peoples inside countries to which they felt little loyalty, and under regimes for which they have little affinity. The leaderships often have the same people, or are from the same stables, as the old Communist dictatorships, but are reprocessed as nationalists. The roots of such conflicts may be religious, ethnic, economic, historic or a combination of all these. Resentments usually run deep, and achieving long-term, viable, stable resolutions to such conflicts is difficult.[5]

The rim of the former Soviet Union has been the location of many post-Cold War conflicts in the 1990s, and could be so again early in the next century. The reimposition of Russian military influence in some new states, such as Georgia, has so far been one answer to instability, but whether this is conducive to long-term security is open to question. The Ukraine, where there is no Russian military presence, is a major source of instability. There is a deep ethnic division between the Russians in eastern Ukraine and the ethnic Ukrainians. Expected economic progress has been virtually non-existent, and for many people living standards have fallen since the disintegration of the Soviet Union. Economic reform has been and remains painfully slow. With a population the size of France and agricultural land as rich as the Canadian prairies, the Ukraine ought to be the 'bread basket' of Europe. In the late 1990s the Ukraine could still not feed itself and was a net importer of food. Among ethnic Ukrainians there is great resentment over Russian economic dominance, especially the supply of fuel. In the east, there are strong sympathies for secession and rejoining Russia. In 1996 there was still no viable currency and government employees were often not paid for lengthy periods. Discontent was rife in the armed services, who often did not receive the coupons which substituted for currency for many months. This is a case where civil conflict could lead to major Russian intervention, with wider, regional security ramifications. Romania is another East European state where political and economic reform have been extremely disappointing, and mismanagement and corruption are widespread. Much of the old apparatus from the Communist era persists and there is deep discontent.

Such tensions and conflicts need not be in Europe to affect European security. The civil war in Algeria has produced terrorist bombs in Paris and London, and should the fundamentalists prevail southern Europe would need to brace itself for an influx of refugees. Serious repercussions could easily spread along the littoral of the southern Mediterranean affecting pro-Western governments, already under militant pressures, in Tunisia and Egypt.[6] In a worst-case analysis, the fall of the Mubarak regime in Egypt would destroy the Arab–Israeli peace process and plunge the region into turmoil. Among other things, the pro-Western, oil-producing Gulf monarchies would become vulnerable to domestic, militant Islamicist forces and external pressures from Iran.

While most risks and challenges arise from actual or prospective civil or ethnic conflicts, these are relatively low-level actual or potential conflicts. The threat least likely to contemporary European security at present, but most dangerous should it occur, is that of traditional, large-scale, interstate war between the Great Powers on the European continent. In this regard the greatest challenge – not yet a threat – to European security is the German–Russian relationship. The enduring, crucial strategic importance of this relationship to European security arrangements constitutes the fourth condition determining the prospects for European security. Russia has a European foreign policy antithetical to the collective defence enjoyed by Germany. Russia's European policy attaches a top priority to transforming NATO from a collective defence organisation to a much weaker collective security organisation, ideally answerable to the OSCE. Such circumstances would dilute American power and German influence in European security arrangements and enhance Russian influence. For axiomatic, geo-strategic reasons, East Europe between Germany and Russia has been an historic arena of German–Russian competition. Since the collapse of the Soviet Union, German influence in East Europe – especially economic influence – has been dominant. By the late 1990s Russian political influence was attempting to stage a comeback in parts of the old Warsaw Pact, and a political offensive is in train.[7] The return of ex-Communists to high political office and the survival of much of the old, civil service power structure in some East European states is conducive to the recovery of some Russian power in the region.[8] As the West European integration process slows and falters, German national political and economic interests will be drawn even more towards that more traditional market place, source of raw materials and cheap labour, and arena of political competition between the German and Russian borders. Regardless of the political nature of the Russian leadership, deep rivalry and competition between Germany and Russia over the medium- to longer-term is inevitable. NATO expansion, even limited to one or two countries, can only exacerbate such potential tensions while, simultaneously, weakening NATO cohesion and diluting its strategic credibility.

The political momentum towards a formal declaration of some NATO expansion may be too great to be stopped, but if it can be halted it would be more in the interest of European security to encourage a local alliance in East Europe. Assuming NATO cohesion as presently structured, the Western Alliance ought to encourage a Central–East European collective defence arrangement. The attraction of NATO and the WEU for the Central and East European states is that there are no such structures in that part of Europe. That being so, one should be created. The Visegrad states, (Poland, the Czech Republic, Slovakia and Hungary) and perhaps the small Baltic republics, have a common anxiety about Russian intentions and common strategic interests in protecting borders and sustaining political stability. If local rivalries and suspicions preclude these states forming their own military alliance, then it is vital that these problems are not imported into any expanded NATO. A local alliance would probably not meet Russian opposition. The Yeltsin/Kozyrev/Primakov foreign policy does not, so far, appear intent in reasserting old-style Soviet hegemony over the former Warsaw Pact states. However, that part of Slav Europe is seen as fertile ground for a new economic and political relationship without the burden of military domination, but susceptible to Russian political influence. Formal NATO expansion to include some of the Visegrad states would preclude such influence. A local regional alliance would not. An alliance based upon the Visegrad states, and perhaps including the Baltic republics and one or two Balkan states, would leave Russia as hegemon in the territory of the former Soviet Union and perhaps part of the Balkans. In practice, this is happening already. The Commonwealth of Independent States (which excludes the Baltic republics) is slowly but certainly taking on the appearance of a confederation with Russia at its heart.

The fifth, and most crucial, condition affecting European security arrangements will be the character of the American commitment to European security. The future stability and security of Europe requires a high-level, visible involvement by the United States in European security arrangements. As was demonstrated in two world wars and the Cold War during the twentieth century, no other state has – given the will – either the political or military capabilities to adjudicate successfully between the competitive continental Great Powers while reassuring the rest of Europe that their liberties and traditions are safe. Sustaining American interest in and commitment to continent-wide, international security in Europe is more important than, and should be given priority over, creating a narrow, parochial West European defence entity. The two may not always be in contradiction, but when they are American leadership in European security must come first.

It is difficult enough to persuade the US Congress and people to perpetuate security guarantees to Europe when no direct ideological or military threat to the United States from Europe exists. In the mid-1980s surveys indicated that more than 66 per cent of Americans supported the use of American military forces to defend West Europe from aggression; by 1994 the figure had dropped to 54 per cent.[9] It will be even more difficult if West Europe is seen to be reluctant to support the United States in tackling instability and threats, often relevant to West Europe as well as the United States, outside continental Europe. Managing 'chaos' when societies break down in strategic parts of the world, protecting markets and raw materials, sustaining free trade and, where realisable, guarding democratic values are the security contingencies most likely to demand Western military effort over the next few years. As the practical distinction between in- and out-of-area fades away for NATO, the United States will increasingly measure NATO's value by what NATO Europe does to assist in safeguarding Washington's trans-Atlantic security interests from the Barents Sea to the Indian Ocean.

The grand strategic challenge facing West Europe is to look outwards from Europe. The great European powers in NATO, including Germany, should adopt a role of commitment – political as well as military – to trans-Atlantic security, not just European security. And to impress the US Congress and voters, West European support does need a visible, credible military dimension. Humanitarian assistance, medical support and economic aid are all perceived as soft options while American service personnel put their lives at risk. As well as encouraging deep, sustained US security involvement in Europe, such perspectives and commitment would add power to West European arguments when there were disagreements with the United States over objectives or strategies. In the most serious contingencies, Washington has made it clear it would act alone if required, but it is also obvious that it would welcome and expect support from long-standing allies.[10] In turn, the United States needs to adopt a more realistic, less idealistic, appreciation of world politics. The first Clinton term was marked by the priority given to perceived moral objectives over strategic and political requirements. Washington's adoption of realistic and realisable political objectives which address vital strategic needs will facilitate West European cooperation.

The next ten years will be crucial for European security. NATO, the vehicle for American commitment, will not survive as a virile, collective defence organisation unless the capable West European states, not just Britain, show the political will to bear a wider military burden alongside the United States. Nor will NATO prosper if collective defence is exchanged for collective security by the over-expansion of formal membership. The framework of European security arrangements will always be untidy as long as the continent is not divided between two hostile blocs, crudely balanced by military power. Contemporary arrangements have an incomplete quality to them but, to a large extent, they reflect the geo-strategic reality of the post-Cold War years. The most valuable bequest of the Cold War to European security is the overarching United States commitment. It settles, stabilises and underpins the formal and informal components of the post-Cold War security regime in Europe. Without it, or with a much-diminished commitment, Europe's prospects will be less secure.

Notes

1. See 'The international order: Situation, mission, execution', *Economist*, 24 December 1994 – 4 January 1995, pp. 17–20, for an analysis of the health of international order and some prescriptions.
2. See *BP Statistical Review of World Energy* (London: BP Group Media and Publications, 1995), p. 7 and p. 16.
3. Henry Kissinger, *Diplomacy* (London: Simon & Schuster, 1995), p. 805.
4. Ronald D. Asmus *et al*. argue strongly for enlargement in 'NATO expansion: The next steps', *Survival*, Vol. 37, No. 1, Spring 1995, p. 7–33. Field Marshal Lord Carver, Sir Michael Howard, and Admiral of the Fleet Lord Hill-Norton deploy a battery of arguments against enlargement in letters to the editor of the *Times*, 23 May 1996, p. 21.
5. See Joseph S. Nye, 'Conflicts after the Cold War', *Washington Quarterly*, Vol. 19, No. 1, Winter 1996, p. 6.
6. See James Wyllie, 'Egypt – A State of Jeopardy', *Jane's Intelligence Review*, Vol. 6, No. 1, January 1994, pp. 29–31; 'Tunisia – In the shadow of fundamentalism', *Jane's Intelligence Review*, Vol. 6, No. 7, July 1994, pp. 312–13; and 'Egypt – staying the course', *Jane's Intelligence Review* , Vol. 7, No. 11, November 1995, pp. 499–501.

7. See George Brock, 'Cold War veterans fret over Europe's fraying links with US', *Times*, 13 May 1996, p. 12.

8. See Anne Applebaum, 'The fall and rise of the Communists', *Foreign Affairs*, Vol. 73, No. 6, November/December 1994, pp. 7–14; and 'A phoenix phenomenon', *Economist*, 25 February 1995, p. 46.

9. See Eugene R. Wittkopf, 'What Americans really think about foreign policy', *Washington Quarterly*, Vol. 19, No. 3, Summer 1996, p. 92.

10. See *A National Security Strategy of Engagement and Enlargement* (Washington: White House, February 1996), p. 14.

Appendix I

The North Atlantic Treaty
Washington DC, 4 April 1949

The Parties to this Treaty reaffirm their faith in the purposes and principles of the Charter of the United Nations and their desire to live in peace with all peoples and all governments.

They are determined to safeguard the freedom, common heritage and civilisation of their peoples, founded on the principles of democracy, individual liberty and the rule of law.

They seek to promote stability and wellbeing in the North Atlantic area.

They are resolved to unite their efforts for collective defence and for the preservation of peace and security.

They therefore agree to this North Atlantic Treaty.

Article 1

The Parties undertake, as set forth in the Charter of the United Nations, to settle any international disputes in which they may be involved by peaceful means in such a manner that international peace and security, and justice, are not endangered, and to refrain in their international relations from the threat or use of force in any manner inconsistent with the purposes of the United Nations.

Article 2

The Parties will contribute toward the further development of peaceful and friendly international relations by strengthening their free institutions, by bringing about a better understanding of the principles upon which these institutions are founded, and by promoting conditions of stability and well-being. They will seek to eliminate conflict in their international economic policies and will encourage economic collaboration between any or all of them.

Article 3

In order more effectively to achieve the objectives of this Treaty, the Parties, separately and jointly, by means of continuous and effective self-help and mutual aid, will maintain and develop their individual and collective capacity to resist armed attack.

Article 4

The Parties will consult together whenever, in the opinion of any of them, the territorial integrity, political independence or security of any of the Parties is threatened.

Article 5

The Parties agree that an armed attack against one or more of them in Europe or North America shall be considered an attack against them all; and consequently they agree that, if such an armed attack occurs, each of them, in exercise of the right of individual or collective self-defence recognised by Article 51 of the Charter of the United Nations, will assist the Party or Parties so attacked by taking forthwith, individually and in concert with the other Parties, such action as it deems necessary, including the use of armed force, to restore and maintain the security of the North Atlantic area.

Any such armed attack and all measures taken as a result thereof shall immediately be reported to the Security Council. Such measures shall be terminated when the Security Council has taken the measures necessary to restore and maintain international peace and security.

Article 6[1]

For the purpose of Article 5, an armed attack on one or more of the Parties is deemed to include an armed attack:

- on the territory of any of the Parties in Europe or North America, on the Algerian Departments of France,[2] on the territory of Turkey or on the islands under the jurisdiction of any of the Parties in the North Atlantic area north of the Tropic of Cancer;
- on the forces, vessels, or aircraft of any of the Parties, when in or over these territories or any other area in Europe in which occupation forces of any of the Parties were stationed on the date when the Treaty entered into force or the Mediterranean Sea or the North Atlantic area north of the Tropic of Cancer.

Article 7

The Treaty does not affect, and shall not be interpreted as affecting, in any way the rights and obligations under the Charter of the Parties which are members of the United Nations, or the primary responsibility of the Security Council for the maintenance of international peace and security.

Article 8

Each Party declares that none of the international engagements now in force between it and any other of the Parties of any third state is in conflict with the provisions of this Treaty, and undertakes not to enter into any international engagement in conflict with this Treaty.

Article 9

The Parties hereby establish a council, on which each of them shall be represented, to consider matters concerning the implementation of this Treaty. The council shall be so organised as to be able to meet promptly at any time. The council shall set up such subsidiary bodies as may be necessary; in particular it shall establish immediately a defence committee which shall recommend measures for the implementation of Articles 3 and 5.

Article 10

The Parties may, by unanimous agreement, invite any other European state in a position to further the principles of this Treaty and to contribute to the security of the North Atlantic area to accede to this Treaty. Any state so invited may become a Party to the Treaty by depositing its instrument of accession with the Government of the United States of America. The Government of the United States of America will inform each of the Parties of the deposit of each such instrument of accession.

Article 11

This Treaty shall be ratified and its provisions carried out by the Parties in accordance with their respective constitutional processes. The instruments of ratification shall be deposited as soon as possible with the Government of the United States of America, which will notify all the other signatories of each deposit. The Treaty shall enter into force between the states which have ratified it as soon as the ratifications of the majority of the signatories, including the ratifications of Belgium, Canada, France, Luxembourg, The Netherlands, the United Kingdom and the United States, have been deposited and shall come into effect with respect to other states on the date of the deposit of their ratifications.[3]

Article 12

After the Treaty has been in force for ten years, or at any time thereafter, the Parties shall, if any of them so requests, consult together for the purpose of reviewing the Treaty, having regard for the factors then affecting peace and security in the North Atlantic area, including the development of universal as well as regional arrangements under the Charter of the United Nations for the maintenance of international peace and security.

Article 13

After the Treaty has been in force for twenty years, any Party may cease to be a Party one year after its notice of denunciation has been given to the Government of the United States of America, which will inform the Governments of the other Parties of the deposit of each notice of denunciation.

Article 14

This Treaty, of which the English and French texts are equally authentic, shall be deposited in the archives of the Government of the United States of America. Duly certified copies thereof will be transmitted by that Government to the Governments of the other signatories.

1. As amended by Article 2 of the Protocol to the North Atlantic Treaty on the accession of Greece and Turkey.
2. On 16 January 1963, the Council noted that insofar as the former Algerian Departments of France were concerned, the relevant clauses of this Treaty had become inapplicable as from 3 July 1962.
3. The Treaty came into force on 24 August 1949, after the deposit of the ratifications of all signatory states.

Appendix II

Membership of international organisations as at 1 April 1996

NATO	WEU	EU	PfP
Belgium	Belgium	Belgium	NATO
Denmark	France	Denmark	+
France	Germany	France	Austria
Germany	Greece	Germany	Sweden
Greece	Italy	Greece	Finland
Italy	Luxembourg	Italy	Bulgaria
Luxembourg	The Netherlands	Luxembourg	Czech Republic
The Netherlands	Portugal	The Netherlands	Estonia
Portugal	Spain	Portugal	Hungary
Spain	UK	Spain	Latvia
UK		UK	Lithuania
Canada	**Observer Status**	Ireland	Poland
USA	Denmark	Austria	Romania
Iceland	Ireland	Sweden	Slovakia
Norway	Austria	Finland	Malta
Turkey	Sweden		Albania
	Finland		Armenia
			Azerbaijan
	Associate Members		Belarus
	Iceland		Macedonia
	Norway		Georgia
	Turkey		Kazakhstan
			Kyrgyzstan
	Associate Partners		Moldova
	Bulgaria		Russia
	Czech Republic		Slovenia
	Estonia		Turkmenistan
	Hungary		Ukraine
	Latvia		Uzbekistan
	Lithuania		
	Poland		
	Romania		
	Slovakia		

OSCE

Ireland	Slovakia
Austria	Albania
Sweden	Armenia
Finland	Azerbaijan
Belgium	Belarus
Denmark	Macedonia
France	Georgia
Germany	Kazakhstan
Greece	Kyrgyzstan
Italy	Moldova
Luxembourg	Russia
The Netherlands	Slovenia
Portugal	Turkmenistan
Spain	Ukraine
UK	Uzbekistan
Iceland	Tajikistan
Norway	Malta
Turkey	Bosnia-Herzegovina
Canada	Croatia
USA	Cyprus
Bulgaria	Fed. Rep. of Yugoslavia[1]
Czech Republic	Holy See
Estonia	Monaco
Hungary	San Marino
Latvia	Switzerland
Lithuania	
Poland	
Romania	

[1] Membership suspended.

Select bibliography

Abshire, David M., 'US global policy: Toward an agile strategy', *Washington Quarterly*, Vol. 19, No. 2, Spring 1996.

Adomeit, Hannes, 'Russia: Partner or risk factor', *European Security after the Cold War Part II* (London: IISS, 1994), Adelphi Paper 285.

Adomeit, Hannes, 'Russia as a "great power" in world affairs: image and reality', *International Affairs*, Vol. 71, No. 1, January 1995.

Almond, Mark, 'The grand abdication', *Wall Street Journal Europe*, 27 April, 1993, p. 6.

Applebaum, Anne, 'The fall and rise of the Communists', *Foreign Affairs*, Vol. 73, No. 6, November/December 1994.

Ash, Timothy Garton, 'Germany's choice', *Foreign Affairs*, Vol. 73, No. 4, July/August 1994.

Aspin, Les, 'Forces and Alliances for a New Era', *European Security after the Cold War Part II* (London: IISS, 1994), Adelphi Paper 285.

Bailes, Alyson, 'Britain's security policy agenda', *Journal of the Royal United Services Institute for Defence Studies*, Vol. 140, No. 1, February 1995.

Bartlett, C. J., *The 'Special Relationship': A Political History of Anglo-American Relations since 1945* (London: Longman, 1992).

Baylis, John, *British Defence Policy: Striking the Right Balance* (London: Macmillan, 1989).

Borawski, John and Khmelevskasa, M., 'The CSCE Helsinki Summit: New Directions for Euro-Atlantic Security', *European Security*, Vol. 1, No. 3, Autumn 1992.

Brown, Harold, 'Transatlantic security in the Pacific century', *Washington Quarterly*, Vol. 18, No. 4, Autumn 1995.

Brown, Michael, 'The flawed logic of NATO expansion', *Survival*, Vol. 37, No. 1, Spring 1995.

Brusstar, James H., 'Russian vital interests and Western security', *ORBIS*, Vol. 38, No. 4, Fall 1994.

Brzezinski, Zbigniew, 'The premature partnership', *Foreign Affairs*, Vol. 73, No. 2, March/April 1994.

Bull, Hedley, *The Anarchical Society* (London: Macmillan, 1977).

Buszynski, Leszek, 'Russia and the West: Towards renewed geopolitical rivalry', *Survival*, Vol. 37 , No. 3, Autumn 1995.

Buzan, Barry, 'Is international security possible? in Booth, K. (ed.) *New Thinking About Strategy and International Security* (London: HarperCollins, 1991).

Calleo, David, *The German Problem Reconsidered* (Cambridge: Cambridge University Press, 1980).

Clarke, Jonathan, 'Replacing NATO', *Foreign Policy 93*, Winter 1993–1994.

Clarke, Jonathan, 'Leaders and followers', *Foreign Policy 101*, Winter 1995–1996.

Cowper-Coles, Sherard, 'From defence to security: British policy in transition', *Survival*, Vol. 36, No. 1, Spring 1994.

De Nevers, Renée, *Russia's Strategic Renovation* (London: IISS, 1994), Adelphi Paper 289.

Deporte, A. W., *Europe between the Superpowers* (New Haven: Yale University Press, 1979).

Dick, Charles, 'The military doctrine of the Russian federation', *Jane's Intelligence Review Special Report No. 1*, January 1994.

Freedman, Lawrence, 'Alliance and the British way in warfare', *Review of International Studies*, Vol. 21, No. 2, April 1995.

Gambles, Ian, *Prospects for West European Security Cooperation* (London, IISS, 1989) Adelphi Paper 244.

Gebhard, Paul R. S., *The United States and European Security* (London: IISS, 1994), Adelphi Paper 286.

Glaser, Charles, 'Why NATO is still best: Future security arrangements for Europe', *International Security*, Vol. 18, No. 1, Spring 1993.

Gnesotto, Nicole, 'Common defence and transatlantic relations', *Survival*, Vol. 38, No. 1, Spring 1996.

Gordon, Philip H., 'Recasting the Atlantic Alliance', *Survival*, Vol. 38, No. 1, Spring 1996.

Grant, Robert P., 'France's new relationship with NATO', *Survival*, Vol. 38, No. 1, Spring 1996.

Greenberger, Robert, 'Dateline Capitol Hill: The new majority's foreign policy', *Foreign Policy 101*, Winter 1995–1996.

Grove, Eric, *The Army and British Security After the Cold War: Defence Planning for a New Era* (Camberley: Strategic and Combat Studies Institute, 1996), Occasional Paper 20.

Huntingdon, Samuel P., 'The clash of civilisations', *Foreign Affairs*, Vol. 72, No. 3, Summer 1993.

Hyland, William G., 'A mediocre record', *Foreign Policy 101*, Winter 1995–1996.

IISS, *Strategic Survey* (London: IISS, published annually).

IISS, *The Military Balance* (London: IISS, published annually).

Inge, Field Marshal Sir Peter, 'The roles and challenges of the British armed forces', *Journal of the Royal United Services Institute for Defence Studies*, Vol. 141, No. 1, February 1996.

Joffe, Josef, 'After bipolarity: Germany and European security', *European Security after the Cold War Part II* (London, IISS, 1994), Adelphi Paper 285.

Jopp, Mathias, *The Strategic Implications of European Integration* (London: IISS, 1994), Adelphi Paper, 290.

Kegley Jr, Charles W. and Wittkopf, Eugene R., *World Politics: Trend and Transformation* (New York: St Martin's Press, 1993).

Kissinger, Henry, *Diplomacy* (London: Simon & Schuster, 1995).

Kielinger, Thomas and Otte, Max, 'Germany: The pressurised power', *Foreign Policy 91*, Summer 1993.

Kozyrev, Andrei, 'The lagging partnership', *Foreign Affairs*, Vol. 73, No. 3, May/June 1994.

Kozyrev, Andrei, 'Partnership or Cold Peace', *Foreign Policy 39*, Summer 1995.

Lepingwell, John W. R., 'The Russian military and security policy in the "Near Abroad" ', *Survival*, Vol. 34, No. 3, Autumn 1992.

Menon, Anand, 'From independence to cooperation: France, NATO and European security', *International Affairs*, Vol. 71, No. 1, January 1995.

Mearsheimer, John J., 'Back to the future', *International Security*, Vol. 15, No. 1, Summer 1990.

Meiers, Franz-Josef, 'Germany: The reluctant power', *Survival*, Vol. 37, No. 3, Autumn 1995.

Nye, Joseph S., 'Conflicts after the Cold War', *Washington Quarterly*, Vol. 19, No. 1, Winter 1996.

Osgood, Robert, *NATO: The Entangling Alliance* (Chicago: University of Chicago Press, 1962).

Pfaff, William, 'Back to history as usual, which means genuine complexity', *International Herald Tribune*, 7 July 1994, p. 6.

Porter, Bruce D. and Saivetz, Carole R., 'Once and future empire: Russia and the "Near Abroad" ', *Washington Quarterly*, Vol. 17, No. 3, Summer 1994.

Powell, Colin L., 'The American commitment to European security', *Survival*, Vol. 34, No. 2, Summer 1992.

Roberts, Adam, 'A new age in international relations', *International Affairs*, Vol. 67, No. 3, July 1991.

Roberts, Adam, 'The United Nations and international security', *Survival*, Vol. 35, No. 2, Summer 1993.

Rubinstein, Alvin, 'The geopolitical pull on Russia', *ORBIS*, Vol. 38, No. 4, Fall 1994.

Ruehl, Lothar, 'European security and NATO's eastward expansion', *Aussenpolitik*, Vol. 45, No. 2, 1994.

Sabin, Philip, *British Strategic Priorities in the 1990s* (London: IISS, 1990), Adelphi Paper 254.

Schlör, Wolfgang, *German Security Policy* (London: IISS, 1993), Adelphi Paper 277.

Shashenkov, Maxim, 'Russian peacekeeping in the "Near Abroad" ', *Survival*, Vol. 36, No. 3, Autumn 1994.

Sherr, James, 'The Russian army's new charter', *Wall Street Journal Europe*, 9 December 1993, p. 6.

Smyser, W. R., 'Dateline Berlin: Germany's new vision', *Foreign Policy 97*, Winter 1994–1995.

Statement on Defence Estimates 1996 (London: HMSO, 1996).

Taylor, Trevor, 'West European security and defence cooperation: Maastricht and beyond', *International Affairs*, Vol. 70, No. 1, January 1994.

Treverton, Gregory, 'America's stakes and choices in Europe', *Survival*, Vol. 34, No. 3, Autumn 1992.

Treverton, Gregory F. (Ed), *The Shape of the New Europe* (New York: Council on Foreign Relations Press, 1992).

Ullman, Richard H., *Securing Europe* (Princeton: Princeton University Press, 1991).

Ullman, Richard H., 'A late recovery', *Foreign Policy 101*, Winter 1995–1996.

United States Security Strategy for Europe and NATO (Washington: Department of Defense, Office of International Security Affairs, June 1995).

Vivekanandan, B., 'Washington must rely on London, not Bonn', *ORBIS*, Vol. 35, No. 3, Summer 1991.

Wettig, Gerhard, 'Moscow's perception of NATO's role', *Aussenpolitik*, Vol. 45, No. 2, 1994.

Wettig, Gerhard, 'Controversial foundations of security in Europe', *Aussenpolitik*, Vol. 46, No. 1, 1995.

Wyllie, James H., *European Security in the Nuclear Age* (Oxford: Blackwell, 1986).

Zelikow, Philip, 'The masque of institutions', *Survival*, Vol. 38, No. 1, 1996.

Index